Readings in Credit Scoring

Readings in Credit Scoring

Foundations, developments, and aims

LYN C. THOMAS

School of Management, University of Southampton

DAVID B. EDELMAN

Direct Line Financial Services

JONATHAN N. CROOK

Credit Research Centre, Management School, University of Edinburgh

OXFORD
UNIVERSITY PRESS

This book has been printed digitally and produced in a standard specification in order to ensure its continuing availability

OXFORD
UNIVERSITY PRESS

Great Clarendon Street, Oxford OX2 6DP

Oxford University Press is a department of the University of Oxford.
It furthers the University's objective of excellence in research, scholarship,
and education by publishing worldwide in

Oxford New York

Auckland Cape Town Dar es Salaam Hong Kong Karachi
Kuala Lumpur Madrid Melbourne Mexico City Nairobi
New Delhi Shanghai Taipei Toronto
With offices in
Argentina Austria Brazil Chile Czech Republic France Greece
Guatemala Hungary Italy Japan South Korea Poland Portugal
Singapore Switzerland Thailand Turkey Ukraine Vietnam

Oxford is a registered trade mark of Oxford University Press
in the UK and in certain other countries

Published in the United States
by Oxford University Press Inc., New York

ISBN 978-0-19-852797-8

Printed and bound by CPI Antony Rowe Ltd., Eastbourne

Readings in credit scoring

At one level, credit scoring comprises a set of mathematical and statistical models that quantify the risk related to lending money; and much research and thinking goes into making these models more accurate and more robust.

At another level, credit scoring is a management tool used by lenders, for example, banks, to deal with large volumes of lending decisions in an efficient, consistent, and controlled manner.

Putting these two together becomes a large enterprise, especially as this involves issues that are normally dealt with by other areas—senior management, finance, marketing, IT, compliance, legal, and human resources. However, the potential benefits from a successful implementation of credit scoring are huge. For a major bank, an improvement in effectiveness of 0.1 per cent say, in whatever measure we choose, could represent millions of pounds. Credit scoring is not a simple matter.

Back in 1987, when the three of us first got together and conceived the notion of working together to advance knowledge in credit scoring and also the dissemination of this knowledge, we had little idea of how much could be achieved.

The first achievement was to set up a conference; and Credit Scoring and Credit Control took place in Edinburgh in September 1989. We were not fully aware of the demand for such a conference and were gratified when we attracted over 40 delegates to what was at the time quite an embryonic and relatively specialized area of concern. As well as planning a repeat of the conference—it has taken place every 2 years since and now attracts well over 200 delegates—we produced and had published a set of proceedings (1) for the first conference. This not only created a lasting record of the conference but was also able to address the lack of publications and published research and thinking in credit scoring.

With none of the seven subsequent conferences—Credit Scoring and Credit Control VIII took place in September 2003—have the proceedings been published although with the increasing numbers of delegates, the printed proceedings given to registered delegates have been distributed further and wider.

To further address the publication issue, with three of the subsequent conferences, we have been fortunate to be able to publish special issues of journals (2–4) for selected papers, and other papers have appeared in the regular editions of journals such as those of the Royal Statistical Society, The Institute of Mathematics and its Applications, and the Operational Research Society.

In terms of cementing the knowledge base, we also wrote a textbook (5) that appeared in 2002. However, while in the throes of pulling together that piece of work, we came to the realization that, following the proceedings of the first conference, of which only 200 copies were ever printed, the area needed a publication that was a more mature version of that first publication and that presented the background and also some current thinking. This text is our attempt to do this.

The book is organized into six part and the title of each part should act as a good pointer to the subject matter within:

  I: Historical development of credit and behavioural scoring
 II: Objectives and measures in credit scoring
III: Practical implementation of scoring systems
 IV: Features of scoring
  V: Other applications of scoring in credit risk
 VI: Alternative approaches to scoring systems

Thus, this book tries to bring together some of the seminal of work of the last 10–15 years along with some state-of-the-art work and also some alternative views and wider applications.

At the beginning of each section appears an editorial comment, explaining the importance and role of the papers within the section. Also, given the time that has elapsed since some of the papers first appeared and the fluid movement of people working in credit scoring, many of the authors have changed their status, employers, etc. The papers will appear in the book with the authors' original affiliation. Where their current affiliation/status is known, we shall add this.

Readers of this book can clearly read it all from cover to cover. Alternatively, they can use the sections and the editorial comments as a set of directions, allowing them to find more easily the parts that are of use and interest to them. However, we think that, in time, most readers will at least try to read through all of the papers.

No book of this type can be produced without the help of many, many people, and it is appropriate that we try to thank some of them and, in particular, four groups. The first group is clearly the authors themselves. They have agreed to this repeat publication of their work, once again putting them and their thinking under the spotlight. The second group is the authors' colleagues and employers who supported them in their research and in allowing the papers to appear in the first place. The third group is the University of Edinburgh who have acted as hosts to the series of conferences that have provided the platform for much of the thinking that appears in this text. Finally, we also thank the Oxford University Press for their courage in publication and also for their patience as we tried to assemble all of the pieces.

September 2003

Lyn C. Thomas
Southampton

David B. Edelman
Glasgow

Jonathan N. Crook
Edinburgh

References

1. *Credit Scoring and Credit Control*, (eds. Thomas, Crook, and Edelman), Oxford University Press, Oxford 1992.
2. *IMA Journal of Mathematics Applied in Business and Industry* 4(1), 1992.
3. *IMA Journal of Mathematics Applied in Business and Industry* 5(1), 1993.
4. Special Issue on Credit Scoring and Data Mining, (eds. Crook, Edelman, and Thomas), *Journal of the Operational Research Society* 52(9), September 2001.
5. *Credit Scoring and its Applications* (eds. Thomas, Edelman and Crook). Society for Industrial and Applied Mathematics, Philadelphia, Pennsylvania, USA 2002.

Contents

List of Contributors   xiii

Part I. Historical Development of Credit and Behavioural Scoring

1. Legal, social, and economic issues in implementing
   scoring in the United States   5

   R. W. Johnson

   In *Credit Scoring and Credit Control*, (eds. Thomas, Crook, and Edelman),
   pp. 19–32. OUP, Oxford 2002.

2. Problems in applying discriminant analysis in
   credit-scoring models   17

   Robert A. Eisenbeis

   Journal of Banking and Finance, 2, 205–19, 1978.

3. Behaviour scoring and adaptive control systems   33

   M. A. Hopper and E. M. Lewis

   In *Credit Scoring and Credit Control*, (eds. Thomas, Crook, and Edelman),
   pp. 257–76. OUP, Oxford 2002.

Part II. Objectives and Measures in Credit Scoring

4. Measures for comparing scoring systems   51

   A. D. Wilkie

   In *Credit Scoring and Credit Control*, (eds. Thomas, Crook, and Edelman),
   pp. 123–38. OUP, Oxford 2002.

5. The use of affordability data—does it add real value?   63

George Wilkinson and Jon Tingay
Proceedings of Credit Scoring and Credit Control VII, Credit Research Centre,
University of Edinburgh, 2001.

6. Improving lender offers using consumer preferences   73

Ralph L. Keeney and Robert M. Oliver
Proceedings of Credit Scoring and Credit Control VIII, Credit Research Centre,
University of Edinburgh, 2003.

Part III. Practical Implementation of Scoring Systems

7. Updating scorecards: removing the mystique   93

Alan Lucas
In *Credit Scoring and Credit Control*, (eds. Thomas, Crook, and Edelman),
pp. 179–96. OUP, Oxford 1992.

8. Efficient frontier cut-off policies in credit portfolios   111

Robert M. Oliver and E. Wells
Journal of Operational Research Society, 52, 1025–33, 2001.

Part IV. Features of Scoring

9. Can reject inference ever work?   133

David J. Hand and William E. Henley
IMA Journal of Mathematics Applied in Business and Industry, 5, 45–55,
1993/4.

10. The flat-maximum effect and generic linear scoring models: a test   147

George A. Overstreet, Jr., Edwin L. Bradley, Jr., and Robert S. Kemp, Jr.
IMA Journal of Mathematics Applied in Business and Industry, 4, 97–109, 1992.

11. The degradation of the scorecard over the business cycle   161

Jonathan N. Crook, Lyn C. Thomas, and Robert Hamilton
In *Credit Scoring and Credit Control*, (eds. Thomas, Crook, and Edelman),
pp. 111–23. OUP, Oxford 2002.

12. Inferring the inferred   177

Gaynor Bennett, Graham Platts, and Jane Crossley
IMA Journal of Mathematics Applied in Business and Industry,
7, 327–38, 1996.

Part V. Other Applications of Scoring in Credit Risk

13. Detecting credit card fraud using expert systems 189

Kevin J. Leonard

Computers and Industrial Engineering, 25 (1–4), 103–6, 1993.

14. A single European scorecard? Does data predict differently across Europe: An Experian Scorex investigation 195

Graham Platts and Ian Howe

Proceedings of Credit Scoring and Credit Control V, Credit Research Centre, University of Edinburgh, 1997.

15. Small sample scoring 205

Alan Lucas and Joanna Powell

Proceedings of Credit Scoring and Credit Control V, Credit Research Centre, University of Edinburgh, 1997.

Part VI. Alternative Approaches to Scoring Systems

16. Survival analysis and the credit-granting decision 235

B. Narain

In *Credit Scoring and Credit Control*, (eds. Thomas, Crook, and Edelman), pp. 109–22. OUP, Oxford 2002.

17. Graphical models in credit scoring 247

Pete Sewart and Joe Whittaker

IMA Journal of Mathematics Applied in Business and Industry, 9, 241–66, 1998.

18. Credit scoring using neural and evolutionary techniques 277

Mumine B. Yobas, Jonathan N. Crook, and Peter Ross

IMA Journal of Mathematics Applied in Business and Industry, 11, 111–25, 2000.

19. Segmentation in Markov chain consumer credit behavioural models 295

Joseph Ho, Lyn C. Thomas, T. A. Pomroy, and William T. Scherer

Proceedings of Credit Scoring and Credit Control VII, Credit Research Centre, University of Edinburgh, 2001.

Index 309

List of Contributors

Bennett, Gaynor
Scorex (UK) Ltd, Bradford, UK

Bradley, Edwin L. Jr.
*Department of Biostatistics and Biomathematics, University of Alabama
at Birmingham, Birmingham, Alabama 35294, USA*
Currently retired

Crook, Jonathan N.
Credit Research Centre, The University of Edinburgh, Edinburgh, UK

Crossley, Jane
Marks and Spencer Financial Services, Chester, UK

Eisenbeis, Robert A.
Federal Reserve System, Washington D.C., USA
[Currently: Federal Reserve Bank of Atlanta, Atlanta, USA]

Hamilton, Robert
Loughborough University Business School

Hand, David J.
Department of Statistics, The Open University, Milton Keynes, UK
[Currently: Department of Mathematics, Imperial College, London, UK]

Henley, William E.
Department of Statistics, The Open University, Milton Keynes MK7 6AA, UK
[Currently: Animal Health Trust, Newmarket, UK]

Ho, Joseph
Edinburgh University Management School, Edinburgh, UK
[Currently: Financial Service Authority, London, UK]

Hopper, M. A.
The Fair, Isaac Companies, San Rafael, USA
[Latterly retired]

Howe, Ian
Scorex SAM UK, Bradford, UK
[Currently: Credit call, UK]

Johnson, R. W.
Purdue University, USA

Keeney, Ralph L.
Fuqua School of Business, Duke University, USA

Kemp, Robert S. Jr.
McIntyre School of Commerce, University of Virginia, USA

Leonard, Kevin J.
School of Business and Economics Wilfrid Laurier University, Canada
[Currently: Department of Health Policy, Management and Evaluation, University of Toronto, Toronto, Canada]

Lewis, E. M.
The Fair, Isaac Companies, USA [deceased]

Lucas, Alan
Barclaycard and Barclay Consumer Lending
[Currently: RhinoRisk Ltd, High Wycombe, UK]

Narain, B.
Scorelink, Berkshire, UK
[Currently: Paragan]

Oliver, Robert M.
Fair, Isaac and Company Inc., San Rafael, CA, USA
[Currently: Emeritus Professor, University of California, Berkeley, USA]

Overstreet, George A. Jr.
McIntyre School of Commerce, University of Virginia, USA

Platts, Graham
Scorex SAM

Pomroy, T. A.
Department of Industrial and Systems Engineering, University of Virginia, USA

Powell, Joanna
Barclaycard and Barclay Consumer lending, Northampton, UK

Ross, Peter
Department of Artificial Intelligence, The University of Edinburgh, Edinburgh, UK
[Currently: School of Computing, Napier University, Edinburgh]

Scherer, William T.
Department of Industrial Engineering, University of Virginia, USA

Sewart, Pete
Department of Mathematics and Statistics, Lancaster University, UK

Thomas, Lyn C.
Edinburgh University Management School, Edinburgh, UK
[Currently: School of Management, University of Southampton, UK]

Tingay, Jon
Scorex (UK) Ltd

Wells, E.
Fair, Isaac and Company Inc., San Rafael, CA, USA

Whittaker, Joe
Department of Mathematics and Statistics, Lancaster University, UK

Wilkie, A. D.
R. Watson and Sons, Reigate

Wilkinson, George
George Wilkinson Associates

Yobas, Mumine B.
Department of Artificial Intelligence, The University of Edinburgh, Edinburgh, UK
[Currently: Central Registry Agency, Istanbul, Turkey]

Part I. Historical Development of Credit and Behavioural Scoring

The first part of this book consists of three chapters concerned with the development of credit and behavioural scoring. What is surprising now is that two of them—Johnson and Eisenbeis—spend a considerable time outlining criticisms of credit scoring and the defence against these criticisms. This reflects the fact that with the phenomenal growth in consumer credit in the 1970s and 1980s, and the concomitant rise in credit scoring some people were concerned about the ethics of using such an approach. This was brought to a head with the arguments and analysis that surrounded the legislation to allow equal opportunities for credit and what that really meant. The third chapter by Hopper and Lewis on behavioural scoring is more practically based. It outlines how to use behavioural scoring as part of a customer relationship system and what benefits it can bring.

Johnson's chapter concentrates on the US environment, which is where credit scoring began and where the industry first established itself. He points out the role Durand played as the first person to put together the then new ideas on statistical classification methods and the fact that the first users were retailers not bankers. Even in the very first applications there was concern that users were seeking to override the system and so there was a need to check the validity of the information provided. A more detailed account of the early history can be found in E. M. Lewis's book, *An Introduction to Credit Scoring* (Lewis 1992). Johnson's chapter points out that the 'empirical evaluation process surely dominates the judgmental approach in most instances' before addressing the challenges that credit scoring has had to address. These are that it is impersonal, that there is no rational explanation of the relationships between the variables and the subsequent credit performance, and that it may be discriminatory. His answer to the first two is essentially pragmatic—credit scoring deals with individuals in smaller groups than subjective judgement does, and it does not claim to explain the association between the important individual characteristics and subsequent behaviour, but if it works, use it. His discussion on discrimination questions, asks what is meant by discrimination and suggests that some of the credit scoring anti-discriminatory laws enacted actually, have the effect of increasing the discrimination. He finishes by speculating on four likely developments in credit scoring—risk based pricing, profit scoring, systems approaches, and the increase in concerns on privacy. The first three are areas where the industry is still working hard to develop practical implementations—if one takes systems to mean that the same optimization model is used for all the credit, operational, and marketing decisions. The impact of privacy concerns on credit scoring is still very much more country dependent than one might have expected.

Robert Eisenbeis's chapter on 'Problems in Applying Discriminant Analysis' is very much of the time of the Equal Credit Opportunity Acts in the 1970s when the philosophical and practical problems in applying credit scoring were very much under discussion. The chapter addresses the methodology of credit scoring, the models involved and the statistical problems with the discriminant approach that was then the predominant way of building scorecards. Eisenbeis identified three elements that he would expect to be part of the consumer credit methodology that were not to be found at that time. First, that the models should be multi-period to allow for the several decision points in a lender's relationship with a consumer. Second, that they should address the question of the cost of acquiring extra information on the consumer and third, that the lender should consider more than just the riskiness of the borrower—that is, a need to move from default scoring to profit scoring. The chapter then looks at the existing models and declares them to be deficient in these features. It even suggests the need for a survival analysis type approach if one wants to deal with profit scoring. Finally, it looks at the statistical problems in using discriminant analysis to create scorecards. It suggests eight areas of difficulty from the non-normality and unequal variances of the characteristics between the goods and the bads to the definition of the groups and the selection of a suitable sample. With hindsight these statistical problems seem almost pedantic. Other classification approaches have emerged—logistic regression, classifications trees, linear programming, nearest neighbours, neural nets, support vector machines, and genetic algorithms which do not suffer the same theoretic limitations as linear regression (which is what discriminant analysis really is) but the results are not that superior. Perhaps it is true that logistic regression has taken over from linear regression as the main statistical tool for credit card building because it is theoretically satisfied by a larger class of problems but empirical investigations have shown that quadratic regressions are not better than linear regressions in practice because they lead to poorer parameter estimates. Similarly, chi-square statistics, entropy, and concordance give some indication of the relative importance of the relevant characteristics, whereas marginal good : bad rates are used to choose suitable cut-offs, which in some way reflect the relative cost of the two types of errors. In fact, none of the statistical criticisms are ones that are heard much today whereas the cry for more sophisticated objectives and models is probably still valid. So in the quarter of a century since the chapter was written one might argue that credit scoring has become much more efficient (meeting the objectives it is set) without becoming much more effective (setting the appropriate objectives).

The chapter by Hooper and Lewis is much more practically based but in some way answers some of the criticisms of the other two chapters. Its title suggests it is on behavioural scoring, a monthly updated risk based score which uses a consumer's repayment and usage performance to assess the likelihood of default within a fixed time period. This is mentioned in passing but the real thrust of the chapter is on adaptive control systems and Champion–Challenger strategies. These are ways of improving and updating lenders' actions as more information about the consumers' performance becomes available. Thus it addresses indirectly both the criticism of no multi-period model and the need to set objectives other than default risk. The illustrative problem in the chapter, for example, is collections scoring, which is how to recover as much as possible from those who have defaulted on their loans. The idea of Champion–Challenger—that one can only assess a new strategy by running it in parallel with the existing one—is something that the industry has taken to heart. Moreover, this chapter points out that there are two separate issues in consumer relationship management concerning credit and behavioural scoring—building a suitable scorecard and then using that scorecard to help determine which of a number of different policies is the one most appropriate for that consumer.

Reference

Lewis, E. M. (1992) *An Introduction to Credit Scoring*. Athena Press, San Rafael.

1. Legal, social, and economic issues in implementing scoring in the United States

R. W. Johnson

1.1 Introduction

This chapter is divided into three main parts. To set the stage, the first and very brief section examines the growth of credit scoring in the United States and the economic reasons for its rapid acceptance over the past decade or so. The second part addresses the challenges to credit scoring, their nature, their rationale, and the manner in which they have been resolved. Next, I will suggest that credit scoring has a long way to go and ultimately will not be viewed as credit scoring but as an important tool of profitability management. Finally, I conclude with a plea that in meeting valid concerns for privacy we should not sap the power of credit-scoring systems.

1.2 Origins and economic rationale

Credit for initiating the concept of credit scoring is generally given to David Durand (1941). His study, published in 1941 by the National Bureau of Economic Research, examined about 7200 reports on good and bad installment loans made by 37 firms. Using a chi-square test, Durand identified the variables that significantly distinguished between good and bad loans and developed an 'efficiency index' designed to show how effective a variable was in differentiating good risks from bad among loan applicants. He then used a discriminant function to develop credit-scoring models. It is perhaps of more than passing interest to record that Durand's bank scoring model allocated 2.72 points if the customer had a bank account and 2.63 points if the applicant was

In *Credit Scoring and Credit Control*, (eds. Thomas, Crook, and Edelman), pp. 19–32. OUP, Oxford 2002.

a woman (Durand 1941: 86, 88). One suspects that the few women who had been admitted to the credit market in those days were exceptionally good at credit risks.

The statistical methodology advocated by Durand did not take the country by storm. As he admitted, 'the theoretical considerations upon which the formulae rest, as well as the methods by which they are determined, are too complex to be understandable to any but trained mathematicians' (Durand 1941).

Spiegel, the large US retailer, used credit scoring at an early stage. One other firm, Household Finance Corp. (HFC) attempted to put Durand's techniques into practice at that time. The president of HFC, E. F. Wonderlic, was well versed in statistics as a result of his training in psychology. By 1946, he had developed a 'Credit Guide Score' for appraisal of new loan applicants. That his academic sophistication was not well received is suggested in a memorandum that he circulated in April 1948. After demonstrating the association of credit scoring and credit losses, he pleaded, 'These figures from actual results should prove conclusively to the most sceptical that the Credit Guide Score is a tool which is consistently able to point out the degree of risk in any personal loan, provided, of course, that it is correctly scored' (Wonderlic 1948). His concern about the accounts being correctly scored was well placed. Some years later one of his former branch managers confided to me that in his office they first made the loans and then, after closing, sat around and scored them so that they would show passing scores.

Most of the credit-scoring systems used during the next decade were based on score cards that had been developed by perusing accounts that had been charged off. The variables selected and scores assigned were basically judgemental. But, at least their use brought some uniformity and predictability to the credit-granting process. In an era of rapidly expanding credit portfolios, they often produced better results than the unrestrained judgement of novice credit analysts.

Economic pressures ultimately forced the acceptance of empirically based and statistically derived credit scoring, in spite of objections from credit analysts who were understandably distraught at 'being replaced by a computer'. The extraordinary growth in consumer-installment credit in the postwar period far outstripped the ability of the industry to hire trained personnel to screen credit applicants. Consolidation in the industry made it economical to develop scoring systems. Perhaps most important of all, computers became available that could handle the tedious calculations needed to develop a credit-scoring system.

Thus it was that economic pressures and computer technology came together during the late 1960s and early 1970s with the result that credit-scoring systems based on empirical valuation methods were developed and gradually gained acceptance. Other speakers at this conference will undoubtedly address the superiority of empirically based and statistically derived credit-scoring systems in judgemental systems. While the empirical evaluation process surely dominates the judgemental approach in most instances (Chandler and Coffman 1979), its use in the United States has raised a number of social and economic issues that must now be addressed.

1.3   Challenges to credit scoring

There have been a variety of challenges to the use of credit scoring in the United States—and not just from sceptical credit managers. Some of these objectives have already been raised in the United Kingdom and have probably been expressed in other countries as well. The issues raised reveal a need for research and education in order that we do not legislate a cure for a nonexistent problem.

1.3.1   Impersonal

As numerical rating systems, credit scoring strikes consumers as dispassionate and highly impersonal. 'Treat me as an individual', is the cry. Another aspect of the same, very natural concern is the admonition: 'Don't treat me as just another member of a group'. This latter 'minus point' for credit scoring was very well expressed in the July, 1989 issue of *Which?*: 'Credit scoring doesn't assess the creditworthiness of individuals, just the risk associated with groups of people. So you might fall into a "bad risk" group, even though you personally are scrupulous about paying'.

How do we respond to these challenges? We should recognize that consumers probably do not really wish to be treated personally in the sense that they can sit down with a credit analyst to discuss their finances and watch while he ruminates over their application. The consumer's real concern is over being treated as a member of a class and not isolated for ad hominem credit analysis. One answer to the challenge is that such individual treatment is unavailable, given the volume of applicants and scarcity of skilled analysts. Even if such talent were available, it would be uneconomical for the credit grantor to provide the service because the cost would be unacceptable to consumers.

But a better response is to point out that, when they are evaluated with a credit-scoring system, consumers are treated more as individuals (i.e. the classes are smaller) than if they had been evaluated by human beings. As I have observed elsewhere (Johnson and Jackson 1982): credit-scoring systems permit creditors to screen hundreds of applicants and sort them into many more categories, which range from non-creditworthy through creditworthy, than would be possible using human judgement. Various studies have shown that most people find it difficult to rank objects or people consistently into more than five or six subgroups.

For example, if 1,000 people were to walk through the door, one by one, how accurately could you, by sight, classify them into more than five groups: very tall, tall, medium, short, very short? In contrast, a credit-scoring system classifies a thousand applicants into a hundred or more subgroups and, therefore, treats them more personally than possible with human judgement.

A variation or extension of the charge that credit grantors should not score credit applicants as members of a group is the assertion that credit applicants should not be scored at all using the information typically provided on an application blank. It is reasoned that, if credit grantors cannot use variables such as time at residence, time on job, home ownership, and so on, they obviously cannot classify an applicant into a group according to those characteristics. Rather than rely on group characteristics, they will be forced to 'treat applicants as individuals'. That is, they will have to rely only on that applicant's past payment behaviour. If it is good, grant the credit; if not, reject.

This challenge to credit scoring has been expressed, for example, by US Senator Joseph Biden, who has been quoted as arguing, 'I am not sure that you should be able to use any statistical data which in fact does not relate specifically to that person . . . namely statistical data as to how often he paid' (Credit Card Redlining 1979: 132). This may also be termed the 'One Free Bite Approach', under which each consumer is given a chance to use credit. Thereafter, future access to credit will depend upon his or her payment record.

The rebuttal of this approach appears to be fairly clear. First, there is not a strong relationship between payment history and future credit performance. William Fair, President, Fair, Isaac and Co., testified before a congressional committee investigating 'credit card redlining' (Credit Card Redlining 1979: 197). 'Previous credit performance is a useful but not a determinative predictor of future performance. It is not uncommon for 80 per cent of the applicants for credit who later fail to pay to have entirely satisfactory credit ratings. At the same time, it is not unusual for a substantial number of applicants who show subsequent creditworthy behaviour to have had various levels of unsatisfactory payment performance in the past.'

Second, it is anti-consumer to deny credit grantors the use of variables that are empirically derived and can be shown to be significantly correlated with payment performance. The greater the discrimination provided by the scoring system, the more credit grantors can avoid type 1 and type 2 errors. On the one hand, they will reject more 'bad' accounts that would have been accepted with less data; on the other hand, they will accept more 'good' accounts that would have otherwise been rejected. Creditors reduce their collection costs and credit losses, while at the same time increasing their revenues.

Consumers, in the aggregate, are also better off. Competition among creditors should force a lowering of rates or a greater availability of credit services. Thus, consumers who desire and deserve credit will receive it. Those who desire it, but who have a low probability of repaying the debt, will not receive credit. Presumably, they will be better off by not suffering the indignities of the collection process. However, we should admit that for those consumers who would not have repaid their debts, the joys of not receiving collection calls is offset, at least in part, by not receiving the income transfers that they would have obtained from consumers who did repay (Peck and Adams 1981).

1.3.2   Face validity

Another challenge to credit scoring is that there should be a rational explanation or a clear and believable relationship between each variable used in a scoring system and credit performance. The foremost proponent of this approach in the United States has been Professor Noel Capon of Columbia University. He attempts to make a distinction 'between characteristics that may show some statistical relationship to credit perform- ance and those that have a genuine explanatory relationship to this performance. An explanatory characteristic is one that bears a clear causal relationship to the behaviour being predicted' (Credit Card Redlining 1979: 129). Only those variables that have an explanatory relationship should be used in credit scoring: 'When predictive decisions regarding individuals need to be made, it has been the tradition in American society to base these decisions on variables that bear an explanatory, rather than a statistical, rela- tionship to the behaviour being predicted' (Credit Card Redlining 1979: 130). Unfortu- nately, 'most of the personal characteristics used make no sense, but advocates of point scoring are unconcerned about such niceties' (*New York Times*, February 21, 1979).

In effect Capon sees type 1 and type 2 errors in designing scoring systems. On the one hand, designers include variables that are statistically related to credit performance, but which are not 'genuine'. He questions the validity of using such variables as rent or own, debt to a finance company, age of automobile owned or financed, and occupation. On the other hand, he finds that genuine variables are missing from scoring systems, presumably because the designers failed to find a statistically significant relationship between the variables and credit performance. He asks why such economic variables as 'income, debts, living expenses and the like' seldom appear (Capon 1982: 86).

Capon also expressed concern that points assigned to variables such as time at present address and time with employer do not display a 'rational' pattern. For example, one scoring system that he examined allowed 30 points for being on the job for less than 6 months but only 24 points for being on the job for 6–17 months (Capon 1982: 86).

The response to these challenges by Capon and others seems fairly straightforward. The mathematical techniques make no assumptions about causality; in fact, users of these procedures carefully adopt terms such as 'association' to avoid any implication that they have uncovered causal relationships. It is too much to require that we identify a causal relationship between each variable and credit performance and between variations in the values of each variable and credit performance. There is a high degree of collinearity among the variables that creates oddities such as the pattern of points assigned to time on the job. There probably is causality, but the relationships are simply too complex for the human mind to grasp.

But the fact that we may not understand the causality or association does not mean we should avoid variables that do not appear to be explanatory. We do not know how aspirin works, but we use it. To impose a requirement that the designer show a causal relationship that would be accepted as genuine by a congressman places a burden on the designer that can only raise the costs of scoring programmes and reduce their efficiency. The hard line on choosing variables to include in a scoring programme is simply: If it works, use it. Obviously, this doctrine must be modified by desires to limit the number of variables used and perhaps to find variables that are verifiable. Within those constraints, we select the subset of variables that provides the greatest separation between the mean scores of 'good' and 'bad'.

1.3.3   Discriminatory

Of course the variables that may be considered in developing a credit-scoring system should exclude race, colour, sex, marital status, and so on, should they not? Does not consideration of these variables involve a social cost that is unacceptable? Legislators in both the United States and the United Kingdom obviously thought so. But, when questioned by Representative Levin during the hearings on credit-card redlining, William Fair made clear that developers of credit-scoring systems should be allowed to consider race, religion, sex, age, ethnic origin, and any other 'prohibited variable' (Credit Card Redlining 1979: 221). (Note that considering a variable does not necessarily mean that it is included in the final scoring system.) Let us explore the thorny issue of whether or not credit scoring is discriminatory.

The core of the issue is how we define 'discrimination'. Granting credit, offering life and fire insurance and admitting students to the University of Edinburgh all involve discrimination. Some people receive the service; others are denied it. The evidence is strong that the US Congress did not intend to hinder creditors from sorting good from bad risks. By preventing the inclusion of the prohibited variables in credit-scoring (and judgemental) systems, Congress believed that it had outlawed differential treatment of consumers having one or more of the prohibited variables, but that it had not interfered with discrimination on the basis of creditworthiness.

Not long after the passage of the Equal Credit Opportunity Act (ECOA) in 1972, concerns arose that discrimination still existed because many of the permitted variables were highly correlated with the prohibited variables. To shore up the statute, Congress passed further amendments in 1976, and added as prohibited variables the receipt of public assistance benefits and good faith exercise of rights under the Consumer Protection Act.

The issue may be illustrated by returning to the July issue of *Which?* (p. 317). 'But credit-scoring systems might still produce "indirect discrimination". For instance, one of our readers has told that she was turned down for instant credit because she worked part-time. If part-time work... attracts a low score, it amounts to "indirect discrimination" against women, because the vast majority of part-timers are female. The Equal Opportunities Commission (EOC) has been encouraging some major credit-scoring companies to design scorecards which don't discriminate indirectly.'

But, if we think about it, we can identify a host of variables currently in use in scoring systems that are correlated with the various prohibited variables. Women are more likely to rent than to own their residence than men, are likely to have fewer credit cards than men, and are more likely to be retail clerks than men. In each case, female applicants would receive fewer credit points than the male applicants who own their own home, have more prestigious credit cards and are senior executives. Sexless scoring systems tend to be male dominated.

One approach to this apparent 'indirect discrimination' is to force an adjustment in credit scoring so that the creditors end up accepting the same proportions of female applicants and male applicants. Any other scoring system would be termed 'discriminatory' in that the effect of the system would be to accept different proportions of female and male applicants. However, research has shown that 'the effects approach will produce a higher acceptance ratio for the low-return [bad] group, a lower acceptance rate for the high-return [good] group, and a less accurate and more costly credit screening process'. The research was conducted by Robert Avery (1981) and the citation is from a recent study by Gregory E. Elliehausen and Thomas A. Durkin (1989: 17).

Our legislative history is that Congress did not intend to apply the effects test to the credit market. Nonetheless the sort of indirect discrimination illustrated earlier continues to trouble legislators. We can expect to see efforts to amend the ECOA in the direction of the effects test—to the consequent detriment of credit-scoring systems and consumers.

There is an alternative approach based on a study by Chandler and Ewert (1976) of 2,000 credit-card applicants, some of whom had been rejected, some of whom did not repay satisfactorily, others who did. Four credit-scoring models were developed.

Model 1 was in full compliance with ECOA; model 2 used all of the same applicant characteristics as the first model, plus a dummy variable for sex: model 3 was developed solely on the basis of female applicants; and model 4 was based solely on the basis of male applicants.

More females (both historically good and historically bad) would have received credit with model 2 than with model 1. Also, more previously rejected female applicants would have received credit. When model 3 (females only) was applied to the sample, about 10 percentage points more female applicants were accepted than under model 1. More applicants who had previously been rejected were accepted under model 3 than under model 1. In the middle range of cut-off scores, 40–60 per cent more females previously rejected were accepted.

Thus this research provides an empirical validation of Avery's theoretical simulations. There is good reason to believe that prohibiting the use of variables, such as sex and race, in credit scoring in an effort to assure non-discriminatory treatment of protected classes has a perverse effect. ECOA is inherently discriminatory in that it denies credit grantors the opportunity to adjust statistically for the differences in life style among the protected classes.

The answer to the problem seems to be astonishingly simple but politically unpalatable—permit designers of credit-scoring systems to consider all of the prohibited variables and to include them if they are statistically valid. Were that done, the female who had been rejected because she was working part-time, would be evaluated in conjunction with other females, among whom part-time work was a common source of income. The 'indirect discrimination' would be muted, and creditors would be granting more loans to females in their own economic self-interest.

1.4   Future role of credit scoring

In spite of legislative limits on its effectiveness, credit scoring has a bright future. There are three potential developments: risk-based pricing, profitability scoring, and a systems approach that contributes to this bright future. The darkest cloud on the horizon is perhaps a regrowth of privacy concerns that may stifle the availability of data for scoring systems.

1.4.1   Risk-based pricing

Unlike grantors of commercial credit, most providers of consumer credit have a single house rate applicable to all customers. Thus, a commercial borrower may pay the bank prime plus one point, but the treasurer of the firm will carry a bank card with a rate of 20 per cent, the same rate charged to all other cardholders from that bank.

In the United States there has been a movement towards risk-based pricing among commercial banks. Thus, Watro (1988) in a study of 148 bank holding companies found that banks grossing a return of 14.9 per cent of average credit-card balances had charge-offs of less than 1 per cent. In contrast, that group of banks having gross revenues amounting to 19.3 per cent of average balances had charge-offs ranging from 4.0 to 8.9 per cent. Thus, as any economist would expect, banks charging high rates were motivated to accept high risks, and vice versa.

Credit scoring provides the basis for grantors of consumer credit to engage in risk-based pricing within their portfolios. Conceptually, the finance rate could be adjusted for each customer, just as banks now do for commercial loans. The policy would benefit consumers across the board. The high-risk applicant would receive credit that he or she would not otherwise receive under a single 'house' rate, albeit at a higher rate of finance charge. The low-risk customer would receive a deservedly lower rate and not partially subsidize high-risk customers under a uniform house rate.

There are at least two barriers to implementing the programme. It may be difficult to explain to a customer why his or her rate is higher than that charged to a neighbour. However, some banks and automobile finance companies have already instituted such programmes without noticeable problems. The other barrier is the threat of suits under the ECOA for discriminatory treatment. Since there have been so few suits under the ECOA to date, this concern may be over-emphasized.

1.4.2 Profitability scoring

Credit-scoring systems predict only payment performance. Essentially, the focus is whether a customer will pay satisfactorily (good versus bad), while the cut-off score reflects in part the relative losses on bad accounts versus the gains to be obtained from good accounts. In the long run, we will develop more sophisticated predictive models that will allow us to screen accounts on the basis of their potential profitability. Specifically, we would accept or reject applications on the basis of the net present value (NPV) of the account. If the NPV is positive, accept; if the NPV is negative, reject.

It is difficult to develop and implement a profitability-scoring model. The design of such a model is very complex, although we are beginning to see some preliminary drafts (Boyes *et al.* 1989). Second, we generally lack the information that we would like to have. Frequently, the necessary back data have not been retained in the files. Often, the application blank has not sought the needed information. Application blanks are still designed primarily to gather information relevant to credit and collections. We need to expand our application forms to collect data relevant to marketing and profitability modelling. Third, the accounting data of most credit grantors is not in a form that readily lends itself to modelling costs and revenues on an economic basis.

Finally, there is an interesting public relations and political problem in the United States. Since credit grantors are required by the ECOA to respond to applicants' requests for reasons for a credit rejection, they will have to generate such reasons under a profitability model. What will we do? If we have only a low annual fee on our credit card, but a reasonably high annual percentage rate, what do we do when somebody applies who will undoubtedly not revolve and not pay a finance charge? If we reject him, do we tell him that his credit record is too good—always pays in full; never generates any delinquency charges? Or do we resort to crass capitalism and bluntly explain that we do not see how we can make any money on him? I suspect that we will do neither. We will change our product mix and our pricing system.

1.4.3   Systems approach

As profitability models are developed, we will have a single risk-management system that is used at every step of the credit process. The same basic model for each product line will be applied to the initial solicitation of the customer, evaluation, and management of the account (credit limit review, authorization, reissue/renewal, collection, assignment to outside collector, and portfolio review).

1.4.4   Privacy thrust

In the United States there has been a considerable revival of concerns about consumer privacy. Evidently, similar interests have been raised in the United Kingdom. At the moment in the United States, the primary threat is to credit reporting agencies. In some cases, the same legislators that urged that credit be granted solely on the basis of consumers' track records now seek to truncate that record. Similar privacy concerns may impede creditors' efforts to gather more data from consumers in an effort to implement profitability modelling.

1.5   Conclusion

Credit scoring offers grantors of consumer credit a far more effective technique of managing risk than is available to lenders in the commercial field. In a freely competitive market, without government intervention, it is a technique whereby the self-interest of the credit grantor coincides closely with that of the consumer. There is no economic incentive for the credit grantor to err in granting credit. At the same time, most consumers have a self-interest in using only the amounts of credit that they can repay. By the same token, credit grantors have no economic incentive to discriminate against applicants according to sex, race, or any of the other prohibited variables under ECOA. Given freedom to innovate, designers of credit-scoring systems can make significant contributions to the credit industry and to the consumers that it serves. Through conferences such as this, we can achieve a better understanding of credit scoring and foster a public policy that will benefit all consumers.

References

Avery, R. B. (1981) Indirect screening and the Equal Credit Opportunity Act. Research Papers in Banking and Financial Economics, Board of Governors of the Federal Reserve System, Washington, DC.

Boyes, W. J., Hoffman, D. L., and Low, S. A. (1989) An econometric analysis of the bank credit scoring problem. *Journal of Econometrics*, 40, 3–14.

Capon, N. (1982) Credit scoring systems: a critical analysis. *Journal of Marketing*, 46, 82–91.

Chandler, G. G. and Coffman, J. Y. (1979) A comparative analysis of empirical vs. judgmental credit evaluation. *Journal of Retail Banking*, 1, 15–26.

Chandler, G. G. and Ewert, D. C. (1976) *Discrimination on Basis of Sex under the Equal Credit Opportunity Act*. Credit Research Center, Purdue University, West Lafayette, IA.

Credit Card Redlining. (1979) Hearings before the Subcommittee on Consumer Affairs of the Committee on Banking, Housing and Urban Affairs, US Senate, 96th Cong., 1st Sess. on S15, June 4th and 5th. US Government Printing Office, Washington, DC.

(1989) Anon. Credit where it's due. *Which?* 317, July.

Durand, D. (1941) *Risk Elements in Consumer Instalment Financing*. National Bureau of Economic Research, New York.

Elliehausen, G. E. and Durkin, T. A. (1989) *Theory and Evidence of the Impact of Equal Credit Opportunity: An Agnostic Review of the Literature*. Credit Research Center, Purdue University, West Lafayette, IA.

Johnson, R. W. and Jackson, D. P. (1982) *The Role of Credit Scoring in Credit Evaluation*. Credit Research Center and Cooperative Extension Service, Purdue University, West Lafayette, IA.

Peck, C. J. and Adams, R. D. (1981) The net social benefits of reducing defaults in the consumer loans industry. *Journal of Economics*, 7.

Watro, P. R. (March 1988) *The Bank Credit-Card Boom: Some Explanations and Consequences, Economic Commentary*. Federal Reserve Bank of Cleveland, Cleveland, OH.

Wonderlic, E. P. (12th April 1948) Small Loan Division Bulletin No. 57, Household Finance Corp. Prospect Heights, IL.

2. Problems in applying discriminant analysis in credit-scoring models

Robert A. Eisenbeis

2.1 Introduction

Since the mid- and late-1960s credit scoring and related loan review procedures have been applied with increasing frequency by financial institutions and other creditors.[1] Chandler and Coffman (1977), for example, report that credit-scoring systems are in wide use today. However, given the proprietary nature of these systems, precious little is known about the specific content of the models. There have been several credit-scoring systems constructed by academics that have appeared in the journals. If these are representative of the types of systems actually being employed in industry, then it would appear that a number of these systems could be expected to suffer from methodological and statistical problems which may have significant implications for the hundreds employing the models.

As Chandler and Coffman (1977) point out, these problems take on increasing importance given (a) the passage of the Equal Credit Opportunity Act (ECOA) in 1974, which prohibited discrimination in the granting of credit on the basis of sex or marital status and the amendments on March 1976, which added seven other prohibited factors including race, colour, religion, national origin, age, receipt of public assistance benefits, and the good faith exercise of rights under the Consumer Credit

The following chapter, which was summarized in the *Federal Reserve Bulletin* for January 1978, was presented at the Financial Management Association Meetings, 14 October 1977. The analyses and conclusions set forth are those of the author and do not necessarily indicate concurrence by other members of the research staffs, by the Board of Governors, or by the Federal Reserve Banks.

[1] A large number of non-technical pieces have appeared discussing the use of quantitative credit-scoring models. See, for example, Abate (1969), Amstutz and Liebman (1966), Biborosch (1965, 1967), Cannellys (1967), Coakley (1970), Gooch, Wagner and Statham (1973), Hammer and Orgler (1969), Harter (1974), McGrath (1960), Roy and Lewis (1970), Roy and Sanderson (1972), Weingartner (1966), Work (1967).

Journal of Banking and Finance, 2, 205–19, 1978.

Protection Act and (b) the implementation of the Act through the Federal Reserve Regulation B. Particularly relevant to the consumer credit area are the provisions under the Act concerning the use of age in scoring models and the related interpretation under Regulation B describing the criteria scoring systems must satisfy with respect to sampling and validation before they would qualify to employ the prohibited age variable. These laws and new regulations place an important burden on any institution employing screening models to ensure that their systems are statistically and methodologically sound.

The purpose of this chapter is to review the types of credit-scoring models that have been developed. Particular emphasis in Section 2.2 is placed on the methodological approaches that have been taken in selecting and developing screening models. Section 2.3 briefly discusses the various types of scoring models that have been developed. Section 2.4 explores the statistical problems associated with those models, which have employed discriminant analysis techniques. Section 2.5 is a summary and conclusion.

2.2   Credit-scoring model methodology

While there have been a number of attempts to derive credit-scoring models, relatively few researchers have devoted specific attention to the underlying objectives one is trying to achieve in formulating or selecting among the alternative models that might be used. Notable exceptions have been Mehta (1968, 1970), Bierman and Hausman (1970), Dirickx and Wakeman (1976), Greer (1967a, b), Edmister and Schlarbaum (1974), and Long (1976).

One of the first to examine the problem of formulating an optimal credit-granting policy was Greer (1967a) who proposed two models. One was designed to determine the optimal number of credit applicants to accept by maximizing 'credit-related profits', which were a function of the present value of the profits from the current period credit sales, the present value of future profits from applicants granted credit in the current period and the present value of profits from cash sales in both the current and future period. The second model also determined the optimal number of loans to market but included consideration of the opportunity costs of granting loans to fewer than all applicants. Since this second model is formulated to differ from the first by only a constant, it is not surprising that Greer finds that the optimal number of loans to grant is the same from either model. It is important to note that this model is in fact a multi-period model in the sense that the decision on the optimal number of loans to grant in a period is dependent upon not only the future value of the loans granted but also the future value and additional business that might be gained as a result of granting a given number of loans. As formulated, the model does, however, have several limitations. First, it is based upon the firm's historical policies and portfolio experience to the extent that it relies on expressions for average default rates, costs of granting credit collections, and purchasing patterns of past customers. As such the proposed optimal policies only aid in deciding at what level to operate a *given* system. It does not aid in actually making an individual credit decision nor is it particularly useful for evaluating alternative systems not yet in operation, at least in its present form.

Shortly following Greer's work Mehta (1968, 1970) presented a series of sequential decision models using different and successively more costly bits of information to refine the credit granting process. Mehta's (1968) approach to the credit-granting process was quite straightforward and based upon two simple assumptions. First, he assumes that an individual's past credit performance serves as a useful guide to project future credit performance. Second, he argues that information is costly and not all information may be needed to make a decision on every applicant. A creditor is thus faced with the problem of deciding how much information to collect before making the credit decision. Three costs become relevant:[2]

acceptance cost = bad debt cost + investment cost + collection cost,

rejection cost = lost sales cost,

cost of further information = cost of acquiring additional information

+ cost of additional decision.

The creditor then has to go through a sequential process attempting, based upon past experience, to select the alternative which minimizes costs. Each time the alternative to seek more information is selected, more costly information is assumed to be acquired.

In this second paper Mehta (1970) extends the earlier static model to take into account optimal decisions for collection, which were previously assumed to be exogenous, and to recognize the value of future sales and credit requests that might result. A Markov process is used to estimate the values of the additional revenues and costs of collecting account, i-periods old.

Bierman and Hausman (1970) focus on the class of models involving multiple requests for single period loans. In each case it is assumed that a loan is granted and is either repaid in full or not collected and written off during the period requested. At the end of each period a new loan may be requested, and so on for n periods. The essential features of the models are that they allow for consideration of estimates of prior probabilities of collection, consideration or valuation of the customer relationship over n periods, revision of the estimates of the probabilities of repayment based upon previous periods' payment performance, incorporation of discounting in valuing future period receipts and collection costs, consideration of the probability that a customer

---

[2] Bad debt cost = (probability of nonpayment)·(variable product cost), lost sales cost = (probability of payment)·(contribution margin).

may terminate the customer relationship at some future date, and allowance for the fact that the amount of credit granted may affect repayment performance. The models are formulated as dynamic programming models in which the revisions in the estimates of collection probabilities are assumed to follow a beta distribution with parameters n and r denoting n periods and r collections. Dirickx and Wakeman (1976) extended the Bierman–Hausman models to allow for collection after the end of the first period and to allow for partial repayments. These models are still limited, however, by representing a loan as essentially a single period instrument. As such they are not particularly applicable to the installment lending area.

Edmister and Schlarbaum (1974) directly address the problems of selection and evaluation of alternative credit granting systems. Under the assumption that management's objective is to maximize the market value of shareholders' equity, they argue that the goal of any credit analysis system should be to maximize the 'expected net present value of granting loans to applicants'. They proceed to construct an objective or criterion function which is shown to be dependent on (a) a credit system's acceptance rate, (b) the expected returns and losses on good and bad loans that have been accepted, and (c) the cost of credit analysis and processing. In addition they recognize that certain dimensions of an institution's credit policies such as interest rates and collection policies will affect not only the number of applications received but also the net present values of good and bad loans. They do not deal with these endogenous components to evaluating credit systems and proceed to illustrate the selection among alternative systems with the *given* net present values and the number of applications. As such, their work is a partial equilibrium approach and non-optimal. Omission of consideration of the endogenous components eliminates the most interesting and relevant behavioural considerations in the loan-granting problem.

Long (1976) extends the Edmister and Schlarbaum approach to explicitly recognize (a) startup and updating costs, (b) variation in system efficiency over time, and (c) changes in the number and quality of loan applicants. He then proceeds to investigate the effects of alternative assumptions about system decay on update policies.

From a review of the various approaches that have been taken to formulate credit-model-selection objectives it would appear that there are several key elements to the credit-granting decision that have important implications for the construction of a credit-scoring model.

First, the credit-granting decision is in fact a multi-period problem that may, depending upon the types of credits involved, have two dimensions. In the context of the Bierman–Hausman type model, the granting of credit in one period is but part of a customer relationship which extends over many periods. The decision to grant credit affects the value of that customer relationship both over the period of a particular loan and also over the life of the customer relationship. Clearly such a view of the credit process is particularly applicable to the business loan activities of a financial institution and has in fact been modelled by Hester and Pierce (1975) and by Hester (1962). It is not, however, without relevance to the consumer lending area where it is quite clear that the provision of credit is tied or linked to the provision of other financial and non-financial services by creditors over periods greater than the life of a loan. It is also clear from the approaches of many of the authors, particularly Edmister and Schlarbaum (1974) and Long (1976), that a credit decision is really a multi-period decision over which a loan generates a flow of revenues until it is either paid off in full or defaults, after which a portion of the value of the principle may be recovered.[3] Thus, the value of a loan is determined not only by whether it is paid in full but also, in the case of default, by the length of time it is current, by collection costs, and the realizable value of any collateral that may remain. In such a framework it could be that, even if it were 100 per cent certain that a loan might not be paid in full, it may still be worthwhile granting the loan if it is current for a sufficient length of time. This is particularly true if collection costs are low, and the collateral has sufficient recovery value. The possibility that a defaulted loan may still be profitable has been given little attention in the published work to date.

Second, Mehta (1968, 1970), Bierman and Hausman (1970), and Greer (1967a, b) make the point that there is a need to consider the cost of information in formulating a credit granting scheme. To the extent that information on past credit performance, while not costless, is relevant to assessing future credit performance, there is a need to weigh the value of collecting additional information against the costs before deciding when is the appropriate time to make the credit decision.[4]

Third, most of the credit-policy models discussed explicitly or implicitly assume that the prospective lender makes a judgement of the riskiness of a borrower in terms of either default probabilities or opportunity costs in deciding whether or not to grant a loan. Greer (1967b) assumes such a ranking. Bierman and Hausman (1970) and Dirickx and Wakeman (1976) employ a Bayesian approach to estimating default probabilities. Edmister and Schlarbaum (1974), Long (1976), and Mehta (1968) rely on average historical loss experience for given categories of loans.

Finally, in multi-period-multi-decision type models, such as the customer relationship approach of Bierman and Hausman (1970) or Mehta (1970), there may be a need to readjust estimates of expected default probabilities over time based upon customer performance.

---

[3] Dirickx and Wakeman (1976) generalize the Bierman–Hausman (1970) model to include partial and/or full pay back over more than one period.

[4] Both Greer (1967b) and Chandler and Ewert (1975) address this problem directly.

Having reviewed the general approaches that have been taken to the credit-granting problem and examined what appear to be the key features that a credit-scoring model might be required to possess, we now turn to a brief review of the types of models that have been proposed in the literature to see how they measure up.

2.3   Review of credit-scoring models

In general, the credit-scoring models developed have focused on two categories of loans: (a) consumer loans including installment type lending credit cards[5] and (b) commercial loans including term loans, regular commercial and industrial loans, and loans to minorities and small businesses.[6] In addition, the models have been developed for application to two distict phases of the lending function. Most of the models have focused on the credit-granting decision, but at least three studies have dealt with the loan servicing and review functions.[7]

The typical approach in the models noted in notes 5 and 6 is to categorize sample loans into two mutually exclusive groups—'good loans' which are those that will be paid or are current and 'bad loans' which are slow paying, delinquent, or in default.[8] The bad loans are viewed as being risky while the good loans are not. Usually a discriminant function or related procedure is estimated from the pool of loans that had already been granted. A classification rule is then formulated, which is designed to distinguish, or discriminate, between the groups of good and bad loans while minimizing the overall error rates or costs of misclassification.

It is interesting to note how few of the models developed (see notes 5 and 6) actually satisfy the criteria noted in Section 2.2. For example, none of the models were specified in such a way so as to be a multi-period model, to take into account the value of the customer relationship, or to recognize that a defaulted loan may still be profitable, albeit more risky, under certain circumstances. On this latter point, the critical analytical question is not simply whether or not a loan will go into default. Rather, the problem centres on assessment of the probability of default in periods $1, 2, ..., t$.[9]

---

[5] Work on consumer lending models includes Apilado *et al.* (1974), Boggess (1967), Chatterjee and Barcun (1970), Durand (1941), Edmister and Schlarbaum (1974), Ewert and Chandler (1974), Hettenhouse and Wentworth (1971), Lane (1972), Myers and Forgy (1963), Pratt and McGhee (1967), Smith (1964).

[6] Work on commercial loans includes Altman *et al.* (1974), Bates (1973), Chesser (1974), Cohen *et al.* (1966), Edelstein (1975), Edmister (1971), Ewert (1969), Orgler (1970).

[7] Ewert and Chandler (1974), Chesser (1974), and Orgler (1970, 1971).

[8] For example, Bates (1973) classified loans more than 60 days past-due 'bad' and current loans as 'good'. Lane (1973) investigated three groups—debt counsellors, bankruptcies, and bankruptcies filed under chapter III. Edelstein (1975) defined good loans as all those whose payments were on schedule and all the others were considered to be bad loans.

[9] The models of Mehta (1968, 1970) and Bierman and Hausman (1970) suggest that the probability of default in period t may not be independent of payment performance in periods $t-1, t-2, ...,$ etc.

The only area where the reported models dealt with the criteria in Section 2.2 was in the area of estimation of default probabilities. Even here there were clear divisions among the models. Those of Lane (1972), Chatterjee and Barcun (1970), and Durand (1941) specifically had as an objective to minimize the probabilities of misclassification.[10] Most of the remaining models are silent on the objectives of their models although it is probably fair to conclude that they are implicitly attempting to minimize classification errors.

With few exceptions, then, the models discussed in this section are essentially directed towards only one dimension of the credit granting function, albeit a critical one, and that is the assessment of the likelihood that loans will default, go 'bad', or experience difficulty over their life. In this sense they are all single-period models with that period being the life of the loan. No attempt is made to determine at what specific intervals over the life of a loan it is more or less likely to default or become slow paying.[11] Within the scope of this narrower objective, we now turn attention to how well it is executed.

2.4   Statistical problems in credit-scoring models

Most of the models reviewed in the previous section suffer from statistical problems which may affect the reliability of the estimates of default probabilities. Particularly for the consumer credit-granting models, it is important to understand the dimensions of these statistical problems, since as Chandler and Coffman (1977) note, only if a credit-scoring model is 'demonstrably and statistically sound' can it satisfy the regulatory standards under the Federal Reserves Regulation B. Moreover, to the extent that a model is subject to criticism on statistical grounds, vulnerability under the 'effects test' is likely to be increased.[12]

Since all but a few of the models that have appeared in the literature have employed discriminant analysis procedures, attention is focused on the problems that can be identified with the use of this technique.[13]

---

[10] Chatterjee and Barcun (1970) did consider costs but only as a device to show how the cut-off points and error rates were shifted and not as an integral part of the model. Durand (1941) also considered costs but not as part of his empirical model.

[11] An exception is the model of Ewert and Chandler (1974) which focused on the likelihood that once a loan becomes slow paying in one period, it would continue to be slow paying in subsequent periods. This model is not, however, a credit granting model; it is a loan review and internal control model. In this respect, it is more closely linked to the work on optimal foreclosure policies of Pye and Tezel (1974) and Mitchner and Peterson (1957).

[12] See Chandler and Coffman (1977) for a discussion of the 'effect test'.

[13] The models of Chatterjee and Barcun (1970), Chesser (1974), Cohen et al. (1966), Edelstein (1975), and Smith (1964) employ other statistical methods. For a general discussion of the theory of dicriminant analysis see Eisenbeis and Avery (1972), Lachenbruch (1975), or Cooley and Lohnes (1962, 1971).

As has been noted elsewhere by Eisenbeis (1977), the statistical problems in the applied discriminant analysis literature may be categorized into about seven different types.[14] These are:

(1) violation of the assumption about the underlying distributions of the variables,
(2) use of linear discriminant functions instead of quadratic functions when the group dispersions are unequal,
(3) improper interpretation of the role of individual variables in the analysis,
(4) reductions in dimensionality,
(5) problems in the definition of the groups,
(6) use of inappropriate a priori probabilities and/or costs of misclassification,
(7) problems in the estimation of classification error rates to assess the performance of the model.

To these, a review of the credit scoring applications suggest that additional problems are associated with:

(8) selection of the analysis samples.

Each of these problem areas will be briefly discussed in turn.

2.4.1   Distributions of the variables

One of the critical assumptions in discriminant analysis is that the variables describing the members of the groups being evaluated are multivariate normally distributed. None of the models referenced in this chapter devote any attention to this problem. Clearly, those models employing categorical variables violate the distributional assumptions,[15] and hence, may be immediately open to challenge. A successful defence would have to rest on a discussion of the robustness of the procedures employed to differing distributional assumptions.[16] Alternatively, models described by Hills (1967), Linhart (1959), and Chang and Afifi (1974) employing nearest neighbour techniques or methods of subdividing the populations might be used.

2.4.2   Equal versus unequal dispersions

The decision to employ linear as opposed to quadratic discriminant analysis techniques, theoretically rest upon tests for the equality of the group dispersions. When

---

[14] Each of these issues are explored in detail in Eisenbeis (1977) with numerous references to the relevant theoretical and applied literature.

[15] See Eisenbeis (1977) for discussion and references.

[16] All of the variables in Edmister (1971) are categorical and all but one in Orgler (1970) are dummy variables.

the dispersions are equal then linear procedures should be employed and when the dispersions are unequal then quadratic procedures are appropriate.[17] Of the credit-scoring models reviewed, only Bates (1973), Lane (1972), Durand (1941), and Ewert and Chandler (1974) devoted any attention to the appropriate functional form of the model. In this connection, it should also be noted that it is easy to show that use of dummy variables in a discriminant analysis model not only implies that the distributional assumptions are violated, but also that a quadratic model should be used.

2.4.3   The role of individual variables

As Chandler and Coffman (1977) point out, there is a high probability that court tests of the validity of credit-scoring models may place constraints on the variables included in a model requiring the user to be able to demonstrate that each variable contributes significantly to the overall discriminatory power of the model. This possibility poses a serious potential problem for users of discriminant analysis procedures since there are no analogous statistical tests to those in regression analysis for the significance of individual coefficients. In the linear case, it is possible to test for the conditional significance of individual variables and presumably analoguous tests could be formulated in the quadratic case. But as of now, these tests are not widely available in usable form.[18] The lack of exact tests and the need to rely on approximations would certainly complicate the defence of many discriminant analysis credit-scoring models in court.[19]

2.4.4   Reductions in dimensionality

The problems associated with reducing the number of variables in a model pose no special problems for credit-scoring models aside from those generally noted in Eisenbeis (1977).

2.4.5   Problems in the definition of the groups

Discriminant analysis assumes that the groups being investigated are discrete and identifiable. As noted previously, in most of the applications, this has been interpreted

---

[17] Monte Carlo studies by Marks and Dunn (1974) suggest that there may be efficiency trade-offs between use of linear and quadratic rules and sample sizes. When samples are small and the number of variables relatively large, linear rules may give more efficient estimates of the expected error rates than quadratic rules even when the population dispersions are unequal.

[18] Martell (1977) and Fitts employ a test proposed by James (1954) to test for the overall significance of the model when the group dispersions are unequal.

[19] At least six alternative methods have been proposed and employed, see Altman and Eisenbeis (1978).

as categorizing loans for the purposes of estimating the scoring models as either 'good', in which case they were either current or had been paid off, or as 'bad' in which case they were in default or in some way delinquent. For the purposes of constructing the models, these groupings appear to satisfy the discriminant analysis assumptions, and pose little difficulties as long as one is willing to regard risk as a discrete rather than a continuous concept and to disregard recovery values or collateral as a means of reducing creditor risk.

2.4.6   Use of inappropriate a priori probabilities and costs of misclassification

The standard discriminant analysis classification rules—both linear and quadratic—incorporate a priori probabilities to account for the fact that the populations or groups being investigated occur with different relative frequencies in the population. Furthermore, it is also possible to adjust for the fact that one type of misclassification may even be more costly than another.[20] Relatively little attention has been paid to the selection of the appropriate a priori probabilities and most have simply assumed that both the a priori probabilities and costs of errors are equal.[21] It can be demonstrated that proper choice of the a priori probabilities is critical to assessment of the performance of the model and estimates of the default rates. Use of a priori probabilities different from the population priors will result in estimates that may bear little relationship to what might be expected when the model is applied to the population or what the true error rates should be. Moreover, it will not result in minimization of the probabilities of misclassification. In the models reviewed in this chapter, most simply assumed equal a priori probabilities or did not even mention what priors were employed.

2.4.7   Estimation of classification error rates

Particularly critical under the ECOA will be the ability to accurately illustrate or estimate the overall performance of the models in terms the objective function employed. For those attempting to minimize classification error rates; the researchers will be forced to trade off the costs of sample size and of expansion of the variance of error estimates. It has been well publicized that employing the samples used to construct the classification rules to estimate expected error rates leads to a biased and optimistic prediction of how well the model will perform. A number of alternative methods have

---

[20] The costs of errors are fixed in that it is assumed that the cost (e.g.) of a default is invariant with the characteristics of the transaction. That is, it assumes that losses or costs are the same for all errors of the same type.

[21] Only Pratt and McGhee (1967) and Hettenhouse and Wentworth (1971) consider costs at all in those models employing discriminant analysis. Chatterjee and Barcun (1970) consider costs in their nearest neighbour scheme.

been proposed, the most widely used and most expensive being the hold-out method. It is also interesting to note, however, that tests indicated that the hold-out method is not clearly superior to these alternate methods.[22] Of the applied work Orgler (1970), Ewert (1969), Ewert and Chandler (1974), Apilado *et al.* (1974), Myers and Forgy (1963), employ the hold-out method, Hettenhouse and Wentworth (1971), Bates (1973) simply allow for user selection of desired error tradeoffs, presumably based upon reclassification of the original samples. Lane (1972), Orgler (1971), and Altman *et al.* (1974) employ the original sample method, and Edmister (1971) used a synthetic method.

2.4.8   Selection of analysis samples

As Chandler (1977) notes a special problem arises in credit-scoring models because they are usually developed from samples of loans that have been granted rather than based upon lending experience with the population of potential borrowers or through-the-door applicants. Short of granting loans to all comers, the potential user of a credit-scoring model is usually forced to estimate a model with the truncated population of approved borrowers. Such a method is, however, subject to severe problems. Avery (1977) has investigated the effects on a scoring model, with known population parameters, of estimating the model with truncated-normal samples. His results are quite alarming. First, he notes, that even when the underlying populations have equal dispersions, use of truncated samples will lead one to reject the equal dispersion hypothesis and employ quadratic rather than linear rules. Furthermore, one obtains biased estimates of the group means and dispersions, the true cut-off point, and true error rates. Furthermore, the direction and extent of the bias is shown to depend upon the original truncation points and hence is not usually known *ex ante*. In most instances then, without knowing the truncation system, it is not possible to estimate which direction the bias lies. The results of Avery's work are of concern for two reasons. First, systems estimated from loans that have been granted are clearly biased, and the direction and size of that bias is not known. Second, even if a lender decided to incur the costs of granting loans to all-through-the door applicants, there is still no assurance that such a sample would be representative of the population of potential borrowers. If borrowers are aware of an institution's credit policies, then there is a self-pre-screening that can take place because of the autoregressive nature of the process so that even the resulting through-the-door samples might be biased.

Chandler and Coffman (1977) discuss several alternatives to this problem of validation including an interesting heuristic method based upon sampling theory.

---

[22] For a discussion of the methods see Eisenbeis and Avery (1972) and also Eisenbeis (1977).

Shinkel (1977) investigates two alternatives. One, employed by Long (1973), uses both 'good' and 'bad' accepted applicants together with the rejected applicants to estimate, based upon reclassification of the applicants, what proportion of the rejects are likely to be 'good' and 'bad'. The second is a method called 'augmentation' developed by Fair, Issac and Company to weight the good and bad applicants in the accepted group by an estimate of the likelihood that each would be accepted. Shinkel (1977) concludes that both methods also yield biased estimates of the predictive ability of the scoring model. Avery (1977) has proposed a maximum likelihood method to correct for the bias in the estimates of the means and dispersions to construct consistent estimates of these parameters, which can be used to construct unbiased estimates of the error rates. This area is, however, as yet a new one for investigation and promises to be important in view of ECOA.

2.5   Summary and conclusion

This chapter has reviewed the methodological foundations for the formulation and selection of credit-scoring models in order to place the applied literature in perspective. It was shown that in fact the scoring models that have appeared have focused primarily on the minimization of default rates which is in fact only one dimension of the more general credit-granting problem. To the extent that profit maximization or cost minimization is, or should be, the objective of a scoring model, then most of the applied work seems incomplete. Even ignoring these problems, it is also shown that the applied work typically suffers from statistical deficiencies. Of equal concern, is that some of the problems seem inherent in the discriminant analysis techniques employed or are not subject to easy remedy given the state of the art concerning estimation and sampling procedures.

References

Abate, Robert P. (1969) Numerical scoring systems for commercial loans. *Journal of Commercial Bank Lending*, July.

Altman, Edward I., Margaine, Michael, Schlosser, Michel, and Vernimmen, Pierre (1974) Financial and statistical analysis for commercial loan evaluation: a French experience. *Journal of Financial and Quantatitive Analysis*, March, 9(2), 195–211.

Altman, Edward I. and Eisenbeis, Robert A. (1978) Financial applications of discriminant analysis: a clarification. *Journal of Financial and Quantitative Analysis*, 13(1), 185–95.

Amstutz, Arnold E. and Liebman, Leon H. (1966) Micro-analytic customer account review. *Industrial Management Review*, Fall, 25–35.

Apilado, V. P., Warner, D. C., and Dauten, J. J. (1974) Evaluative techniques in consumer finance—experimental results and policy implications. *Journal of Financial and Quantitative Analysis*, March, 9(2), 275–83.

Avery, Robert B. (1977) Credit scoring models with discriminant analysis and truncated samples. Unpublished Paper.

Bates, Timothy (1973) An econometric analysis of lending to black businessmen. *Review of Economics and Statistics*, August, 55(3), 272–83.

Biborosch, R. A. (1965) Numerical credit scoring. *Credit World*, June.

Biborosch, R. A. (1967) Credit scoring systems have built-in bonuses. *Bankers Monthly Magazine*, March.

Bierman, H. and Hausman, W. H. (1970) The credit granting decision. *Management Science*, April, v16, 519–32.

Boggess, William P. (1967) Screen-test your credit risks. *Harvard Business Review*, November–December, 113–22.

Cannellys, Nicholas (1967) Automation and computers in commercial lending. *Journal of Commercial Bank Lending*, September.

Chandler, Gary G. and Coffman, John Y. (1977) *Using credit scoring to improve the quality of consumer receivables: legal and statistical implications*. Presented at the Financial Management Association Meetings, Seattle, WA, October 14.

Chandler, Gary G. and Ewert, David C. (1975) The value of credit reports versus their costs. *Proceedings of the Eastern Finance Association Meetings*.

Chang, P. C. and Afifi, A. A. (1974) Classification based on dichotomous and continuous variables. *Journal of the American Statistical Association*, 69(346, June).

Chatterjee, Samput and Barcun, Seymor (1970) A nonparametric approach to credit screening. *Journal of the American Statistical Association*, March, v65, 150–4.

Chesser, Delton (1974) Predicting loan noncompliance. *Journal of Commercial Bank Lending*, August.

Coakley, Wm. D. (1970) *Points for Small Loan Credit Scoring*. Burroughs Clearing House, December.

Cohen, Kalman J., Gilmore, Thomas G., and Singer, Frank A. (1966) Bank procedures for analyzing business loan applications. In *Analytical Methods in Banking* (eds. Kalman J. Cohen and Frederick F. Hammer) Irwin, Homewood IL.

Cooley, William W. and Lohnes, Paul R. (1962) *Multivariate Procedures For Behavioral Sciences*. Wiley, New York.

Cooley, William W. and Lohnes, Paul R. (1971) *Multivariate Data Analysis*. Wiley, New York.

Dirickx, Y. M. and Wakeman, L. (1976) An extension of the Bierman-Hausman model for credit-granting. *Management Science*, July, v22, 1229–37.

Durand, D. (1941) Risk elements in consumer installment lending. *Consumer Installment Financing*, 8, National Bureau of Economic Research, Inc., New York.

Eaton, M. L. (1969) Some remarks on Scheffe's solution to the Behrens–Fisher problem. *Journal of the American Statistical Association*, 64(328), 1318–22.

Eisenbeis, Robert A. (1977) Pitfalls in the application of discriminant analysis in busines, finance, and economics. *Journal of Finance*, June, v32, 875–900.

Eisenbeis, Robert A. and Avery, Robert B. (1972) *Discriminant Analysis And Classification Procedures: Theory And Applications*. D.C. Heath, Lexington, MA.

Edelstein, Robert H. (1975) Improving the selection of credit risks: an analysis of a commercial bank minority lending program. *Journal of Finance*, March, 30(1), 37–55.

Edmister, Robert O. (1971) Financial ratios and credit scoring for small business loans. *Journal of Commercial Bank Lending*, September, 10–23.

Edmister, Robert O. and Schlarbaum, Gary G. (1974) Credit policy in lending institutions. *Journal of Financial and Quantitative Analysis*, June, 9(3), 335–56.

Ewert, David C. (1969) *Trade credit management: selection of accounts receivable using a statistical model*. Paper No. 236, Institute for Research in the Behavioral, Economic, and Management Sciences, Krannert Graduate School of Industrial Administration, Purdue University, March.

Ewert, David C. and Chandler, Gary G. (1974a) Credit formulas for loan extension. *Atlanta Economic Review*, July–August, 34–7.

Ewert, David C. and Chandler, Gary G. (1974b) Monitoring slow-paying credit card accounts to improve collection efficiency. *Proceedings of the Eastern Finance Association Meetings*.

Greer, C. C. (1967a) The optimal credit acceptance policy. *Journal of Financial and Quantitative Analysis*, March, 2(4), 399–415.

Greer, C. C. (1967b) Measuring the value of information in consumer credit screening. *Management Services*, May–June.

Gooch, L. L., Wagner, G. R., and Statham, D. W. (1973) A method for obtaining personalized credit scoring systems. *Credit World*, March.

Hammer, Frederick S. and Orgler, Yair E. (1969) Developments in credit scoring for commercial loans. *Journal of Commercial Bank Lending*, July.

Harter, Thomas R. (1974) Potentials of credit scoring: myth or fact. *Credit and Financial Management*, April.

Hester, D. D. (1962) An empirical examination of a commercial bank loan offer function. *Yale Economic Essays*, Spring, 2(1), 3–57.

Hester, D. D. and Pierce, James C. (1975) *Bank Management And Portfolio Behavior*. Yale University Press, New Haven and London.

Hettenhouse, George W. and Wentworth, Jack R. (1971) Credit analysis model-a new look for credit scoring. *Journal of Commercial Bank Lending*, December.

Hills, M. (1967) Discrimination and allocation with discrete data. *Applied Statistics*, 16(3), 237–50.

James, G. S. (1954) Tests of linear hypotheses in univariate and multivariate analysis when the ratios of the population variances are unknown. *Biometrika* 41.

Lachenbruch, Peter A. (1975) *Discriminant Analysis*. Hafner Press, New York.

Lane, Sylvia (1972) Submarginal credit risk classification. *Journal of Financial and Quantitative Analysis*, January, 7(1), 1379–85.

Linhart, H. (1959) Techniques for discrimination with discrete variables. *Metrica* 2.

Long, Michael S. (1973) *Credit scoring development for optimal credit extension and management control*. Unpublished Doctoral Thesis, Purdue University.

Long, Michael S. (1976) Credit screening system selection. *Journal of Financial and Quantitative Analysis*, June, 11(2), 313–28.

Marks, Sidney and Dunn, Oliver Jean (1974) Discriminant functions when covariance matrices are unequal. *Journal of the American Statistical Association*, 69(346, June), 555–9.

Martell, Terrence and Fitts, Robert L. (1977) *Determinants or bank trust department usage*. Unpublished Paper, University of Alabama.

McGrath, James L. (1960) Improving credit evaluation with a weighted application blank. *Journal of Applied Psychology*, October, 44, 325–8.

Mehta, D. (1968) The formulation of credit policy models. *Management Science*, October, B30–B50.

Mehta, D. (1970) Optimal credit policy selection: a dynamic approach. *Journal of Financial and Quantitative Analysis*, December, 5(4/5), 421–44.

Mitchner, Morton and Peterson, Raymond P. (1957) An operations-research study of the collection of defaulted loans. *Operations Research*, August, 5(4), 522–45.

Myers, J. H. and Forgy, E. W. (1963) The development or numerical credit evaluation systems. *Journal of the American Statistical Association*, September, v58, 799–806.

Orgler, Yair E. (1970) A credit scoring model for commercial loans. *Journal of Money Credit and Banking*, November, 2(4), 435–45.

Orgler, Yair, E. (1971) Evaluation of consumer loan portfolios with credit scoring models. *Journal of Bank Research*, Spring.

Pratt, R. J. A. and McGhee (1967) *An application of multivariate statistical techniques as an aid in decision making with regard to applications for credit*. Investigation of Corporate Credit and Risk Policies Working Paper No. 2, Graduate School of Business, University of Pittsburgh.

Pye, Gordon and Tezel, Ahmet (1974) Optimal foreclosure policies. *Management Science*, October, 141–7.

Roy, Herbert J. H. and Lewis, Edward M. (1970) Overcoming obstacles in using credit scoring systems. *Credit World*, June.

Roy, Herbert J. H. and Sanderson, R. D. (1972) Human judgement vs. credit scoring. *Credit World*, November.

Shinkel, Bernard A. (1977) *Alternative methodologies to reduce selection bias in credit scoring*. Paper presented at the 1977 Financial Management Association Meetings in Seattle, WA, October 14.

Smith, P. F. (1964) Measuring risks on consumer installment credit. *Management Science*, November, 327–40.

Weingartner, H. Martin (1966) Concepts and utilization of credit scoring techniques. *Banking*, February, v58, 51–3.

Work, Gerald R. (1967) Loan decision making and the critical assumption. *Journal of Commercial Bank Lending*, October.

3. Behaviour scoring and adaptive control systems

M. A. Hopper and E. M. Lewis

3.1 Introduction

Every credit grantor has in effect a set of strategies that specify how each aspect of the credit portfolio is to be managed. There is a strategy for handling delinquent accounts; for each stage of delinquency and account condition a specific action is called for. There is a strategy for credit limits, how they are to be set and how they are to be changed. There is a strategy for reissuing credit cards. There is a strategy for handling accounts that are over limit. There are even rules for the treatment of satisfactory accounts and these rules also constitute a strategy.

However, traditional credit strategies fail to take advantage of the power that is available in the data processing system and in modern statistical methods. In consequence, accounts that should, and could, be treated differently because they present different risks are treated alike, to the disadvantage of both the credit grantor and the customer. It is also usually the case that the automated billing systems normally produce reports on each credit portfolio as a whole and do not address the individual aspects of management's strategies. For example, a report may show the total number of accounts that were delinquent on the last cycle and that are now current, but does not show how many delinquent accounts recovered following the application of each of several alternative collection strategies.

Traditional practice, bound as it is by the limitation of the manner in which strategies are expressed and executed, and by the limitations of reporting, does not permit management to examine the effectiveness of its strategies as compared to possible alternative strategies. An Adaptive Control System (ACS) addresses these shortcomings

In *Credit Scoring and Credit Control*, (eds. Thomas, Crook, and Edelman), pp. 257–76. OUP, Oxford 2002.

directly: it permits the rapid and accurate installation of strategies, the prompt evaluation of strategies, and the efficient replacement of strategies whose utility is inferior or is diminishing, with strategies that are more effective. In addition, ACS provides its users with the powerful tool of Behaviour Scoring, a procedure for the determination of the risk presented by each account, which permits accounts to be differentiated more precisely than has been possible in the past, allowing the description and application of powerful and effective strategies in all aspects of credit portfolio management.

3.2   Strategy

Adaptive Control System, being able to differentiate sharply among accounts, permits management to express its strategies regarding many account risk groups with a precision never before possible. An example will illustrate this point.

Consider the following strategy, described here in words and schematically in Fig. 3.1:

1. For all accounts now one cycle delinquent, send Reminder Letter # 1 at 45 days delinquent.
2. For all accounts now two cycles delinquent, with a balance of less than $300, send reminder letter # 2 at 75 days delinquent.
3. For all accounts now two cycles delinquent, with a balance of $300 or more, send to collectors queue at 75 days delinquent.
4. For all accounts now three or more cycles delinquent, send to collectors queue.

Note that this strategy, like most traditional delinquent account strategies, does not consider the history of an account or the degree of risk that it presents. However,

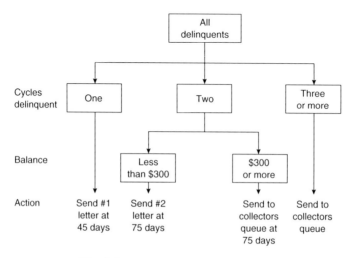

Fig. 3.1   Traditional collection strategy.

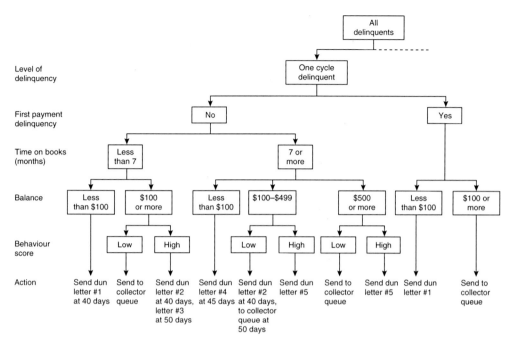

Fig. 3.2 Example of collection strategy.

even this rather simple strategy illustrates that each strategy consists of two major parts: the division of the whole body of accounts under consideration into groups, and the specific treatment that is to be applied to each of the differentiated groups.

Consider as an alternative, the following strategy, described in schematic form in Fig. 3.2. A schematic description is appropriate, since a prose description is both cumbersome and is liable to be incomplete. (The strategy in the figure covers only one of the three branches shown in Fig. 3.1, the remainder of the strategy applies to the other branches but is not shown in this illustration.)

While the strategy shown in Fig. 3.2 appears complicated, once it has been stated, its installation and execution adds no burden to management since the load is absorbed by the data processing facility; computers are allowed to do what they are designed for.

Note that the strategy illustrated in Fig. 3.1 showed that all one-cycle delinquents are to be treated in the same way. In this new strategy, accounts are differentiated into 10 separate groups, and these receive not one, but six separate treatments.

3.3 Champion versus challenger

After the strategy illustrated in Fig. 3.2 has been in effect for some time, the financial reports will show the status of the delinquent accounts. Are the figures for numbers of accounts delinquent and total dollars delinquent acceptable? While any level of delinquency might be considered unsatisfactory, reality tells us that some level of delinquency is to be expected. Each management will have its own view of this matter, but it is important to ask the question: Would a different strategy produce better results?

The central feature of the ACS is that management has the power to address this question and to find the answer. The best way to find out if it is possible to reduce delinquencies is to try another collection strategy and then compare the results. The collection strategy that is in place, that is, what is currently considered to be the best strategy, is called the Champion, and the alternative strategy that will be compared to the Champion is, naturally, the Challenger.

To find out which of the two produces better results, the Champion and the Challenger are permitted to operate and the reports of the results are compared as soon as they are available. Sufficient time must be permitted to pass so that transient results do not mask the real power of the two contenders. If the Champion produces superior results, then the Challenger is discarded and a new Challenger is invented and the test is repeated. The results that are produced by the original Challenger will probably suggest the direction in which changes should be made to improve performance. If the Challenger proves superior to the Champion, then it becomes the new Champion. In this case, too, a new Challenger is invented and the test procedure is continued, since any Champion may be unseated at any time.

The operation of two competing strategies at the same time requires some attention, since it is impossible to submit all accounts to both of the competitors. Furthermore, since the results of the operation of the Challenger cannot be predicted with accuracy, management may quite reasonably be unwilling to send more than a small fraction of the accounts to that untested strategy.

3.3.1   Management controls Champion–Challenger contest rules

Adaptive Control System has two features that let management test Challenger strategies with confidence and with minimum risk. The first of these features lets management designate the percentage of the accounts that are to be submitted to the Challenger strategy. If the Challenger is a minor variant of the Champion, management might be willing to send 25 or even 50 per cent of the accounts to the Challenger. If on the other hand, the Challenger is dramatically different from the Champion, management may prefer to send only 4 or 5 per cent of the accounts in its direction.

When only a very small fraction of the accounts are initially sent to the Challenger, it may turn out that management develops confidence in the Challenger as soon as the first reports on the results become available. ACS lets management change the percentage of accounts treated by the various strategies at any time, so that as confidence in a strategy grows, a larger fraction of accounts can be sent to the strategy.

3.3.2   The ACS random digits

The second feature provided by ACS addresses the problem of insuring that the fractions of accounts sent to each of the contending strategies are statistically equivalent. For the performance of two strategies to be validly compared, the sets of accounts treated by the strategies must be of similar composition. The ACS random digits feature makes the necessary statistical analysis of the whole body of accounts and devises the manner in which that body can be split into two streams of statistically equivalent accounts.

3.3.3   Management may test several Challengers at once

The Champion–Challenger contest is not restricted to only one Challenger. Management can elect to have several Challengers under test at the same time, directing management-chosen fractions of the total account stream to each. This procedure produces more rapid results since it is not necessary to wait for the completion of one Champion–Challenger experiment before beginning the next.

3.3.4   Reports

When a Champion and one or more Challengers are in operation, reports are produced that allow management to assess the comparative effectiveness of each of the contenders. Reports showing the performance of two contenders, allow management to observe the results of its efforts. On the basis of such reports management might decide to send a larger fraction of the accounts to one or another of the contenders or to completely eliminate a contender that has proved to be ineffective.

3.4   The adaptive control system—ACS

The ability to experiment with the strategies used for delinquent account collection, overlimit account collection, credit limit changes, authorizations, and card reissue allows management to conduct its credit operations as an ACS.

   An ACS recognizes that the world in which we live is constantly changing, and that the solutions to yesterday's problems may not be appropriate to the problems that face us today, nor will they be adequate to those that will come in the future. Furthermore, human behaviour is an enormously complex phenomenon, and it has been shown repeatedly that to treat as the same, all individuals who are in some particular condition, such as one cycle delinquent or 10 per cent over-limit, fails to take advantage of the improvements that are attainable by a more detailed differentiation among accounts.

3.4.1   ACS—tools for dealing with complexity and change

The ACS provides the tools for dealing with complexity and change. By constantly testing the possibility that a current Champion no longer produces the best results, changes in the make-up of the customer population and in the economic environment can be detected and productive actions can be taken. The credit function can adapt to the new conditions. Note that it is not necessary to know whether it is the customer population that has changed or the economy that has developed some new characteristics; what is important is the detection of the fact of a change and the adaptation of the system in such a way as to benefit from the change, or at worst to avoid damage from it. (Investigation of the nature of detected changes is a useful process, and much guidance can be derived from it, but that type of analysis is not an integral part of the ACS.)

Since change and complexity are always with us, an ACS is an on-going process, not a temporary expedient. However, since the expression and installation of new Challenger strategies is easy, and the production of the appropriate reports entirely under the control of credit management without calling for programming changes by systems staff, the on-going nature of Adaptive Control should quickly become a normal part of the routine of the credit operation. The most demanding part of the process is the invention of new strategies, especially at first. It is not always easy to invent new ways by which to differentiate accounts, nor is it always simple to devise new account treatments. Proposed Challengers will appear enormously complex compared with current practice, but as management becomes familiar with the ease with which new strategies are expressed and installed, subsequent Challengers will be invented freely.

3.5   Account differentiation by risk-behaviour scoring

Accounts can be differentiated one from the other by many account attributes. In considering delinquent accounts, the differentiation can include, among other items, the level of delinquency, whether a payment ever made, time on books, amount of delinquency, whether the account is over limit or not, whether or not the account has ever been delinquent in the past, and the highest previous delinquency, both in level and dollar amount.

```
Score              Odds
 440  ........... 80/1
 420  ........... 40/1
 400  ........... 20/1
 380  ........... 10/1
 360  ...........  5/1
 340  ...........  2/1
```

Fig. 3.3 Behaviour score and odds.

Adaptive Control System provides one additional means for the differentiation of accounts: the measure of the risk of continued delinquency that is presented by the account. This is done through the use of the risk calculation tool known as behaviour scoring.

Behaviour scoring is a tool that establishes the probability that an account will remain in, or return to, a satisfactory condition. Every credit manager, when examining an account, attempts to predict whether or not that account will remain satisfactory or, if currently unsatisfactory, will return to a satisfactory condition. Behaviour scoring allows credit managers to determine the numerical value for the probability that an account will be satisfactory in the future. A high score, such as 440 in Fig. 3.3, might indicate that the odds are 80 to 1 that the account will prove to be a good one, while a score of 360 might mean that the odds are only 5 to 1.

Note that behaviour scores cannot identify with certainty which individual accounts will prove satisfactory and which will not, the complexities of human behaviour and the nature of the physical world making absolute prediction impossible in any area. Behaviour scoring can only establish the probability of satisfactory performance.

The calculation of a behaviour score at every billing cycle gives management a precise measure of the current risk presented by each account, making it possible to design and to execute effective strategies for the control of the portfolio.

Behaviour scoring plays a critical role in an ACS. It provides one of the principal means of differentiating accounts by measuring the risk that each account presents. Almost every strategy expression treats high and low scoring accounts differently, many use multiple behaviour score intervals as account.

Behaviour scores are calculated by the application of a table such as is shown in Fig. 3.4.

A particular account may contain information as shown in Fig. 3.5, leading to the calculation of a score of 440, representing in this example the odds of 80 to 1 that it will remain in (or return to) a satisfactory condition.

Total payments as % of total balance for last 6 months	0–3% 60	4–8% 74	9–12% 81	13–35% 90	36–100% 81
Months since delinquency	0–3 21	4–5 54	6–9 67	10+ 79	Never 90
Purchases this period as % of balance	1–19 60	20–49 67	50–89 71	90–99 77	100+ 71
Average balance for last 6 months	<$250 62	$250–499 75	$500–3499 85	$3500+ 49	
% of balance that is cash advance	0 85	1–19 68	20–49 50	50+ 43	
Current balance as % of highest balance	1–39 95	40–69 87	70–79 80	80–89 75	90–100 71

Fig. 3.4 Score card example.

Score

Total payments as % of total balance for last 6 months	0–3% 60	4–8% 74	9–12% 81	13–35% 90	36–100% 81	74
Months since delinquency	0–3 21	4–5 54	6–9 67	10+ 79	Never 90	79
Purchases this period as % of balance	1–19 60	20–49 67	50–89 71	90–99 77	100+ 71	77
Average balance for last 6 months	<$250 62	$250–499 75	$500–3499 85	$3500+ 49		85
% of balance that is cash advance	0 85	1–19 68	20–49 50	50+ 43		50
Current balance as % of highest balance	1–39 95	40–69 87	70–79 80	80–89 75	90–100 71	75

440

Fig. 3.5 Sample score.

3.5.1 Behaviour scoring table construction

Behaviour scoring tables are constructed through an analysis of the data contained in master billing files. The analysis required for the construction of a behaviour scoring table is technically and mathematically of considerable complexity, but it is conceptually quite straightforward. The process begins by defining what is meant by a satisfactory and an unsatisfactory account. Then two groups of accounts are identified, one group consisting of accounts that were satisfactory at a specific starting date and remained satisfactory 6 months later (called Goods, for convenience), and the second group being accounts that were satisfactory on the starting date but were unsatisfactory 6 months later (called Bads, for convenience).

Account balance	% of good accounts	% of bad accounts	Odds
Less than $100	11	22	0.5/1
$100–$299	13	12	1.1/1
$300–$699	20	7	2.9/1
$700–$999	31	13	2.4/1
$1000–$1999	18	19	0.9/1
$2000 and over	7	27	0.3/1

Fig. 3.6   Example statistics.

A comparison is then made between what was known about Good accounts and Bad accounts on the starting date. Every field in the records of the two groups of accounts is considered; no preconceived notions as to what is predictive or what is not are applied.

For example, account balance, on examination, might show the percentages in Fig. 3.6. Some fields will be seen to show a considerable range of odds, and are therefore useful in prediction, while others may show very little range and will not be useful. (Figure 3.6 is an entirely fictitious example intended only to illustrate how account statistics can be examined.)

Note that in the example in Fig. 3.6, accounts with a balance between $300 and $699 show, on the basis of this fact alone, odds of almost 3 to 1 to be Good, while those with high balances have odds of only 0.3 to 1, and are nearly 10 times less likely to be Good. It must be remembered that no item is determinative of future performance and no one item is dominant in establishing a probability. It is the combination of probabilities, some of which may be quite low, that produces the final behaviour score.

The task of the builder of a behaviour scoring table is to combine the most effective set of account fields in such a way as to make the separation of the average scores of the Good and the Bad accounts as large as possible.

Behaviour scoring tables are constructed by considering every field in the account records. Behaviour score measures risk presented by an account after considering not only its current status, but also considering its history. As a result, it may classify two accounts with exactly the same current status as regards balance, delinquency, and activity, as presenting very different risks due to the importance of the account histories in predicting future behaviour. This ability to differentiate among accounts in apparently similar status is critical to ACS, since the ability to differentiate among accounts permits users to take action appropriate to risk rather than to base action on current account status alone.

3.6 Glossary

The definitions in the following Glossary are in an order that follows, as well as it can, the logic of the ACS. However, the alphabetical index given below shows the number of each item for quick reference.

Action set	6
Champion–Challenger	7
Client portfolio ID	1
Decision area	3
Differentiators	11
Exceptions scores	2.1
Exclusions	2.2
Global parameters	2
Portfolio	1
Random digit groups	8
Scenario table	6.1
Strategy	5
Strategy assignment table	10
Strategy definition tree	5.1
Strategy table	9
Tree leaf	5.3
Tree level	5.2
Triggering event	4

Portfolio and client portfolio ID. Each creditor offers one or more credit products to the public. These include various kinds of Mastercards, various Visa cards, Affinity cards, instalment loans, and various retail plans. A creditor may elect to treat each of these products differently as regards one or more of the decision areas, or it may group several for similar treatment. Any product or group of products that is treated according to the creditors' specified rules is called a portfolio. Each portfolio is identified by a unique portfolio ID.

Global parameters. Any creditor may elect to treat some accounts or some class of accounts (such as employees or special customers) in a way independent of the status of those accounts in each of the decision areas. Such accounts are identified by global parameters that override all other account conditions.

Decision area. One of the five areas in which ACS implements client strategy. The five areas are:

- Delinquent account collections
- Over limit account collections
- Credit limit changes
- Reissue
- Authorizations.

Triggering event. The condition of an account that causes that account to be sent for treatment in one or more of the decision areas. For example, an account becoming one cycle delinquent will cause it to be sent to the delinquent account collections area for treatment according to the client's strategy in such cases.

Strategy. A strategy for the treatment of accounts in any of the four account conditions consists of two parts; first, the manner in which the portfolio is divided into account condition subsets and second, the treatment to be given to each account in each account condition subset. Figure 3.7 illustrates a simple strategy. Figures 3.8–3.11 show the names given to parts of the strategy.

- Strategy definition tree: The top half of Figs 3.7–3.11, the part that separates the accounts into account condition subsets, is called the strategy definition tree.
- Tree level (Account conditions key, differentiators): The horizontal rows are called tree levels. In this case there are three levels.
- Tree leaf: Account condition subsets are also called tree leaves.

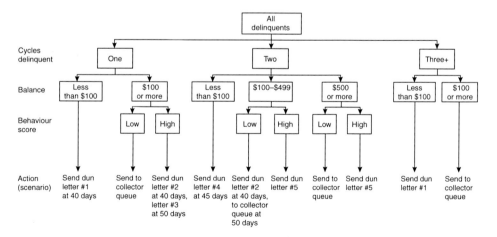

Fig. 3.7 Example of strategy.

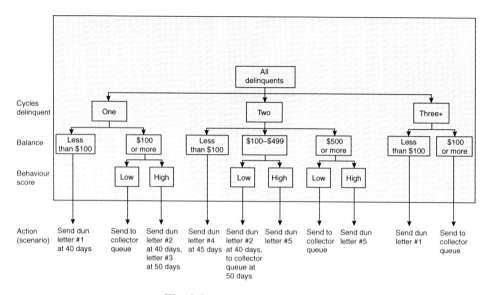

Fig. 3.8   Strategy definition tree.

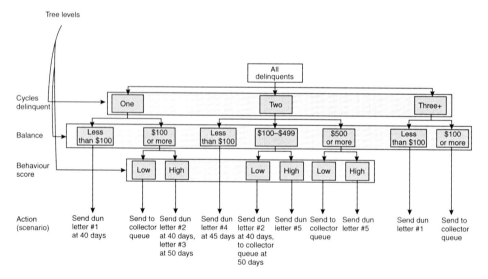

Fig. 3.9   Tree levels.

Action set.   The lower part of Figs 3.7–3.11, shows the second component of a strategy, the action set. This is the totality of actions that are taken on the accounts in that decision area.

- Scenario table: A special case of the action set applies to the treatment of accounts in the delinquent account collections decision area. Such accounts may receive

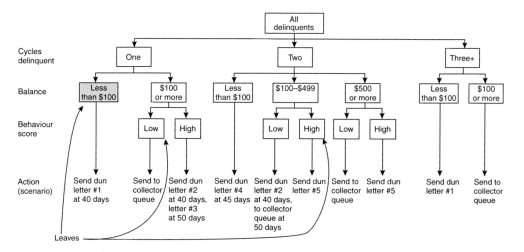

Fig. 3.10

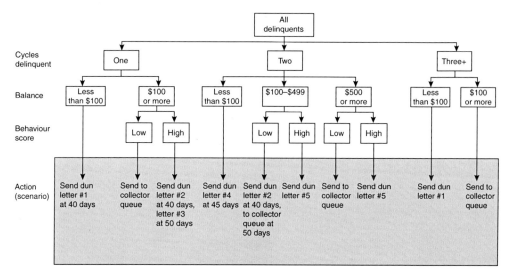

Fig. 3.11 Action set.

more than one action. For example, if an account becomes one cycle delinquent, a statement message may be sent, followed, if the account does not cure the delinquency, by a collection letter, followed by other actions if called for. The set of such sequences of actions applied in the collection case is called a scenario table.

Champion–Challenger. In conducting experiments on alternative strategies, one strategy (the one currently in place) is called the Champion and all others under test are called Challengers.

Stream splitter. In conducting experiments with Champions and Challengers, the accounts are divided in to several streams, one for the Champion and one for each Challenger. The client specifies what fractions are to be sent to each of the contenders using random digits.

Strategy table. A creditor may define many strategies for each of the decision areas. Not all of the defined strategies may be in use at any one time. The full list of all of these strategies for the five decision areas is the strategy table.

Strategy assignment table. The manner in which the account stream is split is by means of the strategy assignment table. This table assigns accounts to strategies. For example, accounts with certain random digits containing number 00 to 08 may be assigned to Challenger number I, those with number 09 to 19 to Challenger number 2, and the remainder (82t) to the Champion. These assignments are under creditor control.

Differentiators. See tree level.

Part II.   Objectives and Measures in Credit Scoring

The three chapters in this part, although they all deal with ways, 'objectives', of scoring systems are quite distinct in their intentions. Wilkie's chapter brings together a number of measures that are used to assess how well classification systems perform and explains how they are used in the credit-scoring context. Wilkinson and Tingay's chapter discusses whether one should use affordability as a criterion in consumer-credit granting. This is of relevance since in some countries like Australia legislation demands that such a criterion is used. Finally, Keeney and Oliver's chapter is the first to start building models, where the objective is the profit to the lender and the lender is able not only to accept or reject a consumer but also adjust some of the factors of the loan product so as to improve profitability. Their chapter shows though that in such cases one also needs to model the consumer's preferences, here by using a utility function, since the consumer can decide not to accept the offer. Thus it is one of the first models to address the issues that there are two decision-makers involved in the problem—the lender and the borrowing consumer.

David Wilkie had a distinguished career in the insurance industry, but is recently semi-retired, and so his chapter on measures for comparing scoring systems looks at measures that are used in other industries as well as consumer credit. He distinguishes between measures that depend on the numbers of goods and bads in the population and those that do not, and then concentrates on those that work if the score distributions are normally distributed. Nowadays one would perhaps differentiate more between those that describe the scorecards general properties and those that describe how it performs with a specific cut-off score. Wilkie's Lorenz diagram is nowadays more usually called a receiver operating curve (ROC) from its use in communications and is probably the main measure used to describe the general fit of a scorecard. It is also the case that the area between the curve and the diagonal is the concordance statistic (the chance that a good picked at random will have a higher score than a bad picked at random) and so there is a direct relationship between this and the Gini coefficient. The relationships that hold if the scores are normally distributed are interesting but not used much in reality because practitioners do not often assume the scores have such a distribution.

The chapter by Wilkinson and Tingay is quite different in that it asks whether one should ask at least two questions in credit scoring. As well as asking, 'will the consumer default on the loan', it addresses the question, 'can the consumer afford the loan?'. The chapter recounts one lender's attempts, through analysis and scorecard development—and against the current background with its UK Government-inspired focus on affordability and tackling over-indebtedness—to answer one simple question: 'does an affordability assessment add real value to the credit assessment?'.

The simple answer, and one that the uninitiated might offer, is a resounding yes. However, credit-scoring works, amongst other reasons, because of the strong correlations between scorecards and the other factors used in credit assessment. Thus, while a scorecard might look at a variety of factors not directly connected with the applicant's ability to repay—age, marital status, time at current employment—there are some strong correlations between these and affordability. Clearly, when the scorecard also takes into account income, existing credit commitments, and recent arrears history (if any), then the strong correlations are to be expected.

Before summarizing the conclusions, we should highlight one statement that is included in the chapter. The authors refer to 'quality and quantity of data across a stable lending environment—the basis for sound analytical research'. First, this is a desired state of affairs, rarely achieved, but it should still be sought. Second, when it cannot be achieved, appropriate steps should be taken to modify the analysis and/or the expectations. Too often we hear of cases where the right data was not available and so no analysis could be performed.

The authors state that affordability factors are to an extent predictive of credit risk. However, their benefit, over and above the scorecard development, is marginal and may not be justifiable against the increased costs. They close leaving us with a practical and perhaps moral, question. In some operations, an application is scored and has the affordability assessed in two separate steps. If a customer passes the score but is declined on a subjective affordability rule where we have established that affordability adds very little value to the decision process, is this responsible lending? Each lender must strive to find a balance between scoring and affordability assessment.

The last chapter in this part, by Oliver and Keeney, looks at how to model the situation where one can adjust the features of the loan product so as to try and improve the profitability of the consumer to the lender. It argues that the obvious assumption that a better deal for the company must be worse for the consumer is not necessarily the case, because they are interested in different objectives and so there may be win–win alternatives which are optimal for both.

The chapter is utility theory based and argues mainly by diagram rather than detailed mathematics and concentrates on a product like credit cards, where the two dominant features are the credit limit and the annual percentage rate (APR) on the interest charged. It starts by looking at the preferences to an individual consumer over the different features of the loan offer (APR and credit limit) and then translates these into the effect of the different offers to the lender, in terms of expected profit and percentage of the population accepting the offers made. This allows the lender to identify a set of undominated offers (in Pareto optimality terms), which are best for him; the chapter then looks at what these offers mean for the consumers. It also considers what extra information is needed to implement such strategies, namely the consumers' preferences, the probabilities that they will accept various offers and the effect of the lender on consumers accepting the various offers. Some of this information will require lenders to acquire utility preference information from their customers, like would you prefer a credit line of £5,000 with an interest rate of 14 per cent or one of £2,500 with an interest rate of 9 per cent? One also needs information about the lenders preferences between profit and market share but these should be easier to elicit as most organizations have strategies that in some sense identify their view of these tradeoffs.

Although this chapter is essentially a theoretical one it does map out how lenders can start to move to building consumer relationship management systems that are profit based and can deal with more complex questions than, 'shall we offer this consumer a loan?'. Certainly, the move to models that allow one to customize the loan (and where appropriate the price of the loan) will be one of the major advances in scoring methodology in the next decade.

4. Measures for comparing scoring systems

A. D. Wilkie

4.1 Introduction

The purpose of this note is to describe a variety of measures that can be used to compare different scoring systems with one another. A description of these measures may assist practitioners in deciding which they may find useful for their own purposes and also when discussing scoring systems with clients. It may also help clients to understand what practitioners mean when discussing what may be described as the 'relative power' of different scoring systems, when applied to the same data or to different populations. Different individuals may find some measures more intuitively appealing than others.

In every case it is assumed that each 'case' in a given data set can be classified either as 'good' or as 'bad'. For each case a number of characteristics are recorded, each of which is usually subdivided into discrete categories.

A scoring system is a set of (usually integer) scores, one score being associated with each possible category within each relevant characteristic. The score for the case is the sum of the appropriate scores for the categories applicable to that case.

In practice credit scores are usually based on such categorical attributes, but in principle there is no reason why they should not be based on numeric attributes, in which case the scoring system would consist of 'weights' to be applied to these numeric attributes, so that the score is the weighted sum of the values of the relevant attributes.

In either case the result is a 'score' for each case, by means of which it is hoped to discriminate between good and bad cases. It is usual to scale the scores so that good

In *Credit Scoring and Credit Control*, (eds. Thomas, Crook, and Edelman), pp. 123–38. OUP, Oxford 2002.

cases typically have higher scores and bad cases typically have lower scores, all within a finite positive range, which for the sake of example we may take as $0-100$.

Once a scoring system has been devised, it can be used with a 'cut-off' score, so that applications for credit whose scores exceed the cut-off score are accepted, whereas those applications whose scores equal or fall below the cut-off score are rejected.

In Section 4.2 we describe a number of measures which depend only on the distributions of scores of the good cases and bad cases, and do not depend on the proportions of good and bad cases in the total population. In Section 4.3 we describe other measures which do depend on the particular numbers of goods and bads in the population, and on other specific features. In Section 4.4 we discuss certain results that apply if the distributions of scores of good cases and of bad cases can each be approximated by a normal distribution. We make no attempt to be comprehensive in our description, nor do we consider whether the same results might apply if scores were not distributed approximately normally. In Section 4.5 we draw some conclusions.

4.2   Measures for comparing distributions of goods and bads

We start with some definitions.

Let i be the score, in the range $L-H$, that is, $L \le i \le H$ (e.g. $0 \le i \le 100$). Let $n_g(i)$, $n_b(i)$ be the numbers of good cases and bad cases with score i in a given population. Let $N_g(i)$, $N_b(i)$ be the numbers good and bad in the population with scores less than or equal to i so that

$$N_g(i) = \sum_{j=L}^{i} n_g(j)$$

and

$$N_b(i) = \sum_{j=L}^{i} N_b(j).$$

Let $N_g = N_g(H)$ and $N_b = N_b(H)$ be the total numbers of goods and bads in the population.

Let $p_g(i)$, $p_b(i)$ be the proportions of goods with score i and bads with score i in the population, so that

$$p_g(i) = n_g(i)/N_g \quad \text{and} \quad p_b(i) = n_b(i)/N_b.$$

Let $P_g(i)$, $P_b(i)$ be the proportions good and bad with scores less than or equal to i in the population so that

$$P_g(i) = N_g(i)/N_g = \sum_{j=L}^{i} p_g(j)$$

and

$$P_b(i) = N_b(i)/N_b = \sum_{j=L}^{i} p_b(j).$$

Let M_g, M_b be the mean scores of the goods and bads respectively, calculated as

$$M_g = \sum_{i=L}^{H} i p_g(i) \quad \text{and} \quad M_b = \sum_{i=L}^{H} i p_b(i).$$

Let S_g, S_b be the standard deviations of the scores of goods and bads respectively, calculated as

$$S_g = \left\{ \sum_{i=L}^{H} i^2 p_g(i) - M_g^2 \right\}^{1/2} \quad \text{and} \quad S_b = \left\{ \sum_{i=L}^{H} i^2 p_b(i) - M_b^2 \right\}^{1/2}.$$

Let S be the pooled standard deviation of the goods and bads, measured from their respective means and calculated as

$$S = \frac{\{N_g^2 S_g + N_b^2 S_b\}^{1/2}}{N_g + N_b}.$$

Note that the value of S does depend on the relative numbers of good and bad in the particular population. However, in many practical cases the values of S_b and S_g are approximately equal, in which case the value of S is not sensitive to the relative numbers of goods and bads in the population.

We can now define the first of our measures for comparing distributions of goods and bads. This measure is the standardized difference between the means of the two distributions, or the 'mean difference', which we shall denote by D, calculated as

$$D = (M_g - M_b)/S.$$

Note that the mean difference is not affected by the scaling chosen for the scores. Thus, if we replace each score i by an alternative score $k = a + bi$, with $b > 0$, and carry out all the previous calculations using k instead of i, then the calculated value of the mean difference will be unchanged.

We have already noted that in general good cases are supposed to get high scores and bad cases low scores, so that we would expect the mean score of the goods to be greater than the mean score of the bads, that is, $M_g > M_b$, so that D is positive. The higher the value of D the more the distributions of goods and bads are separated. This can be seen in Fig. 4.1 in which the value of $p_g(i)$ and $p_b(i)$ are plotted against i for a specimen population.

The scores for goods and bads show two typical (though irregular) bell-shaped distributions, and the further apart these distributions lie the greater the discrimination between goods and bads.

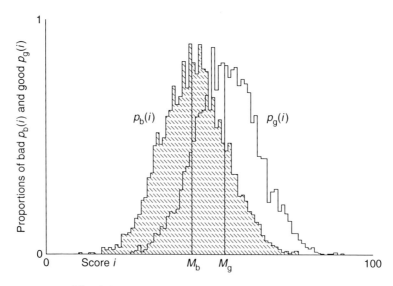

Fig. 4.1   Proportions of bad and good at each score.

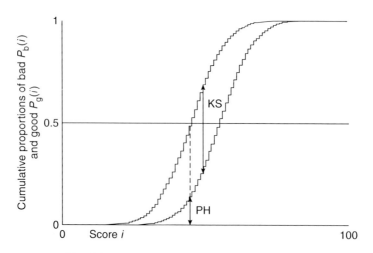

Fig. 4.2   Cumulative proportions of bad and good.

We now discuss a number of measures which depend on the cumulative distributions of goods and bads, $P_g(i)$ and $P_b(i)$.

These are plotted in Fig. 4.2 for the same specimen population as in Fig. 4.1. Note that for a given score, $P_b(i)$ is generally greater than $P_g(i)$, except at the extremes of the range of scores where they are both 0 at low scores, and both 1 at high scores.

We now define the medians of the distributions of goods and bads. The median of a distribution is the score which divides the distribution in half, with 50 per cent of cases having a score below the median, and 50 per cent above. We denote the medians of the distributions of goods and bads by Med_g and Med_b and we calculate, for example,

$$Med_g = i_{m+1} \quad \text{when} \quad P(i_m) < 0.5 < P(i_{m+1}),$$

Med_b is calculated similarly. We assume here that scores take only integer values; obvious modifications are necessary otherwise.

The medians of the distributions of goods and bads can be seen on Fig. 4.2, being the scores at which the cumulative distributions cross the horizontal line through 0.5, that is, where the cumulative distribution has reached 50 per cent.

A measure that could now be defined is the median difference, or $(Med_g - Med_b)/S$, but the value of this is likely to be very close to that of the mean difference.

A convenient specific measure of the difference between the cumulative distributions is the 'percentage of good for 50 per cent of the bads', which we shall denote 100PH.

This can be calculated from

$$PH = P_g(Med_b) = P_g(i_g) + (Med_b - i_g)P_g(i_{g+1}),$$

where $i_g < Med = b < i_{g+1}$.

The value of PH leads to a statement like: 'if the cut-off scores were set at about Med_g, 50 per cent of the present bads would be rejected and 100PH per cent of the present goods'. The lower the value of PH the more satisfactory is the discrimination between goods and bads.

The value of PH can be read off on Fig. 4.2 as the vertical coordinate of the point on the distribution of goods corresponding to the median of the bads.

A third measure of deviation between cumulative distributions is the 'maximum deviation', which is related to the Smirnov statistic used in the Kolmogorov–Smirnov test. We denote this by KS, and it is given by

$$KS = Max_i(P_b(i) - P_g(i)).$$

Let the score at which this occurs be denoted i_k. The value of i_k, and of KS can be found by calculating the values of $P_b(i) - P_g(i)$ and looking for the largest value. It is portrayed in Fig. 4.2 as the point where the cumulative distributions are furthest apart in a vertical direction. Provided that the distribution of scores is sufficiently regular, i_k can also be discovered from the point at which

$$p_b(i_k) > p_g(i_k) \quad \text{and} \quad p_b(i_{k+1}) < p_g(i_{k+1}),$$

or seen from Fig. 4.1 as the score at which the two frequency distributions cross.

A third geometrical way of displaying the distributions of goods and bads is with a 'Lorenz diagram', as shown in Fig. 4.3. In this diagram the horizontal axis represents the cumulative proportion bad, $P_b(i)$ running from 0 to 1, and the vertical axis represents the cumulative proportion good, $P_g(i)$, also running from 0 to 1. The points

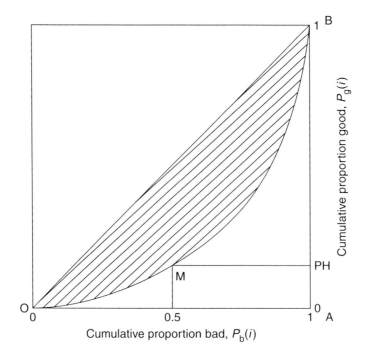

Fig. 4.3   Lorenz diagram.

$O(0, 0)$, $A(0, 1)$, and $B(1, 1)$ are marked on the diagram. One point is plotted for each score, with coordinates $P_b(i)$ and $P_g(i)$. The points for successive scores are then joined to give a 'curved' line running from O to B. The point M is also marked in the diagram, at which $P = 0.5$ and $P = PH$, the proportion good for 50 per cent of the bads.

The Gini coefficient is defined as the ratio of the area of the segment OMB to the area of the triangle OAB, that is,

$$G = \text{Area OMB/Area OAB}.$$

Since the area of the triangle OAB is $1/2$, we find that

$$G = 2 \text{ Area OMB}$$

and it is more readily calculated by calculating the area of the region below the curve, OMBA and subtracting it from the area of the triangle, giving

$$G = 1 - 2 \text{ Area OMBA}.$$

Since the points representing neighbouring scores have been joined by straight lines, we can calculate the area OMBA by the formula

$$\text{Area OMBA} = \sum_{i=L}^{H} P_b(i)(P_g(i-1) + P_g(i))/2,$$

with $P_g(L-1) = 0$.

The better the scoring system discriminates between good and bad, the larger the area of the segment OMB, and the smaller the area OMBA. At one extreme, for a 'useless' scoring system, the line OMB would coincide with the diagonal OB, and at the other extreme, for a 'perfect' scoring system, in which 100 per cent of the bads were scored before any of the goods, the line OMB would run along the lines OA and AB. The range of the Gini coefficient is therefore from 0 to 1. It may be convenient to express it as a percentage.

A measure that is particularly appropriate when a log-linear model has been fitted to derive the scoring scheme, but which is nevertheless useful in any circumstances, is the information statistic I, defined by

$$I = \sum_{i=L}^{H} (p_g(i) - p_b(i)) \log(p_g(i)/p_b(i)).$$

Provided that the scoring system is not useless, the value of I is always positive. However, if the scoring system is 'perverse', that is, gives bad cases generally higher scores than good cases, the information statistic will also be positive, so that it lacks 'direction'. This is not true of the measures we have discussed above, which will produce negative or otherwise anomalous values for a perverse scoring system. Further, sampling irregularities in scoring actual populations will increase the value of the information statistic without reflecting the true effectiveness of the scoring system. This makes it a dangerous statistic to rely on when the population sizes are small.

4.3 Measures for comparing within specific populations

The measures described in this section depend explicitly on the proportion of bads in the total population. We denote the number of cases in the total population as N_t, given by

$$N_t = N_g + N_b$$

and the proportion of bads in the total population as r, given by

$$r = N_b/N_t.$$

The proportion of goods in the population is $1 - r$.

We now consider the proportion of cases misclassified at a given score i. We assume that all cases with a score less than or equal to i are rejected, and cases with a score greater than i are accepted. The number of good cases rejected is $N_g(i)$, and the number of bad cases accepted is $N_b - N_b(i)$. The total proportion misclassified at score i, denoted $PM(i)$, is therefore given by:

$$PM(i) = (N_g(i) + (N_b - N_b(i)))/N_t$$
$$= (1-r)P_g(i) + r(1 - P_b(i)).$$

For all possible cut-off scores, i, there is one that gives the minimum value of $PM(i)$. Assuming that the number of cases in each score are sufficiently regular, this will be at the score at which the number of goods at score i equals the number of bads at score i, $n_g(i) = n_b(i)$. However, in a real population it is possible that this is at or near the lowest possible score, particularly if the proportion of bad cases in the population is fairly small. It may therefore be preferable to take into account the relative costs of rejecting a good case and accepting a bad case, as is considered below.

Let the cost of rejecting a good case, in terms of profit foregone, be C_g, and let the cost of accepting a bad case, taking account both the loss of capital and interest and administrative costs of collection, be C_b. Assume that these amounts are the same for all cases, irrespective of score, or any other feature. Then the loss incurred if the cut-off score, is chosen as i, denoted by $Loss(i)$, is given by

$$Loss(i) = (1-r)P_g(i)C_g + r(1 - P_b(i))C_b.$$

Assuming a sufficiently smooth progression of numbers, the loss is minimized at the score at which approximately

$$\frac{n_g(i)}{n_b(i)} = \frac{C_b}{C_g},$$

that is, the score at which the odds of goods versus bads is equal to the ratio of the costs of goods and bads.

It is likely that both the profit foregone for goods rejected and the costs incurred for bads accepted depends on the amount of the loan, and on the 'degree' of badness, for example, how quickly a loan falls into arrears, what proportion is recovered, what expenses are incurred in collecting or attempting to collect arrears. If such information is available then different ways of finding optimum scoring systems are appropriate, and a measure which minimizes loss is appropriate; but such methods are outside the scope of this note.

4.4   Some results when scores are normally distributed

We now make the assumption that the scores of good cases and of bad cases are each approximately normally distributed. A normal distribution applies to a variable which can take any value, x, not limited to integers, and positive or negative, with an infinite range. This cannot exactly represent scores in a practical scoring system, but the approximation may nevertheless be extremely close, and certainly useful for practical purposes.

We now denote the score by x, with $-\infty \leq x \leq \infty$. We denote the distribution functions of the goods and bads by $F_g(x)$ and $F_b(x)$, respectively, with corresponding densities $f_g(x)$ and $f_b(x)$. These correspond in concept to $P_g(i)$, $P_b(i)$, $p_g(i)$, and $p_b(i)$, respectively.

We denote the means of the distributions of goods and bads by μ_g and μ_b respectively, and the standard deviations by σ_g and σ_b. We assume that the standard deviations are equal to a common value σ.

The mean difference, D, is calculated as before as

$$D = (\mu_g - \mu_b)/\sigma.$$

Since, the scaling of the scoring system is arbitrary, we see that the difference between the distributions of goods and bads is determined wholly by the value of D, and hence that all other measures of difference, under the assumption of normality and equal standard deviation, depend only on D.

The median of a normal distribution is identical with the mean, so the median difference, defined in Section 4.2, is identical with the mean difference.

The proportion good for 50 per cent of the bads, PH, is given by the proportion of the distribution of goods that lies below the mean of the bads. This can be calculated as $N(-D)$, where $N(\cdot)$ is the normal distribution function for a unit normal variable, that is, a normally distributed variable with zero mean and unit standard deviation.

The maximum difference between the cumulative distributions, denoted KS in Section 4.2, is calculated at the point where the distributions cross, halfway between the means. The value of KS is therefore given by,

$$KS = N(D/2) - N(-D/2)$$
$$= 2N(D/2) - 1.$$

The Gini coefficient, G, is calculated as $G = 1 - 2$ Area OMBA, where OMBA is the area in Fig. 4.3. The area of OMBA is given by any of the rather cumbersome

Table 4.1   Values of selected measures for specimen values of the mean difference, D, assuming that the scores of goods and bads are normally distributed with a common standard deviation.

Mean difference, D	% good for 50% of bads, $PH = N(-D)$ ($\times 100$)	Maximum deviation, $KS = 2N(D/2) - 1$ ($\times 100$)	Gini coefficient, G (approximate) ($\times 100$)	Information statistic, $I = D^2$
0.25	40.1	9.9	14.0	0.06
0.5	30.9	19.7	27.6	0.25
0.75	22.7	29.2	40.4	0.56
1.0	15.9	38.3	52.0	1.00
1.25	10.6	46.8	62.3	1.56
1.5	6.7	54.7	71.1	2.25
1.75	4.0	61.8	78.4	3.06
2.0	2.3	68.3	84.3	4.00

functions

$$\text{Area OMBA} = \int_0^1 F_g(F_b^{-1}(b))\, db = \int_{-\infty}^{\infty} F_g(x) f_b(x)\, dx$$

$$= 1 - \int_{-\infty}^{\infty} f_g(x) F_b(x)\, dx.$$

Any of these, however, can be calculated numerically, with the results shown in Table 4.1, which also shows the numerical values of some other measures for specimen values of D.

The information statistic, I, was defined in Section 4.2 for discrete scores. When the score is treated as continuous the appropriate formula is similar, requiring an integral rather than a summation, viz.:

$$I = \int_{-\infty}^{\infty} (f_g(x) - f_b(x)) \log(f_g(x)/f_b(x))\, dx.$$

Some straightforward calculations using the formula for the normal density function show that this is equal to D^2.

One measure that relates the numbers of goods and bads at any particular score is the rate bad out of the total at that score, given by

$$n_b(i)/(n_b(i) + n_g(i)).$$

This corresponds to the probability that a case with score i will turn out to be bad. Another measure is the odds of goods versus bads, given by $n_g(i)/n_b(i)$.

We define the total odds, $TO = N_g/N_b = (1 - r)/r$, where r is the overall rate of bad defined in Section 4.3. We then define the odds at score x, $O(x)$, assuming a continuous distribution of scores, by

$$O(x) = (1 - r) f_g(x)/r f_b(x).$$

From the odds value we derive the log odds. The total log odds, LO, is given by $\log((1-r)/r)$. The log odds at score x, $LO(x)$, is given by

$$LO(x) = \log((1-r)/r) + \log(f_g(x)/f_b(x)).$$

If the scores of the goods and bads are both normally distributed, with common standard deviation σ, then the log odds at score x can be shown to be given by

$$LO(x) = LO + (xD/\sigma) - (\mu_g + \mu_b)/2\sigma,$$

so when log odds is plotted against score, it is represented by a straight line, with slope D/σ. If all scoring systems are scaled to have a common standard deviation, then the higher the value of D, the steeper is the log odds line.

Although normality of the distributions of goods and bads, along with a common standard deviation, is a sufficient condition for the log odds line to be linear, it is not a necessary one. Other possible distributions also lead to a linear log odds result. A simple example is the exponential distribution.

4.5 Conclusions

In Section 4.2 we presented a number of measures by which different scoring systems applied to the same population or different populations, could be compared. In Section 4.4 we showed that, under the assumption of normal distributions with equal standard deviations, the measures defined in Section 4.2 were all functions of one statistic, the mean difference, and so were mathematically equivalent. Scoring systems would be ranked in the same order of discriminatory power, whichever measure was used. However, even though the scores of goods and bads in any population may be approximately normally distributed, the irregularities of sampling errors and the discreteness of integer scores means that it is possible that different measures will rank scoring systems in a different sequence. In practice this is unlikely to be a problem.

A more practical problem arises where a rigid cut-off score has been applied before the population is investigated. If only cases with a score higher than the cut-off are accepted and their performance as good or bad subsequently is recorded, then the distribution of scores, at least according to the scoring system used on application, will be truncated at the cut-off point. It is possible to make inferences about what the behaviour of rejected cases might have been if they had been accepted, but it is not possible to count the results case by case.

For practical decisions about what cut-off score to use, the measures discussed in Section 4.3 may be appropriate. These, however, are dependent on the proportions of bad in a specific population, and also possibly on the financial consequences to the lender of misclassification. They are therefore not suitable for comparing scoring systems applied to different populations.

The discriminatory power of a scoring system depends not only on the methods used to construct it, which are not considered here, but also on the discriminatory power inherent in the characteristics available. If sufficiently pertinent characteristics are available, then it should be possible to devise a powerful scoring system using them. If the characteristics themselves are weak or irrelevant, they can lead only to a weak scoring system.

References

There seem to be no published references to these methods, which are nevertheless familiar to some practitioners. The Gini coefficient and Lorenz diagram are discussed in a different context in:

Kendall, Sir Maurice and Stuart, A. (1977) *The Advanced Theory of Statistics*. Vol. 1, 4th edn. Griffin, London, pp. 47–50.

5. The use of affordability data—does it add real value?

George Wilkinson and Jon Tingay

Affordability is a high profile issue. This is a case study of an unsecured personal loan operation that wanted to understand the impact of affordability data on decision-making. Four scorecards were built, including and excluding affordability information, to assess the real value that income and expenditure data adds. Ability to repay is often treated as a subjective rule. Is that right for your business and is it responsible?

5.1 Introduction

Regulators and industry practitioners have, for some time, been debating the importance and means of assessing *affordability* in the credit-granting process. Indeed, the report published by the UK Government-inspired industry taskforce on *tackling overindebtedness (July 2001)* concluded that 'Lenders should continue to invest in the development of more sophisticated scoring techniques to better identify over-commitment . . .'. It went on to say that 'Lenders who use data scoring should consider during the development of decision systems making use of all available data to assess ability to repay'.

Regulators in the United Kingdom and other countries may believe that a customer's disposable income should be the main factor in granting credit. In practice, some lenders treat the ability to repay as the *overriding* factor in the lending decision. But does a detailed assessment of a customer's income and expenditure always lead to a responsible lending decision?

Practitioners themselves have looked at various methodologies to define and assess affordability—the data used and methods of analysis vary from company to company.

Proceedings of Credit Scoring and Credit Control VII, Credit Research Centre, University of Edinburgh, 2001.

Determining income is not an exact science. Do we take basic salary (gross or net)? Do we add a percentage of overtime/commission? And what about the annual bonus? The problems with defining income aside, the common area of real difficulty is the pinning down of what constitutes expenditure. Is this just mortgage/rent? Are fixed term credit agreements included? If so, is it only when the agreement has more than 6 months still to run? What about revolving facilities—is the limit itself counted or the minimum monthly payment, or average balance over say the last 3 months? Then we get on to areas such as life assurance payments, endowments, maintenance—where does this stop? And, by the way, how does the lender verify all this information that the customer gives over the telephone, without them having last month's salary slip and bills to hand, and still give an instant and responsible decision?

So, all in all, defining affordability, let alone verifying and assessing it, gives a very hazy picture. But does it really matter? Can a simple assessment of income and expenditure give as a good a guide as a complex ratio that demands to know every last detail on bonus, overtime, household bills, investments, and occasionally even entertainment? Also, how do we allow for wide variations experienced in reality on many live cases? After all we know that income and expenditure is cumbersome to collect, almost impossible to verify and perhaps even prone to exaggeration.

Ultimately, does affordability add *real* value to the lending decision?

There is an apparent lack of empirical evidence to answer this fundamental question, but for one lender it has been partially answered and the approach and findings are now discussed.

5.2   The organization

The lender who commissioned this piece of work is a major organization with a size-able unsecured personal loan book, drawing customers from what could be described as the mass market. They are fully committed to automated decision systems wit-nessed over a number of generations of scorecards, with segmentation focusing on homogenous subpopulations. Reject rates are high as the applicant risk is significant and customers are offered terms through risk based pricing. They currently apply affordability checks to a significant number of applicants and this is costly. Not all organizations are provided with complete income and expenditure facts, or are in a position to accept their accuracy.

The portfolio selected for the analysis had a mass-market high-risk customer base. This was chosen because it was thought to have the type of customer who would be most susceptible to affordability problems.

Any major changes to the marketing of loans, the size of the loan offered, and the interest rate used could change the conclusions reached here.

5.2.1   Analysis foundations

The data available for assessing the added value of affordability was of good quality, even on elusive income and expenditure because of the efforts made by the company staff. Samples available for analysis contained several thousand bad customers and tens of thousands of rejected and good customers. The applicant population and scorecard performance has remained fairly stable, with business seeing gradual improvements in bad rates over time due to scoring and collections improvements.

So, quality and quantity of data across a stable lending environment—the basis for sound analytical research.

5.2.2   Analysis objectives

The primary aim of the analysis was to assess objectively the added value of affordability information in determining the likelihood that a loan would be repaid.

Of secondary consideration was the influence of credit bureau data, specifically credit searches, electoral roll information, and full payment history records (CAIS/ Insight) on assessing credit risk. The findings from this part of the analysis are not discussed here, but will be in a subsequent paper.

5.3   Affordability in its own right

The first question to answer is whether or not affordability factors are predictive of credit risk, *in their own right*.

A number of affordability factors were devised and calculated ranging from basic income declared on the application form and outstanding balances obtained via the credit bureaux, to more complex calculations involving many facets of income and expenditure. Each factor was assessed individually and a measure of predictive value established. With varying degrees of effectiveness each of these confirmed that affordability factors are to an extent predictive of credit risk.

As income increased, credit risk reduced. The larger the outstanding balance on other credit commitments registered with the bureaux, the less likely the customer is to repay the loan they are applying for; and the larger the 'free income' the more likely the lender is in having their loan repaid by the customer. This is illustrated in Fig. 5.1.

To give some perspective to the relative strength of affordability factors with more traditional risk indicators, the analysis revealed that knowing the customer's residential status was more predictive of credit risk than *any* of the affordability factors, simple or complex.

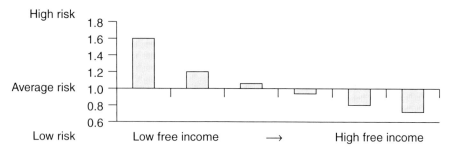

Fig. 5.1   Risk to 'free income' relationship.

Without knowing anything else about a customer that applies for a loan, knowing their income and expenditure information will give some (albeit weak) indication of their likelihood of repayment. So yes, in its own right, affordability is a 'reasonable' guide to determining likelihood of repayment.

5.4   Affordability—added value

Having established that affordability factors do have a degree of predictive value, the next and key question to answer then is, do they add value *over and above* more established indicators of risk such as an applicant's age or conduct on other existing credit agreements?

To answer this question four models were built utilizing proprietary scorecard development software. Each model had a different objective, the sum of which would enable conclusions to be drawn, objectively, as to the added value of affordability in the particular credit granting process being considered.

The first model focused solely on affordability factors. Individually, affordability factors are predictive of credit risk to varying degrees, but could a scorecard based on affordability alone provide a viable solution to the business?

The second model built on the results of the first model. Taking the 'affordability-only' scorecard as its base, model two then considered adding non-affordability factors to it—that is, their contribution was minimized.

The third model ignored affordability factors. Built purely on applicant and bureau criteria without any reference to income or expenditure.

The fourth model built on the results of the third model. Taking the 'non-affordability-only' scorecard as its base, model four then considered adding affordability factors to it, *after* all non-affordability factors had been considered—that is, the affordability contribution is minimized.

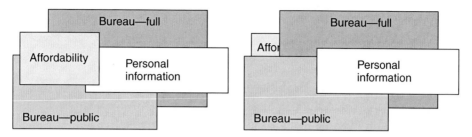

Fig. 5.2 Representation of scorecard predictive strength.

This approach would reveal how closely matched affordability was with non-affordability criteria and consequently the true added value affordability brings.

In summary, the models were built on:

- Affordability only
- Affordability (maximized) + non-affordability (minimized)
- Non-affordability only
- Non-affordability (maximized) + affordability (minimized).

The consequence of maximizing and minimizing criteria within models can probably best be described pictorially. Figure 5.2 represents two scorecards. The area of the scorecards represents their overall predictive strength (referred to as 'discrimination'). The composition of the scorecard, in terms of criteria influence, is represented by the size and visible area of the rectangles within the perimeter.

The overall area (or perimeter) of both scorecards is the same. Therefore they have equal predictive strength and would both deliver the same overall benefit to business.

The scorecard on the left is, in effect, our model two—affordability factors are maximized. We know this because we can see all its shape therefore all its predictive value has been allowed to influence the model.

The scorecard on the right is our model four—affordability factors are minimized. All other factors have been considered, with affordability factors only able to contribute to the model at the final step.

5.4.1 Measuring added value

The measures used to allow comparison between the models and assess the added value of affordability were through:

1. Scorecard discrimination (or divergence): measuring impact across the full score range. This is common practice and is an objective measure.

2. Operational tradeoff: the point at which business would be most interested in—answering the question, how many *fewer bad accounts* are taken on for the same level of business accepted?

5.4.1.1   Scorecard one: affordability factors only. Upward of 30 affordability criteria were considered for the model, of which five were significant enough to be added. The five affordability factors included income and monthly mortgage/rent payments, plus outstanding unsecured credit balances.

Of important note and interest was that only the simple affordability factors entered the scorecard. Several complex equation based affordability factors were tested here (as used by some lenders) but did not add value over and above the more simple affordability factors.

The results showed that if the lender granted loans on the basis of the 'affordability-only' scorecard they would see a *significant increase* in bad rate and bad business taken on, without any change in the volume of business accepted. Clearly this was not a viable business solution.

5.4.1.2   Scorecard two: affordability   maximized   and   non-affordability minimized. Building on the previous model containing five affordability factors, all other criteria were then considered. These were the more traditional credit-risk indicators taken from the application form and credit bureaux.

The resultant model increased in number of criteria from 5 to 14, equating to 9 non-affordability criteria.

In terms of the increase in predictive strength—taking scorecard one as our base position with a predictive strength index of say 100, scorecard two's predictive strength index increased to over 500. Looking at it the other way round, the five affordability factors contributed to only 20 per cent of the total predictive strength of model two.

Considering the impact of model two on the lender's ability to improve their accept rate versus bad rate tradeoff, this scorecard delivered operational improvements, that is to say the previous lending benchmark of bad rate could be reduced without impacting on acceptance rate.

5.4.1.3   Scorecard three: affordability factors ignored. Building the model on non-affordability factors only resulted in a weaker overall scorecard than that achieved in model two—that is, scorecard three's ability to discriminate between good and bad credit risks was reduced, when compared to scorecard two.

When criteria are removed from a model those remaining generally increase their contribution to take up some of the 'gaps' created. That is what has happened here. Although in model two affordability factors contributed around 20 per cent of the overall model strength, by removing them from model three the other criteria increased their own contribution, plus additional non-affordability criteria were added to the model, such that the overall loss of affordability factors have to an extent been mitigated. The net drop in model strength by losing the five affordability factors is around 6 per cent.

Based on the measure of overall discrimination, model two is stronger than model three hence affordability adds some value. Although, when considering the accept rate versus bad rate tradeoff for scorecard three, this shows that the lender *would* be able to reduce their bad rate position while maintaining their level of business taken on—that is, model three delivers operational improvements over the previous decision process.

So, if we can deliver an 'affordability-free' scorecard with operational tradeoff improvements (in an environment that is mature in its use of scorecards), why do we need affordability at all? This question is particularly germane since there are many issues regarding the quality of income and expenditure information.

5.4.1.4   Scorecard four: 'minimize' affordability factors. This is where the true added value of affordability is determined. Model four took scorecard three as its base and only then considered affordability factors.

The results revealed that three affordability factors were added to the model increasing the overall scorecard strength (model three to model four) by some 7 per cent.

Model four would enable the lender to achieve a reduction in bad rate from accepted business, without reducing the volumes of new accounts taken on.

5.5   Comparison of models

Using the two key measures the analysis reveals, for this lender:

Model one: the 'affordability-only' scorecard did not deliver business benefits—bad rates increased for the same level of accepted business. Therefore the 'affordability-only' scorecard is not a viable method of credit-risk assessment in its own right.

Models two, three, and four: all three scorecards delivered acceptable improvements in business tradeoff. Bad rates reduced without loss of business taken on.

Models two and four: both included a combination of affordability and non-affordability factors. Both were slightly stronger than model three, which considered no affordability at all. Both had the same overall scorecard strengths and business tradeoff results. This means that affordability factors could be minimized without detriment to the model or business decision.

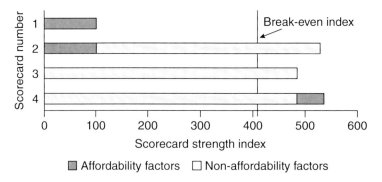

Fig. 5.3   Comparison of contributions of affordability and non-affordability factors.

These conclusions are shown in Fig. 5.3. The vertical axis represents the scorecard model number and horizontal axis, the scorecard strength. Affordability factors are the dark/solid bars and non-affordability the lighter/shaded bars.

It is easy to see the relative weakness of model one 'affordability-only' as it falls way short of the 'break-even index' of 405. This is the minimum strength the model would have to achieve to deliver a benefit to the business. It is only at this point and above that a reduction in bad rate could be achieved while maintaining the level of new accounts taken on. Below this point business would increase their bad rate for the same level of business accepted.

The difference between models three and four is the addition (minimization) of affordability factors. Again Fig. 5.3 helps to visualize its added value.

5.6   Conclusions

In conclusion, affordability does add to the lending decision, albeit marginally. Due to the demands, suspect-nature, and cost of achieving quality data capture for income and expenditure; then if it were to be used within a scorecard, model four would be preferred. Implementing model four (minimizing affordability) rather than model three (no affordability) would give the lender an improved accept rate versus bad rate tradeoff. For every 100 bad accounts taken on by model three, 96 would have been taken on by model four. This gives perspective into the *real added value* that affordability brings. This is perhaps not as much value as some would believe. Nor does it imply that subjective affordability checks have operational importance.

To further qualify this seemingly marginal benefit, it should be pointed out that the portfolio used in the analysis was chosen as it represented a mass-market high-risk customer base, perhaps the type of customer who would be most susceptible to affordability problems.

So, this then is the decision to be made by lenders—the reduction in bad rate at a cost of what, in terms of achieving good quality data capture on income and expenditure? For this lender this has been achieved through the continued efforts of staff, and time spent collecting and checking income and expenditure information is time not spent on other operational tasks.

The reason why affordability added only marginally was because its predictive value is closely correlated to more traditional and reliable assessment factors from the application form and credit bureaux. So, as scorecard developers and business practitioners we can influence the impact and use of affordability without adversely affecting the resultant lending decision.

Affordability should be minimized within scorecards giving the lender an indication of the true added value of affordability.

5.7   Closing thoughts

Lenders typically score and assess affordability independently. The lending decision is often a combination of these two factors. For example, the customer may pass the scorecard cut-off but 'fail' a subjective affordability rule and be declined. To answer a question posed at the outset, this is not necessarily responsible lending. We know from this analysis that affordability can have limited use in determining the likelihood of repayment, so its use should be balanced to reflect this and used objectively within scorecards, rather than in isolation in a subjective manner. The customer who is acceptable to the lender from the risk perspective but not the subjective ability to repay perspective is likely to seek credit elsewhere. They may be forced to get credit from a lender charging higher interest rates that would put additional financial strain on the individual. Is that responsible lending?

There is undoubtedly a tradeoff between subjective affordability rules and objective well-defined risk assessment techniques such as scorecards. Each lender needs to assess the importance and definition of affordability within their own portfolios and aim to find an equitable balance.

6. Improving lender offers using consumer preferences

Ralph L. Keeney and Robert M. Oliver

6.1 Introduction

Acquiring and managing financial loan portfolios are major components of the retail credit business in the United States. Such portfolios include household mortgages, automobile loans, equity lines of all types, and credit cards. The total amount loaned is estimated to be between 8 and 13 trillions of dollars in the United States alone (Federal Reserve 2002). It is obviously important to manage those portfolios in a way, that is, consistent with portfolio objectives.

Different lenders may naturally have different objectives that they hope to achieve in managing their portfolios. Many are means objectives, such as minimize required loan loss reserves, minimize the cost per new customer acquired, maximize the response rate on acquisitions mailings to acquire new customers, minimize time from billing to collection, and minimize the default rate on loans. Means objectives matter because they eventually have an impact on the economic performance of the portfolio. Two fundamental objectives for the economic performance of many loan portfolios are maximize profits and maximize market share.

Everyone seems to accept profit as a fundamental objective, but some are not sure that market share is. There are several reasons why it should be. First, in evaluating decisions that will affect profits over several years, one cannot with any accuracy predict what the profits will be more than 2 or 3 years into the future. One can predict profits due to different alternatives over the next 2 years, for example, and then use

Much of the basic work on this model was supported by Fair Isaac Corporation, a provider of analytics and software for the financial services industry. The work of Keeney in preparing this chapter was supported in part by Grant DMI-0003298 from the National Science Foundation.

Proceedings of Credit Scoring and Credit Control VIII, Credit Research Centre, University of Edinburgh, 2003.

market share at the end of the period to indicate the ability of the organization to make decisions to address whatever the situation is at that time. With larger market share, a sagging product can be revised or a new product introduced and sold to existing customers to improve future profits. Second, there are opportunities to cross-sell other products to existing customers and increase profits of the institution without changing the profits directly attributed to the original loan portfolio. For example, customers who currently have an auto loan with a given lender may get offers to use a credit-card. If successful, this cross-sell may increase both overall lender profits and the market-share of the credit-card portfolio. Third, existing customers become more profitable because the average cost to manage an existing loan will drop as market share (i.e. number of customers) increases and management efficiencies are introduced. Note that the reasons to include market share as an objective along with profits are the same reasons an organization might offer potential customers a product with negative expected profit. Finally, in the model developed here, the lender organization should eventually weight profits versus market share to evaluate prospective product offers. If zero weight is placed on market share, the offers that are predicted to lead to maximum expected profits are selected; analogously, a zero weight on profit focuses attention entirely on market share.

In this chapter, we develop and illustrate an effective procedure to enhance loan portfolio performance in terms of profit and market share. The general concepts can be extended to include other objectives that a loan manager may consider important. To place our work in context, consider the broad picture of a lender's financial perform-ance in Fig. 6.1. One can imagine an existing loan portfolio with an efficient frontier and a current operating point as indicated in the figure. It would be useful to improve

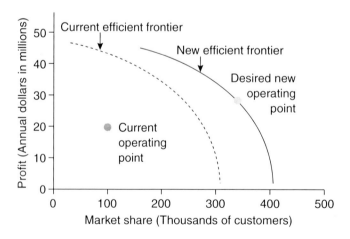

Fig. 6.1   Lender's perspective of financial performance.

the current operating point by increasing both profits and market share. In general, there are three ways to improve performance in such a situation. One needs to make decisions to achieve the following:

(1) move the current operating point towards the current efficient frontier by improving profits and/or market share,

(2) move the new operating point along the efficient frontier to find the best balance of profits and market share, and

(3) move the efficient frontier up and to the right and then follow steps one and two.

By developing a model of offers for potential new customers (i.e. consumers) that are tailored to individual preferences, we identify offers that both move the current operating point towards the efficient frontier and push the efficient frontier up and to the right. We then indicate how to select the specific offers for individual consumers that will guide the operating point to one desired by the lender on the new efficient frontier.

The focus in developing offers to consumers is to account for the preferences of each individual consumer. We examine the contributions of each of the potential offers to the profit and market share objectives of the organization. Our analysis indicates how to improve offers to individuals that simultaneously improve the potential contribution of that individual to organizational lending objectives. Collectively, all of the individuals to whom the methodology is applied will enhance the organizational profits and market share performance.

Information about consumer preferences has been used for a long time in numerous situations to guide the design of new products (Green and Wind 1973; Urban and Hauser 1980). A combination of structured qualitative information about design attributes and quantitative information about priorities can stimulate the creation of innovative and better products (Griffin and Hauser 1993; Keeney 1994; Kim and Mauborgne 1997; Ulwick 2002). There are also cases where detailed multiattribute objective functions have been assessed (Keeney and Lilien 1987) for the design of expensive business products. All of this experience has been for situations where the same product would be purchased or used by a large class of consumers. In situations such as this, a reasonable amount of time can be taken to assess each individual's preferences, since only a representative set of consumer preferences is needed.

There are three aspects of this chapter that are innovative. First, each individual consumer's preferences are explicitly used in developing appropriate product offers for that consumer only. Second, the individual's preferences and the corporate preferences for the achievement of its objectives are combined in evaluating the desirability of the prospective product offers. Third, a small class of 'win–win' offers is identified that represents the dominant set of offers for the organization and also the dominant set of offers for the individual consumer.

In Sections 6.2 and 6.3 we consider the consequences of potential product offers to an individual consumer and to a lender respectively. In Section 6.4, the set of win–win offers is identified. Implementation and application issues are considered in Section 6.5, and Section 6.6 is a summary. The ideas in this chapter are described using logic and graphical illustrations rather than mathematical formulas. It is easier to understand the concepts using a specific example. For this purpose, we have chosen a credit card. Again, however, it is important to stress that the ideas are applicable to many types of loan product and can be readily extended to include different or more objectives of both consumers and lenders.

6.2   Consequences of product offers to consumers

Consumers are interested in the quality and price of almost anything they purchase. Regarding loans, a major feature and indicator of quality is the loan amount and of price is the interest rate. Hence, in our model, the two consumer objectives are to maximize the available credit line and minimize the interest rate. Measures to indicate the degree to which these objectives are achieved are thousands of dollars for the loan amount and annual percentage rate (APR) for the interest rates. The set of all possible products to an individual consumer is illustrated in Fig. 6.2. Each specific point in the figure represents a specific product. For instance, point A represents a loan of $25,000 at a 15 per cent interest rate. Point B is a $10,000 loan at a 20 per cent interest rate.

Some aspects of consumer preferences for these potential products are obvious. Specifically, we would expect that any consumer would prefer a higher loan amount to borrow against and a lower interest rate. Figure 6.2 illustrates two iso-preference

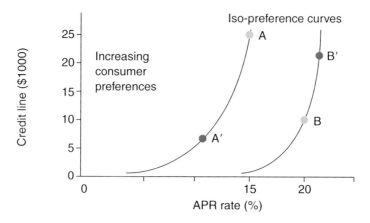

Fig. 6.2   Iso-preference curves for a single consumer for offers.

lines, which are lines composed of offers that are equally preferred by a consumer. Naturally, the consumer would prefer either offer A or A′ to either offer B or B′. Hence, the consumer's preferences increase as offers move up and to the left in the credit line–APR space.

Even though the iso-preference curves for each consumer represent more desirable offers as they move upward and to the left, they could vary greatly among consumers. The steepness of those curves would depend on the value tradeoff that the individual consumer makes between increasing the loan amount and decreasing the interest rate. A consumer who was more sensitive to the interest rate would have iso-preference curves that were much more vertical than a consumer who was more sensitive to the amount of the loan and whose iso-preference curves would be more horizontal.

6.3   Lender consequences of offers

Since the fundamental objectives of the lender are to maximize profits and market share, the contribution of any offer is the degree to which the lender's objectives are eventually affected. Let us measure profits by dollars and market share by the number of customers as indicated in Fig. 6.1. The contribution that an individual consumer might make to achieving those objectives are the expected profits contributed by the individual and the likelihood that that individual will become a customer.

To understand the consequences to the lender, we view the consumer consequence space of offers and consider the implications of different offers on lender profits and the likelihood of taking them. We first assume that the consumer will accept any product, that is, offered and then account for the likelihood that the product is really accepted (i.e. taken).

Any offer that falls on a consumer's iso-preference curve in Fig. 6.3 is, by definition, equally desirable to that particular consumer. Hence, it is reasonable to assume that any offer along that curve has an equal probability of being taken.

Now, consider contribution to profits. As one begins at the bottom of the iso-preference curve and moves up to the right, three changes occur. There is increasing revenue to the lender if there is no default on the loan. There are increasing losses to the lender if there is default, because a larger amount can be in default. Also, the default risk increases as the loan amount and interest rate both increase along the given iso-preference curve. At the lower part of the curve, there is little contribution to profit as the amount borrowed is small. As the amount increases, we would expect profit to increase before the default risk increases significantly. However, at some point, the default losses begin to contribute more than the increasing revenue without default; as a result contribution to profit would again decrease as you move up along the iso-preference curve. In summary, we find that a contribution to expected profits

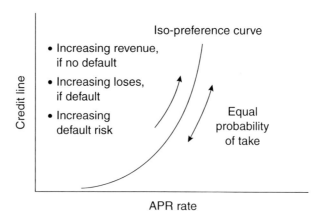

Fig. 6.3   Consumer performance along an iso-preference curve.

is initially small, increases to a single high point and then decreases monotonically along any individual iso-preference curve in Fig. 6.3.

What happens as one moves across different iso-preference curves from left to right? At the far left, the offer would not be profitable to the lending organization as the interest rate would simply be too low. At the far right, the offers would also not be profitable as credit lines with a very high interest rate would rarely be used; besides, the chance of default would be much higher. Furthermore, we expect that the likelihood of taking such an offer would be very low. Hence, if accepted, the loan might contribute negatively to expected profits, and it certainly contributes nothing if it is not taken. The same type of reasoning applies as you go from bottom to top and vary the credit line in Fig. 6.3. If the credit line is very low, there is little opportunity to make any profit. On the other hand, if the credit line is very high, the possibilities of default and large losses lead to expected negative profits if the offer is accepted.

The reasoning above indicates that the expected profit contribution to a lender from a prospective customer can be represented by a hill over the consequence space of the consumer where the height at any point on the hill corresponds to expected profit. The top of that hill represents the offer that contributes the most to expected profit. Because some individuals are poor credit risks, the top of that hill may actually be a negative value. In general, there are sophisticated models that use indicators such as the credit worthiness and financial situation of the prospective customer to determine the consequences of different offers. The determination of accept/reject cut-off scores for acquisition appears to have been first described by Lewis (1992); more recently, Hoadley and Oliver (1998) explored cut-off policies that maximize expected profit. Oliver and Wells (2001) have explicitly analysed the two objectives of expected profit and market share in retail credit portfolios and shown how the tradeoffs between these two measures affect the optimal cut-off policies. We will say more about how to determine this hill and the expected profit contours in Section 6.5 on implementation.

We now examine the implications of specific offers made by a lender in terms of the probability of take and the expected profits given that the offer is taken. Because the probability of accepting an offer along a given iso-preference curve is the same, these curves in Fig. 6.4 correspond to vertical lines in the lender consequence space of Fig. 6.5. The maximum expected profit offer on the corresponding iso-preference curve is the top of the vertical line. For this illustration, we have assumed that offers A and B are those with the maximum expected profits along the respective consumer iso-preference curves and that the expected profit of offer B is greater than that of offer A. It is perhaps worth noting that except for those offers at the top of the lines in Fig. 6.5, the other points do not represent a unique offer. For instance, there would be an offer below B on the same iso-preference curve that has the same probability of take and expected profits given take as offer B′.

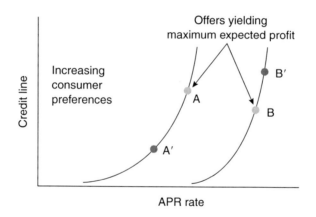

Fig. 6.4   Maximum profit offers on different iso-preferences curves.

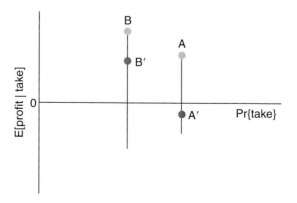

Fig. 6.5   Lender consequences of offers on iso-preference curves.

Continuing in this same fashion, by analyzing different iso-preference curves in the consumer space, we could develop the associated curves for the lender as illustrated in Fig. 6.6. The set of offers that correspond to the tops of the lines are those where the expected profits given the offer is taken is maximized for each particular level of the probability of take. It is worth noting that the maximum expected profit for some probabilities of take would be negative. Those correspond to iso-preference curves that are further to the left and up in Fig. 6.4. Offers that have a higher credit line and lower interest rates are more preferable to the consumer and are, hence, more likely to be taken.

It is of course not the expected profit given the offer is accepted that an organization is concerned about maximizing, but rather the expected profit given the offer. We can easily convert the information in Fig. 6.6 for the conditional maximum expected profit given take to the unconditional expected profit. We illustrate this change in Fig. 6.7, which simply involves multiplying the probability of take times the expected

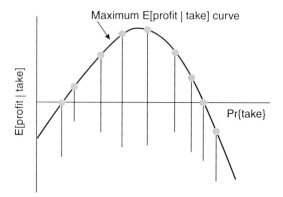

Fig. 6.6   The profile of most profitable accepted offers for lender.

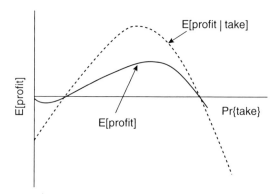

Fig. 6.7   Deriving unconditional expected profit per offer.

profit given a take to get the unconditional expected profit. Here we assume that if the offer was not taken, the expected profit is zero. Although we have not explicitly included acquisition costs in this graphical explanation of the model, it can and should be included in deciding how a loan organization should make acquisitions. However, once the acquisition is contacted and the lender is at the stage of what offer to make, the acquisition cost is essentially a sunk cost. The expected profit curve indicated in Fig. 6.7 is the one to examine for potential offers. All offers under that curve would correspond to lower contribution to expected profit with the same probability of take and expected contribution to market share.

6.4   Deriving the set of win–win offers

The expected profit line in Fig. 6.7 is redrawn in Fig. 6.8, where the dominant set of offers from the lender's perspective are those corresponding to the thicker part of that expected profit line. Quite obviously, any offer that does not translate to a point on that line is inferior to some offers that are on that line. In general, an offer with a higher probability of take and higher expected profit is dominant, from the lender's perspective, to one with a lower probability of take and lower expected profits. Thus, the only offers a lender should seriously consider for a prospective customer are those in this dominant set.

We want to examine the consequences of this dominant set of offers for the consumer. To do this, let us consider the numerical example represented by Fig. 6.9, where the capital letters refer to specific offers that have the corresponding expected profits and probabilities of take. The implications for consequences to the consumer are illustrated in Fig. 6.10. Let us go through the logic that makes this translation.

At some point (i.e. offer) in the consumer's consequence space, there is a maximum expected profit offer C as indicated. It is the top of the hill of expected profits to the lender of the different offers. As one moves in all directions from offer C, the expected profit decreases monotonically.

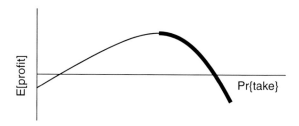

Fig. 6.8   Consequences of the set of dominant offers to the lender.

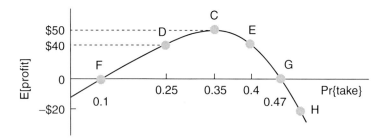

Fig. 6.9   Lender consequences of different offers.

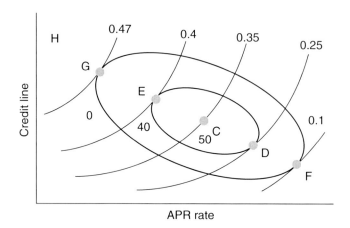

Fig. 6.10   Set of iso-profit offers for lender.

From Fig. 6.9, one can see that offers D and E each have an expected profit of $40 with different probabilities of take. These are illustrated in Fig. 6.10 on the consumer space. As one goes up the iso-preference curve that includes offer C in Fig. 6.10, there must be some point that also has an expected profit of $40 for the lender. As one decreases along that same iso-preference curve, there must be another point with an expected profit of $40 to the lender. Hence, in general, there is a shape represented by the oval here that corresponds to a contour on the expected profit hill where the expected profit is $40.

If one considers offers F and G in Fig. 6.9, the same type of logic will lead to the larger contour in Fig. 6.10. That larger contour includes offers F and G and has an expected profit of zero in our example. Offer H in Fig. 6.9, which has an expected profit of $-$20, is also shown in Fig. 6.10.

By comparing Figs 6.8 and 6.9, one sees that the set of dominant offers corresponds to those that begin with offer C and continues to offers E, G, H, and beyond to offers with a higher probability of take and a greater negative expected contribution

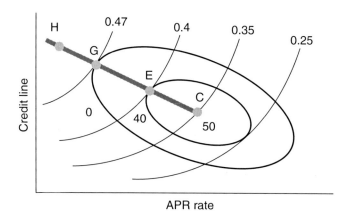

Fig. 6.11   Lender's set of dominant offers for one consumer.

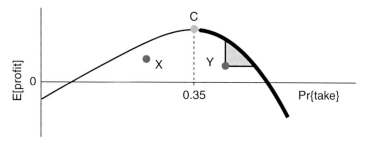

Fig. 6.12   Offers X and Y are less profitable and has a lower Pr{take} than dominant offers.

to profits. This set of dominant offers to the lender is indicated in Fig. 6.11 in the consumer consequence space.

Consider offers X and Y in Fig. 6.12 of the lender consequences space. Let's look at their implications for the consumer, as we know they are less desirable for the lender than offers on the dominant set. Offer X represents a general offer to the left of offer C in Fig. 6.12 that naturally corresponds to a lower probability of take, which indicates that offer X is also less desirable to the consumer than offer C. Thus, any offer to the right or below the 0.35 iso-preference curve in Fig. 6.13 is inferior to offer C from the customer's point of view.

Now consider offer Y indicated in Fig. 6.12. From the lender's perspective, Y is inferior to a set of offers corresponding to higher probabilities of take and higher expected profits that are up and to the right on the dominant set in Fig. 6.12. An offer Y would have the consequences to the consumer as indicated in Fig. 6.13. The vertical and horizontal lines through offer Y in Fig. 6.12 translate into the iso-preference curve and the iso-profit curve drawn through offer Y in Fig. 6.13. The offers between where the iso-preference line and iso-profit line cross the line from offer C to offer G are preferred by the consumer to offer Y. This is because they are all to the left of the

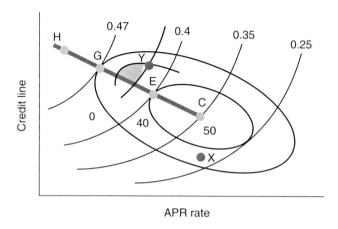

Fig. 6.13   The set of win–win offers for lender and consumer.

iso-preference curve through offer Y. These are the same offers that correspond to those that are dominant over offer Y for the lender in Fig. 6.12.

This demonstrates that the lender's set of dominant offers from C to H and beyond represented by the boldface line in Fig. 6.12 is also a set of dominant offers for the consumer represented in Fig. 6.13. In other words, this set of offers is a win–win set of offers. Given the preferences of the consumer and the objectives of profit and market share for the lender, these are the only offers that should be considered. Which of these specific offers the lender should make depends on the lender's value tradeoffs between profits and market share. These tradeoffs are discussed in the next section.

6.5   Implementation and use issues

Conceptually, the model has identified the set of offers that represent a 'sweet spot' for each consumer. Relative to all possible offers represented by the set of points in Fig. 6.13, the sweet spot of win–win offers is quite small. We now discuss how to implement the model to identify the win–win set of offers and then indicate how to select an appropriate offer for each individual consumer from this set.

To implement this model, we need three types of information: the consumer's preferences, the probabilities that consumers will accept various offers, and estimates of the consequences to the lender of various offers accepted by the consumer. We want to collect relevant data for assessing consumer preferences so that we can predict the consequences Models (references needed) in current use predict the expected profitability of a consumer given the consumer accepts a given offer. These calculations take into account the credit worthiness of the consumer, the amount of the loan and interest rate, the economic conditions that prevail at the time the loan is made, how these conditions may change in the future, and other information about the consumer's credit record, financial situation, and personal management style. It is, of course, an additional step to gain information on consumer preferences and the probability that individuals will accept the offer, but that step is one that can and should be taken.

Consumer preferences have been assessed in numerous situations with success. Typically, the experience has been with expensive items, where an individual could take a reasonable amount of time to express their preferences. When one has products like loans where hundreds may be made in a given day, one can't take a lengthy period of time to determine preferences. However, it might be only relevant to determine a couple key components of a consumer's preferences. Specifically, the most important information regarding the model here is the relative importance that an individual consumer places on increments of the loan amount and increments of the interest level. This indicates whether the consumer iso-preference curves in Fig. 6.2 are relatively steep (i.e. more vertical) or relatively flat (i.e. more horizontal) and the degree of curvature. It would be reasonable to parameterize a set of perhaps ten representations of iso-preference curves and then categorize individual consumers by asking questions to identify which set best represents their preferences. A typical question about credit-card preferences may be something like the following: 'Would you prefer a credit line of $25,000 with an interest rate of 14% or a credit line of $10,000 with an interest rate of 9%?' With the responses to a few good questions, one could identify a reasonably set of iso-preference curves.

To estimate the probability that individuals would accept different offers, one could directly ask the consumer or use general information of credit card portfolio managers about classes of consumers. Over time, by monitoring what offers individuals did accept and by categorizing individuals into types (i.e. such as by sets of iso-preference curves and financial status), one could build a useful model for the probability of acceptance.

It would be useful to assess more detailed information about corporate portfolio preferences than those for an individual consumer. On the other hand, one needs to make this assessment only once as it can be used repeatedly for evaluating offers to all prospective customers. Hence, it makes sense to spend a little effort generating this information. It is not unreasonable for an organization to think carefully about its tradeoffs between profits and market share of a credit-card portfolio. There is significant experience in assessing such organizational preferences (Keeney 1992) including preferences for the performance of card portfolios at American Express (Keeney and Lin 2000).

For use of this model, a lender might proceed as follows. First, the institution must clearly define measures for the objectives of profits and market share. Suppose the chosen measures were 'next year's profits' and 'number of customers in the portfolio at the end of the year'. Second, they should specify the operating point of their loan portfolio in terms of these measures. Then they can ask unambiguous value tradeoff questions such as: 'Suppose that over the next year you could increase your loan portfolio by 10,000 customers and maintain your expected profit, or you could keep the size of your current portfolio fixed and increase your profit by amount M. How much would M have to be in order to be indifferent between these two changes?' Suppose M was determined to be $1 million. This tradeoff indicates that an increase of 10,000 customers is equally as important as an increase in $1 million profit to the lender organization.

By translating this value tradeoff from significant amounts down to the individual level, this information implies that each additional customer added to the portfolio is as important as each additional $100 of expected profit added to the portfolio. This further implies that a 0.5 probability of gaining a customer is equally valuable as an increase profit of $50. It is this value tradeoff, that is, used in evaluating which of the alternative offers from the win–win set is best for the lender to offer.

Suppose a financial loan portfolio was currently quite profitable and the lender wished to stress the objective of increasing the size of the portfolio. Their tradeoff may be $200 per gained customer. This suggests that an offer closer to G in Fig. 6.12, and perhaps even an offer that corresponded to H with a negative contribution to expected profits, would be the preferred offer. If another organization wished to stress expected profit and was not particularly concerned about their market share, they may have a value tradeoff of $25 per increased customer. This would lead one to make offers that corresponded closely to those of offer C in Fig. 6.12. If an organization said that its only objective was to maximize profits, its value tradeoff would de facto be $0 per additional customer, and the best offer to make would be offer C.

The assessed corporate value tradeoff implies the slope of linear iso-preference curves appropriate for individual consumer offers that can be used with the win–win set of offers in Fig. 6.12 to select the optimum offer for each individual consumer. This offer is where the iso-preference curve is tangent to the win–win set of offers. However, the appropriate offer for the lender to make to an individual consumer might not necessarily be the optimum offer, as the lender may wish to have only a specific set of available offers (e.g. forty offers). In this case, the lender's value tradeoff will indicate the best offer from the specific set to better satisfy the consumer and to best contribute to the lender's portfolio objectives. If the set of available offers is sufficiently rich, this tailoring should lead to a significant contribution to the profits and market share of the lender's portfolio.

To effectively implement such a model, one would obviously need to automate it with software. Conceptually, this would not be difficult given the information on the lender organization's preferences and consumer preferences. It may naturally be a difficult task in practice. Again, the component parts of the model that estimate the potential performance of consumers are available in many cases. What is needed is to gather the information on consumer preferences and have that automatically input to the model, similar to the way that the information on the consumers' financial status gathered in interviews and from data sources is input. Also, one needs to incorporate the value tradeoffs of the lending organization into the model. One could adjust the corporate tradeoffs over time as the status on the loan portfolio performance changed and as the relative contribution of this portfolio to the operation of the organization as a whole changed.

6.6 Summary

Methodologies and procedures currently exist for the assessments of preferences required by our model (Keeney and Raiffa 1993). Utility analysis can be used to quantify company preferences for different profit and market share levels. For consumers, individuals can be asked a few questions on their application forms for loan products that would provide very useful information. Alternatively, a website could be designed to help individuals express their consumer preferences. Software could then naturally integrate these preferences with the technical analysis of the various potential products that could be offered, a market analysis that describes the likelihood of different consumers accepting different offers, and a financial analysis that examines the implications of those offers for the contribution to company profits and market share. Based on this integrative analysis, a set of win–win offers could be identified and specific offers selected for individual consumers that met their priorities and best contributed to the bottom line concerns of the lender organization.

The benefits of such a model for the consumer are obvious. Quite simply, they can get more desirable offers. Also, there can be faster response to consumers requesting a credit card.

There are numerous benefits to the lender. The overall benefit is that the model could significantly contribute to the bottom line performance of the portfolio. It can help identify the offers that are going to allow one to better increase profits and market share. It can make better offers to consumers and thereby improve one's reputation with consumers. It would be significant to be known as a company who is explicitly responsive to the preferences of individual consumers. This would naturally allow an organization to be more competitive in their offers and make better offers more quickly since the entire system could be automated. This would also reduce the costs inherent in that process.

When this methodology is used for situations with more than two objectives, the likelihood of identifying creative desireable alternatives increases. These concepts are relevant to many classes of consumer as well as business products. The greatest advantage may be for products that can be easily custom designed to meet consumer desires. One general situation where this design is very easy is when the quality characteristics of a product can be changed electronically, as with personal financial products. Other examples would involve telecommunication services (i.e. phone and online service plans) and airline travel, where quality is perhaps indicated by the time and route available to fly for a given price.

References

Federal Reserve (2002) Balance Sheet Tables- Household Debt, September, 16, p.102.

Green, P. E. and Wind, Y. (1973) *Multi-Attribute Decisions in Marketing*. Dryden Press, Hinsdale, IL.

Griffin, A. and Hauser, J. R. (1993) The voice of the customer. *Marketing Science*, 12(1), 1–27.

Hoadley, B. and Oliver, R. M. (1998) Business measures of scorecard benefit. *IMA Journal of Mathematics Applied in Business and Industry*, 9, 55–64.

Keeney, R. L. (1992) *Value-Focused Thinking*. Harvard University Press, Cambridge, MA.

Keeney, R. L. (1994) Creativity in decision making with value-focused thinking. *Sloan Management Review*, 35(4), 33–41.

Keeney, R. L. and Lilien, G. L. (1987) New industrial product design and evaluation using multiattribute value analysis. *Journal of Product Innovation Management*, 4, 185–98.

Keeney, R. L. and Lin, O. (2000) Evaluating customer acquisition at American Express using multiple objectives. *Interfaces*, 30, 31–3.

Keeney, R. L. and Raiffa, H. (1993) *Decisions with Multiple Objectives*. Cambridge University Press.

Kim, W. C. and Mauborgne, R. (1997) Value innovation: The strategic logic of high growth. *Harvard Business Review*, January–February, 103–12.

Lewis, E. M. (1992) *An Introduction to Credit Scoring*. Fair Isaac and Co., San Rafael, CA.

Oliver, R. M. and Wells, E. (2001) Efficient frontier cutoff policies in credit portfolios. *Operational Research*, 52, 1025–33.

Ulwick, A. W. (2002) Churned Customer Input Into Innovation. *Harvard Business Review*, January, 5–11.

Urban, G. L. and Hauser, J. R. (1980) *Design and Marketing of New Products*. Prentice-Hall, Englewood Cliffs, NJ.

Part III. Practical Implementation of Scoring Systems

That there are only two chapters in this part on the Practical Implementation of Scoring Systems should not be taken as a sign that scoring is all very theoretical. In fact, the converse is probably true—that scoring is full of many interesting applications. However, many of these applications have commercial value and are rarely published.

This part's two chapters are quite different. In the first, Lucas delivers a fairly practical discussion on scorecard development and monitoring. In the second, Oliver and Wells extend some basic ideas, through the use of some mathematics, to begin to address some practical problems. Together, these chapters present some strong glimpses of what is possible and what is being achieved currently within many risk management teams.

In the introductory section of his chapter, Alan Lucas refers to it as an 'essay'. The essay covers several topics as it briefly runs through some basics of scorecard development before discussing some issues of scorecard monitoring. In developing the scorecard, he considers the use of Multiple Linear Regression. While this is not necessarily the method of choice for the purists, it is used often in practice and some of its strengths and weaknesses are evident in the chapter.

Through scorecard monitoring, in which a number of scenarios is considered, Lucas discusses how one might adjust scorecards in the light of this monitoring information, introducing both statistical considerations and some practical common sense. He also considers much of the practical side of scorecard monitoring, covering the methods and the different options available when trying to make early adjustments with a new lending product or when one has some early or even mature delinquency information.

The chapter also contains some simple 'gems of wisdom', based on the author's experience and the following statement is typical:

policy rules tends to result in increased reject rates, because the rules are usually on the negative side and because they do not take account of the correlations inherent in the data.

With a chapter that was originally published in 1992, presented at a conference in 1989 and is, therefore, based on experience during the 1980s, one might reasonably question the continuing validity of the advice. The editors' response to that is that, while some aspects of the chapter are certainly dated—for example, what is described as a large development data set could now be considered small—the advice in the chapter is certainly not out of date. In fact, with the much greater computing power of the twenty-first century, it is sometimes easy to 'turn the handle' without a proper and thorough consideration and understanding of the data. To do so may result in missing a key piece of information; and following the procedures in or referred to in the chapter will help to avoid such omissions as well as allow the appropriate next steps to be taken.

In Oliver and Wells' chapter, the authors examine the process behind setting score-card cut-offs and begin to challenge existing practice. Existing practice based on arbitrary acceptance rates or marginal bad rates has come about because it is simple to understand and implement and requires little data, theory, or modelling. However, it is far from optimal. This suboptimality has been known for some time and this chapter is a good attempt to establish an alternative framework.

While the chapter is quite theoretical in parts, it also addresses and is aware of some of the practical concerns. For example, they discuss a lending business where there are two possible cut-off settings yielding the same profit. One has a high acceptance rate and one has a low acceptance rate. Lenders in practice go for the former. While it does expose the lender to much greater losses in absolute terms, which may require larger reserves to be set aside, it also presents much greater opportunities to cross-sell to the accepted applicants and for repeat business. The authors try to build this benefit into their modelling. Many other papers have extended the ideas or the practical applications, and two worth referring to are by Hoadley and Oliver and by Brown and Edelman.

Some of the mathematics and thinking that is applied to establishing cut-off policies and efficient frontiers in retail credit portfolios is quite naïve compared with the mathematics used in corporate lending and especially treasury functions. Perhaps, there is an indication here that large banks are beginning to be aware of the fact that aspects of their retail portfolios ought to be managed in the same way as their commercial and wholesale portfolios.

References

Brown, D. and Edelman, D. (2001) *Some views on setting scorecard cut-off's*. Proceedings of Credit Scoring and Credit Control VII, Credit Research Centre, University of Edinburgh.

Hoadley, B. and Oliver, R. M. (1998) Business measures of scorecard benefit. *IMA Journal of Mathematics Applied in Business and Industry*, 9, 55–64.

7. Updating scorecards: removing the mystique

Alan Lucas

7.1 Introduction and objectives

In what follows it is assumed that we are examining a credit book with one scorecard either in place or about to be installed, operating on the whole book or on a well defined subpopulation. The objectives of this chapter are threefold:

(1) to expound on a monitoring theme which will determine whether the scorecard is working 'optimally';
(2) to suggest ways of updating the scorecard if it is not perfect;
(3) third, if the scorecard is deemed to need amendment, to explain how the basic principle embodied within this chapter can be used to quantify expert opinion in situations where there is not enough data to undertake a full statistical inference (including new book situations).

At the kernel of this essay is a relationship between scorecard points and estimates of bad rates. This will be explored in some detail. The main inspiration comes from some simple mathematics behind a statistical method of scorecard building called multiple linear regression. The maths allows estimates of bad rates to be changed according to experience and gives a method for altering the associated points on the scorecard. For this reason I am going to explore regression in some detail to draw out the relevant equations.

In the following section I highlight the reasons why scorecard adjustments may be necessary and then follow up with some definitions. After this I examine scorecard

Mathematical details of the assertion that the logistic formula is the only function (of a score) with range 0–100% that satisfies both maximum likelihood constraints and good rate 'matching' are available from the author on request.

In *Credit Scoring and Credit Control*, (eds. Thomas, Crook, and Edelman), pp. 179–96. OUP, Oxford 1992.

building to establish some basic principles, subsequently moving on to techniques for monitoring scorecard misbehaviour and subsequently adjusting the scorecards, which make use of these principles. Finally I look at some time series reports that can be used as early warning indication of future troubles.

7.2   Why do scorecards need adjusting?

There are many reasons why the scorecard might not be working as effectively as it could. Typically it would have been developed on a sample of accounts that are on average 18 months old, and the development process and subsequent installation will take a further 9 months. Thus the scorecard will be over 2 years old on implementation. This means that 6 months after implementation when sufficient arrears information is available to begin drawing some tentative conclusions, the development sample will be almost 3 years old. The use of scorecards is based on the assumption that the future will be similar to the past. Often, in today's changing credit climate, this assumption will not be completely valid, and 3 years is a long time nowadays.

Some of the factors that may cause degradation of scientific models of account performance are outlined below. Some of these are under the control of the credit grantor, but most are not. The Credit Grantor can have an impact through Credit Policy, Collections Policy, and Marketing Policy. The areas outside his control are

(1) the increasing number of credit sources and credit products/facilities from competitors;
(2) legislation and credit controls (or the lack of them);
(3) the economy, especially unemployment figures and interest rates;
(4) over-commitment and changing consumer perceptions about borrowing;
(5) higher divorce rates and changes in moral values.

In parallel with these changing domains, new and enhanced data sources are becoming available (especially on large mainframe computers), which can be beneficial in appraising the creditworthiness of applicants.

Despite these factors, I would recommend that without monitoring systems that are geared up to handling adaptive scorecard adjustments, one should be wary of making changes early in the life of a card. If amendments have to be made it is obviously beneficial to make the minimal adjustments necessary rather than change the look of the whole scorecard (especially as early arrears information may be an unreliable guide). It is, however, often better to make these adjustments rather than to rely on policy rules; the reason being that increasing the number of policy rules tends to result in increased reject rates, because the rules are usually on the negative side and because they do not take account of the correlations inherent in the data.

There are two different types of situation where one might want to make scorecard adjustments. The first is where one has account delinquency information available, and the second is where there is no such information. I will deal with these separately in the following sections, but the same amendment principles are embodied in both.

As well as making changes to points values for existing characteristics, one may wish to enhance the power of one's scorecard in the light of the availability of additional sources of data, or when important data is no longer available.

These situations can arise for the following reasons:

1. When the original scorecard was developed some of the data may have been unuseable for model building but is now deemed to be important. This can have happened, for example, because the data was not available for rejects, or perhaps because certain policy rules were over-restrictive.
2. Since the scorecard was developed new data sources have become available; for example, INFOLINK's payment profile database is a valuable and predictive source of extra information describing credit history.
3. The inclusion of certain characteristics that have been found to be manipulable or illogical may no longer be practical.
4. Certain characteristics may even need refining.
5. The monitoring techniques and adjustment methods work just as well for existing and new characteristics, whether or not full or partial, or indeed no delinquency information can be obtained. If full delinquency data is available and a scorecard amendment is necessary then it may well be better to rebuild the scorecard rather than just make adjustments.

7.3 Traditional scorecard development—some pertinent features

Before launching into turbulent waters, I will relate some features one encounters when building traditional credit scorecards, which may only be obvious to those in the credit industry. These features are important in what follows.

7.3.1 Goods, bads, and rejects

Accounts are normally divided into Goods (creditworthy accounts), Bads (uncreditworthy accounts), and indeterminates. (Indeterminates are those accounts that cannot be classified as good or bad, in the main because (a) they are inactive or (b) they are not bad but insufficient time has elapsed to classify them as good). Rejected credit applications also play a role; each reject is considered to be part good and part bad. The process whereby the rejects are split into these parts is called 'reject inference'.

When building a scorecard the aim is to provide a model which distinguishes the goods from the bads. Indeterminates are normally excluded from the scorecard building process.

7.3.2   Categorical characteristics

The data on a credit applicant, obtained from application forms and other sources, can be described by a set of characteristics. A characteristic is a question about the data with mutually exclusive answers, which describes the profile of the credit applicant. Each characteristic can be either continuous or categorical (i.e. have continuous or discrete values).

For building credit scorecards, the set of possible values from a characteristic is partitioned into mutually exclusive subsets called Attributes. This partitioning is carried out for both categorical and continuous characteristics, thus effectively turning continuous characteristics into categorical ones. This grouping of continuous characteristics is a legacy from the first days of credit scoring and is an effective means of not making assumptions about the functional forms of variables. Only once have I incorporated a continuous characteristic directly within a scorecard, and I did that, after building the scorecard, by extrapolation.

Only categorical characteristics will be examined in the subsequent mathematical analyses.

7.3.3   Time lag

There is a time lag between when the data is collected and when account performance is known. It typically takes a minimum of 6 months before sufficient performance information is available on a set of accounts for it to be worthwhile making scorecard adjustments.

7.3.4   Large development data sets

Development data sets usually consist of 500–10,000 each of good, bad, and rejected accounts with typically 15–25 characteristics entering the final scorecard. The large data sets usually mean that one has at one's disposal large validation samples.

7.3.5   Stages

In practice scorecards are often built in two or three stages, where the points are frozen at each stage. The first stage might contain characteristics referred to on the application form, whereas subsequent stages might be for characteristics that require a reference to be obtained on the credit applicant. The points from the characteristics on the subsequent stages would only be utilized if a credit decision could not be made using the first-stage score alone.

7.4   The mechanics of regression

The reason I am examining linear regression is not just because it is a powerful technique that is in common use in building scorecards, but because it is the method that suggests the monitoring technique, which I am recommending to detect scorecard deficiencies. Figure 7.1 shows a scorecard built on three typical characteristics, which I will use as my example throughout.

All those credit managers here who have scorecards in place will have noticed that

(1) the points in my example are not whole numbers;
(2) a fixed value, called the 'intercept point', is added to each case's score (in this case 83.62);
(3) there is always an attribute of each characteristic that has zero points.

This is because my numbers have come straight from a regression run and have not been scaled or transformed in any way to make them all positive. The traditional scaling in fact obscures an important feature of regression, which I will highlight subsequently.

Each variable in the regression model is an attribute of a characteristic. For example, in Fig. 7.1 the variables obtained from the characteristics are numbered 1–4 (N.B.: For each characteristic one leaves one attribute out, because one can infer the

	Variable number	Goods	Bads	Good rate	Points
Overall	(0)	5448	453	92.32	83.62
Residence					
Owner	1	4878	328	93.70	11.23
Tenant		570	125	87.01	0.00
Phone					
Yes	2	5220	422	92.52	3.22
No		228	31	88.03	0.00
Age					
18–40	3	3519	366	90.58	−5.91
41–50	4	1107	60	94.86	−1.98
51+		822	27	96.82	0.00

Fig. 7.1   An example scorecard.

information on it from the other attributes and from the overall details associated with variable 0).

It can be seen that the Good Rates rather than the more common Bad Rates or Odds, have been printed. This is because it makes much of the following discussion easier to understand, as score is an indicator of good rate, that is, the higher the score the higher the expected good rate, whereas bads rates have the opposite relationship. (The bad rate is '100 —the good rate', that is, a bad rate of 8 per cent means a good rate of 92 per cent).

In order to undertake the regression procedure goods are deemed to have an actual good rate of 100 per cent and bads are given a good rate of 0 per cent (each reject would be given a value between 0 and 100 per cent, depending on the details of the method used to infer reject behaviour). The aim of the regression procedure is to obtain an estimate of the probability of good for each data point in the sample; obviously, a perfect model assigns an estimate of 100 to each good account and an estimate of 0 to each bad account. This good rate estimate, or prediction, is in fact the [unadjusted] score for the account. That is, the Predicted Good Rate for the case is obtained by summing the points in the unadjusted scorecard. This is shown in the following example.

An applicant who is on the phone, age 23 and a tenant would have a score, or estimated good rate from Fig. 7.1, of

$$83.62 + 0.00 + 3.22 - 5.91 = 80.93\%$$

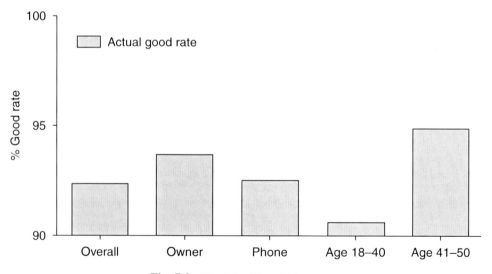

Fig. 7.2   The 'Good Rates' histogram.

The Predicted Good Rate for an Attribute (e.g. Home Owner) is obtained by averaging the case level predictions. It is thus equal to the average score for that attribute (i.e. averaged over all home owners).

The essence of the regression methodology is to use calculus to minimize a sum of squares function that brings the estimated good rates and the actual good rates as close as possible for Each Account. However, we are going to view it in a more intuitive fashion, and at attribute level rather than account level. Figure 7.2 shows the good rates (goods/total) for each attribute in a graphical form.

7.5   Regression from a new unbiased angle

All statisticians here will remember that regression boils down to

$$\text{a matrix} \times \text{points vector} = \text{another vector.}$$

In fact, a bit of simple mathematical juggling with the standard textbook equation reveals that

$$\text{conditional probabilities} \times \text{points} = \text{good rates} \tag{7.1}$$

for each variable (i.e. for each attribute of each characteristic, and overall)

There are three elements to this equation. The Points is just a list of points for each variable, variable 0 holding the intercept points. The Good Rates is a list of good rates for each variable, with the variable good rates being the overall value. The conditional probability matrix contains all two way probabilities of the form:- prob [variable a| variable b].

For example, a typical element is prob [Age 41–50 | House Owner]. The top row of the matrix contains the marginal probabilities such as prob [Age 41–50].

One further point to note about the regression equation is that unless the matrix is non-singular, one can solve it for the points. This gives:

$$\text{Points} = (\text{conditional probabilities})^{-1} \times \text{good rates} \tag{7.2}$$

An interesting philosophical point about the equation is that for a regression model all that the computer program needs to know about the data is encapsulated in pairs of attribute probabilities, that is, not triples, nor quadruples etc.

Another straightforward piece of maths shows that the following equation is universally true:

$$\text{conditional probabilities} \times \text{points} = \text{average scores} \tag{7.3}$$

Therefore equations 7.1 and 7.3 together show that regression is equivalent to:

$$\text{average scores} = \text{good rates} \tag{7.4}$$

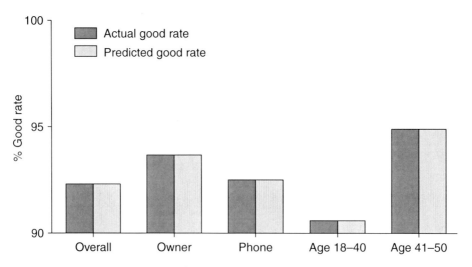

Fig. 7.3   The theory demonstrated.

but as explained in the previous section

$$\text{average scores} = \text{predicted good rates} \tag{7.5}$$

therefore regression is equivalent to

$$\text{predicted good rates} = \text{actual good rates} \tag{7.6}$$

and this is true for each attribute of each characteristic and for the population as a whole. Figure 7.3 shows this relationship for our example scorecard.

Obviously matching on good rates implies matching on bad rates (i.e. if the predicted good rates equal the actual good rates then the predicted bad rates will equal the actual bad rates).

Re-examining equation (7.6), one might ask the question 'Have we the perfect scorecard?' At first glance it might seem that regression provides a perfect linear model (i.e. scorecard). After all, if one were presented with a scorecard that purportedly gave the best possible estimates of good rates, but that understated the overall good rate for house owners and said that they were worse than tenants, one might, with some justification, remark that owners had been given too few points, and that by increasing the points one would have a better scorecard.

It seems obvious that any 'good' scorecard should be unbiased in that it should get the bad rates at least approximately correct for each attribute.

However, there is a practical observation about regression that highlights a hidden difficulty. Regression estimates can lie outside the 0–100 per cent range. That is, there is no constraint on the individual (account level) estimates of 'probability of being good'. Typically, probabilities of −30 per cent or +130 per cent are common. Some research undertaken for a typical personal loan book showed that over 20 per cent of cases had estimates outside the correct range.

The traditional way of handling this is not ideal as can be seen from the following analogy. If a lady wants to purchase a dress, but finds that it is too small for her she might consider the following options:

(1) measure herself halfway round so that she appears to be slimmer than she really is;
(2) use a stretched tape measure, again so that she appears to be slimmer than she really is;

These options represent the two popular ways of handling estimates outside 0−100 per cent, viz:

(1) regard all scores above 100 per cent as being 100 per cent and those below 0 per cent as being 0 per cent;
(2) shrink all scores into the 0−100 per cent range.

Whichever of these methods are chosen, the regression score cannot now be used as a direct predictor of good rate; but instead the good rates need re-estimating from a distribution of good and bad cases by score (for cases in the development sample). This usually involves a curve fitting exercise. Unfortunately, this re-estimation destroys the attribute level good rate matching, just as in a similar vein neither of the measurement options will make the dress fit the lady.

So, going back to the lady in the dress shop, what is the solution, (apart from dieting—which is analogous to decreasing the accept rate)? The solution for the lady is to wear a corset, that is, squeeze herself to the right size before she tries the dress on.

A similar solution exists for building scorecards. Rather than the score being an estimator of good rate, a function of the score can be used to estimate it. The function used needs to be 'monotonically increasing' and have a range of 0−100 per cent. A standard approach is to use Logistic Regression to constrain the range to 0–100 per cent. This method has the good rate matching property we desire (and in fact it can be shown that the logistic function is the only maximum likelihood estimator that is within the range 0−100 per cent and is a function of a score that allows such matching). However, for simplicity of exposition I will confine the analysis to standard regression.

7.6   The usual methods of monitoring

Once the scorecard is operational, there are three commonly used methods for monitoring accounts at characteristic/attribute level. All of these are useful, but each method has its drawbacks. I won't go into details on the methods, as most people who have scorecards will know about these and 'monitoring techniques' feature in other chapters at the conference. However, I will just summarise their use.

7.6.1   Characteristic analysis

This does not look at delinquency information or at characteristics not on the scorecard, but is aimed at detecting population shifts for scored characteristics only, and so it is not useful for examining new data sources.

7.6.2   Score distributions for each characteristic

This is an informative type of report, but contains too much information for decision making.

7.6.3   Alignment of Odds report

This is a table of bad rates by characteristic/attribute and by score band. Its major use is for spotting if a linear model is appropriate—that is, it looks for interactions between each characteristic and score. The report requires large numbers of bad accounts to be useful, for if the score is split into too few bands a bias is introduced into the figures.

In addition to the fact that the third method cannot work on low numbers of delinquent accounts, the first two of these reports do not suggest methods for making changes once anomalies are noticed.

7.7   Monitoring and adjustments in the light of known delinquency

The first situation I am going to examine is where a scorecard has been in place sufficiently long for the credit manager to obtain some statistics on the delinquency of the appropriate credit book.

Figure 7.4 shows a scorecard that is not working well. In particular the prediction for residential status is way off-beam.

The definition of a bad account in the example does not have to be the same as when the scorecard was developed. The sample window will have changed in any case; but, typically, the scorecard might not have been in place for very long and a bad definition which incorporates accounts at a less severe delinquent position may be more appropriate.

For these reasons one needs to refit a 'score' × 'good rate' curve to re-estimate the good rate for each score, before comparing predicted and actual attribute good rates.

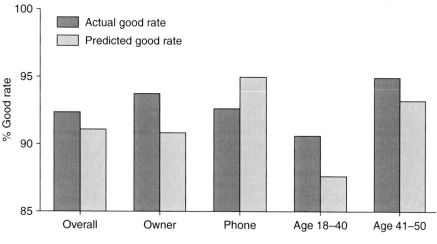

100
95
90
85

% Good rate

■ Actual good rate
□ Predicted good rate

Overall   Owner   Phone   Age 18–40   Age 41–50

Fig. 7.4   The loose fit.

When doing this exercise my colleagues and I have found that a good fit is obtained with the exponential curve

$$\text{estimated good rate at score} = 100 - a*\exp\{[-\text{score}/b]^c\}$$

where a, b, and c are parameters which adjust the intercept, the point of inflexion and the steepness, respectively.

(Alternatively, were one using logistic regression rather than standard regression, one would use a logistic formula. This is the most consistent approach).

The method has been found to be very effective in practice. For example, for one particular scorecard all scored characteristics bar one were found to match on good rates, but non-scored payment profile characteristics (i.e. characteristics obtained from examining past loans of the applicant), which were not available for scorecard development, did not match at all. This indicated that inclusion of the payment profile characteristics would increase the scorecard power. This was confirmed to be the case when my colleagues produced a new scorecard which included the payment profile data and was a significant improvement.

Let us suppose that one's decision to amend one's scorecard is based on

(1) early delinquency results that indicate that bank reference characteristics are more powerful than they were during the scorecard development;
(2) known reasons why this should be the case.

There are three possible stances here:

(1) change no points on the existing scorecard other than for the suspect characteristics;

(2) allow points to change but include no extra characteristics;
(3) allow points and characteristics to change.

The early delinquency figures will be indicative of the changes one should make, but one may not wish to rely on them wholeheartedly. I will explain my suggested approach to a scorecard amendment with reference to the second and third of the above stances. It should be noted that as most scorecards are developed in stages, any modification to the scorecard will upset, somewhat, the staging relationship. For this reason, amongst others, it is beneficial to make modifications that do not radically change the nature of the scorecard.

The modifications involve the use of (7.2) (obtained from equation 7.1). The Good Rates for each attribute of the suspect characteristic are manually adjusted and then equation (7.2) is used to re-estimate the points. In practice, this equation is only appropriate when the good rate by score curve is linear. (In other situations, the iterative logistic approach mentioned earlier needs to be used instead to obtain the points vector from the good rates vector. In fact a similar formulation for manual good rate modifications is available for the logistic regression).

For the characteristics that one is happy with, no adjustment is made. However, the good rates for the bank reference characteristics should be adjusted so they reside between the predicted values and the actual values. There are some typical rules of thumb that can be used when making these adjustments:

1. Do not change values unless estimates and actual values are further than a predetermined distance apart (use a confidence interval approach).
2. Err on the cautious side (especially early in the life of the scorecard) and do not adjust by more than two-thirds of the separation between actual and estimated good rates.
3. Make adjustments that are logical, that is, attributes should be in the right order (e.g. home owners should never be worse than tenants).
4. Examine rejects to ensure that one is being representative on the accepts.
5. Compare one characteristic with another, looking particularly at maximum spread of good rates across attributes.
6. Etc.

Figure 7.5 can be used as an aid in making these adjustments.

One diagram should be produced for predicted good rates, and a transparent overlay produced for actual good rates. One can then see at a glance how all the characteristics in the scorecard (and others) are working together. This example just shows the predicted good rates; the actual good rates would be on an overlay.

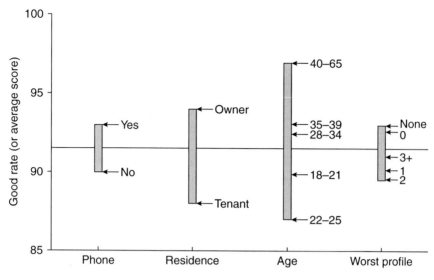

Fig. 7.5   A working diagram.

In the example, our three scorecard characteristics are working as expected. However, the predicted good rates for the 'worst arrears of current loans' (a characteristic not in the scorecard) obviously have an aberration in them, as applicants with a current loan that had reached three instalments in arrears have a better predicted good rate than those applicants with a loan that had never exceeded one instalment in arrears. This is obviously wrong, as the former will almost certainly be less creditworthy than the latter. The scorecard is thus not coping effectively with the characteristic 'worst arrears'. It would almost certainly be beneficial to include this characteristic in the scorecard, in order that applicants with a worst arrears position of 3+ be downgraded. This inclusion could be effected by applying the method outlined above.

In practice the procedure may be more difficult than described above because if the adjustments are not relatively minor then the rejected applications have to be catered for. The way that these are handled is that the decision on (a) which adjustments to make and (b) the scope of the adjustments, should be made on the known attribute good rates, whereas the application of equation 7.2 to recalculate the points should be undertaken on the total population. In fact, this is not directly possible because the rejects have no 'actual good rates' associated with them. There are three methods to circumvent this problem:

1. Having used the good rates to measure the scope of the adjustments, actually make the adjustments on average scores (this procedure is explained in the next section). This is an approximate solution which will give reasonable results that can be checked out when the revised scorecard is reapplied.

2. Assign a 'pseudo-actual' good rate to each rejected account based upon the current scorecard and the 'good rate × score' curve (effectively doing a biased reject inference): then apply equation 7.2. This is a conservative method that will suggest less radical amendments.
3. Use equation (7.2) to adjust the scorecard on the accepts, and then undertake a formal reject inference to obtain pseudo-actual good rates for the rejects. Finally, apply equation (7.2) again on accepts and rejects combined.

When minor adjustments are being made and the rejects are being considered then the first method should prove perfectly adequate.

7.8 Monitoring and adjustments in the case of the new book

When any new product is launched it is a high risk situation. All high risk situations need to have flexible control systems in place that are simple to understand and operate. They also require very close monitoring, and proceeding from this an adaptive approach towards control.

Credit facilities are no exception to this. The control systems are usually scorecards plus policy rules. To increase flexibility and provide 'adaptive' features, the traditional credit scoring system of one scorecard that is fixed for 3 years is inadequate. What is required is a statistical method for changing the scorecard more frequently.

In order to home in on a final scorecard rather than fluctuate wildly between cards that bear no resemblance to each other, the adaptive features should make minimal changes consistent with the aim of accounting for the quality of the credit applicants.

My recommendations for a new product being launched, or for an existing product being sold within a new or different market, are:

1. A generic scorecard be created, which provides an untried score. This scorecard should be based on experience and the examination of similar products and should be operated in conjunction with policy rules.
2. An update of the scorecard should be undertaken after one has data on the first 2,000 applicants.
3. A further update should be undertaken once early delinquency figures are known, using the principles already outlined.
4. Finally, when there is sufficient bad business on the books the scorecard should be redeveloped.

At stage 2 there is no performance information whatsoever, but equation (7.7), obtained from equation (7.3), can be used to make scorecard amendments, viz:

$$\text{points} = (\text{conditional probabilities})^{-1} \times \text{average scores} \qquad (7.7)$$

By adjusting the average scores the points can be recreated using equation (7.7). The two main rules of thumb to be observed when making the adjustments are

1. Make adjustments that are logical, that is, attributes should be in the right order.
2. Ensure that the spread of average scores across the attributes of any given characteristic are what one might expect.

The adjustments should be continued iteratively until both the scorecard points and the average scores are satisfactory.

The fact that this sort of approach is possible is because of the features of credit granting already mentioned, that one knows the application information long before the performance data comes to light and because the regression procedure separates out 'good rate estimates' from 'the matrix which represents just the application data'.

7.9   Population dynamics and monitoring

It is crucial to monitor very closely, once adjustments have been made to a scorecard, and some very useful reports which highlight trends are the following time series graphs, which I will describe in detail. They are both based on the principles already outlined.

Figure 7.6 shows average scores by characteristic and by week or month. (Weekly is possible because averages are reasonably stable for small sample sizes.) This report can be used to spot trends in population movements. It is especially useful if applied to certain characteristics that one has operational control over such as source of business, or dealer (for indirect loans).

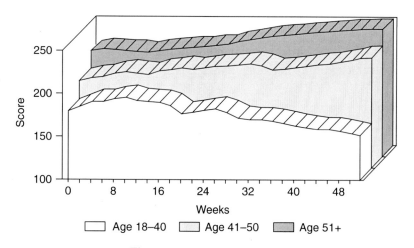

Fig. 7.6   Average score trends.

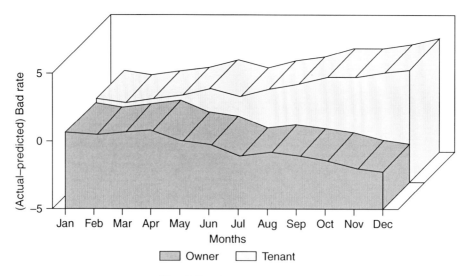

Fig. 7.7   Discrepancy report.

As an example, the characteristic '% delinquency of the dealers business' is a popular way of monitoring dealer quality. However, average scores are often a much more effective way of monitoring and controlling the quality of business obtained through small dealer outlets. The reasons for this are average scores are immediately available; average scores are more stable statistically, (principally because the averages are taken across good accounts as well as delinquent accounts).

Figure 7.7 is again by characteristic and by time tranche. It is only applicable if account performance data is available, and shows whether the scorecard is becoming progressively less effective as time goes on, and which characteristics are being affected. It can be applied to both scored and non-scored characteristics, and can show whether data that was not used in scorecard development is now coming into its own. The vertical axis can be either the magnitude of the difference between the predicted and actual bad rates, or the percentage increase/decrease of the predicted value from the actual value.

7.10   Summary

A number of points have been made in this chapter:

1. To determine whether or not one's scorecard is working well one needs to compare actual and predicted bad rates, overall and by every attribute. Their equality, or near equality is a crucial property of a good scorecard.

2. If there are no actual bad rates, one should examine the average scores for their consistency.
3. Good rates and average scores can be adjusted to re-evaluate scorecard points, by using an iterative technique based upon principles embodied in regression. The adjustments can be made in the light of expert opinion utilizing some simple rules of thumb to ensure that the changes are reasonable (Garthwaite and Dickey 1988).
4. Both average scores and predicted bad rates are an effective means of monitoring and controlling one's business, especially when trends are examined.
5. I would suggest that if the trend reports show serious misalignments over many characteristics, it is worth considering a full scorecard rebuild rather than just making adjustments. This is so that characteristic groupings can be re-examined, new data sources can be critically looked at and, importantly, a revised reject inference can be done.

Reference

Garthwaite, P. H. and Dickey, J. M. (1988) Quantifying expert opinion in linear regression problems. *Journal of the Royal Statistical Society*, B 50(3), 462–74.

8. Efficient frontier cut-off policies in credit portfolios

Robert M. Oliver and E. Wells

Historically, account acquisition in scored retail credit and loan portfolios has focused on risk management in the sense of minimizing default losses. We believe that acquisition policies should focus on a broader set of business measures that explicitly recognize tradeoffs between conflicting objectives of losses, volume and profit. Typical business challenges are: 'How do I maximize portfolio profit while keeping acceptance rate (volume, size) at acceptable levels?' 'How do I minimize the risk of large loss exposures for a given market share?' In this chapter we are concerned with which combination of objectives are appropriate, but rather focus on the cut-off policies that allow us to capture a number of different portfolio objectives. When there are conflicting objectives we show that optimal policies yield meaningful tradeoffs between profit and market share. Some of the graphical solutions that we obtain are simple to derive and easy to understand without explicit mathematical formulations but even simple constraints may require formal use of non-linear programming techniques. We concentrate on models and insights that yield decision strategies and cut-off policies rather than the techniques for developing good predictors.

8.1 Introduction

In this chapter the authors analyse the problem of account acquisition using cut-off policies in scored credit and loan portfolios. Although it has been common practice to use quantitative measures and predictors of individual account risk, much less attention has been given to the development of portfolio acquisition policies to achieve desirable business performance. A common decision rule is a score cut-off where individuals

Journal of Operational Research Society, 52, 1025–33, 2001.

with risk scores greater than or equal to a specified score, say s_C, are accepted and others below this cut-off are rejected. In this chapter we focus on a single-stage decision policy; a more complex policy can be based on a two-stage decision rule (Capon 1982). The first stage is to 'Accept' (above an upper cut-off), 'Reject' (below a lower cut-off) or 'Leave Undecided' (between the lower and upper cut-offs). In the second stage a decision of 'Accept' or 'Reject' is based on further information gathered for the 'Undecided' group. In practice sharp cut-offs cannot always be implemented as there may be additional information available about an individual that causes the institution to override the cut-off. Low side overrides admit applicants below the cut-off score that would normally be rejected and high side overrides reject applicants above the cut-off that would normally be accepted. A cut-off policy is often obtained by considering judgmental tradeoffs between account risk and portfolio size. Throughout we assume a binary performance variable yields either Good accounts that pay on time, do not default or do not prepay, and Bad accounts that prepay, default, or pay late.

8.2   Notation

Traditionally, risk scores are used to assess the relative odds of binary Good/Bad outcomes of the random performance of an individual. In this chapter risk (default, late payment, bankruptcy) decreases as score increases. We denote risk score by $s = s(x)$ where the information or data vector x is observed for a single individual or account; x is assumed to contain data relevant to the assessment of the Good/Bad outcomes. The Good/Bad definition usually depends on the portfolio of interest and may be default, late payment, prepayment, fraud, or bankruptcy. There are many techniques for estimating scores; these include linear and non-linear regression, Bayesian and neural net prediction techniques as well as proprietary algorithms. In a population of applicants a priori Good/Bad probabilities and a priori PopOdds (Population odds) are denoted by

$$p_G, \ p_B \text{ and } \omega_0 = \omega(G) = p_G/p_B.$$

The conditional (posterior) probabilities of Good and Bad are given by $p(G|x)$ and $p(B|x)$ so that the posterior odds of an individual being Good is

$$\omega(G|x) = p(G|x)/p(B|x) = p_G f_G(x)/p_B f_B(x) = \omega_0 I(x),$$

where $f_G(x)$ ($f_B(x)$) is the likelihood of the data x conditioned on being Good (Bad) and cumulative conditional and marginal score distributions are denoted by $F_G(s)$, $F_B(s)$ and $F(s)$. The ratio of the conditional density functions in this expression is known as the information odds, $I(x)$; throughout this chapter the score of an individual is the log of posterior odds, that is,

$$s(x) = \ln \omega(G|x) = \ln (p_G f_G(x)/p_B f_B(x)) = \ln \omega_0 + \ln I(x).$$

If the score of an individual includes the constant $s_0 = \ln \omega_0$, the logarithm of the information odds or likelihood ratios measure the risk of an individual relative to that of the overall population, that is,

$$s(x) - s_0 = \ln I(x) = \ln (f_G(x)/f_B(x)).$$

Conditional probabilities, odds and scores are used interchangeably throughout the chapter. Also, we refer to odds or score cut-offs that optimize a measure of expected profits or losses by: ω' the optimal cut-off odds for an unconstrained profit-maximizing problem, ω^* the optimal cut-off odds for a constrained problem.

All numerical calculations in this chapter are based on the score distributions and fitted odds data in the Appendix Table 8.A1, corresponding to an unnamed Bank Z.

8.3   Strategy curves—expected bad rate versus expected acceptance rate

Strategy is a misnomer in this context suggesting a sequence of actions over time— nevertheless, we adopt the standard terminology. Although there are many different ways in which a scoring predictor can be used to influence decisions that reduce risk and increase profitability of a portfolio of accounts, many popular policies do not require the direct use of economic data. A typical use of a score is illustrated in Fig. 8.1 where the expected Bad Rate $p_B(1 - F_B(s))$, is plotted against the acceptance rate, $1 - F(s)$, to obtain what is often referred to as a strategy curve. (Note that bad and

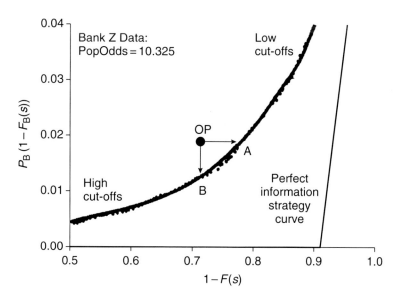

Fig. 8.1   A strategy curve and OP for Bank Z.

acceptance rates suggest number per unit time; a more correct interpretation is fraction bad or fraction accepted. Also, in many applications the vertical axis is the probability of being a Bad conditional on being accepted. The arguments for tradeoffs between risk and volume are essentially the same as the ones presented in this chapter). The strategy curve predicts the various Bad rates one can expect if one uses a cut-off score that results in an acceptance rate measured on the horizontal axis. The bottom left-hand part of the curve in Fig. 8.1 corresponds to large cut-offs and small acceptance rates, whereas the upper right-hand portion corresponds to small cut-offs and large acceptance rates. Different scoring technologies produce different strategy curves. A predictor that discriminates perfectly leads to the solid line that has a horizontal segment with zero Bad rate followed by a straight line when all new acceptances are Bad, that is, the count of Bads increases linearly with the number admitted. The proximity of the strategy curve to the solid line is one measure of the departure of the scoring predictor from that of a predictor with perfect discrimination of Goods and Bads, that is, perfect information on Good/Bad outcomes.

The current operating point for an institution seldom lies on the strategy curve, hence the obvious usefulness of the latter to show how a scoring predictor improves account and portfolio performance. In Fig. 8.1 the operating point (OP) corresponds to an expected bad rate of 1.87 per cent and acceptance rate of 72 per cent. We point out that the strategy curve can also be interpreted as the solution of two different optimization problems, one being to minimize the expected bad rate subject to the constraint that the expected volume of business (alternatively, size of accepted portfolio) exceeds a given level. Alternatively, one maximizes the expected acceptance rate (number of acceptances) subject to the constraint that the expected bad rate lie below a specified value. Thus the entire strategy curve is an efficient frontier (which is a set of reachable OPs that are not dominated by other OPs. See Keeney and Raiffa (1976) for a formal development of dominance and efficient frontiers) that quantifies the positive tradeoff between expected number of bads and expected number of accepted accounts that result as one decreases the cut-off. The efficient frontier is denoted by shading.

It is common practice to suggest new OPs to clients by considering two special cases that relate directly to current operations: either move to a new OP that maintains the same expected bad rate and increases the expected acceptance rate (point A in Fig. 8.1) or maintain the same expected acceptance rate while lowering the expected bad rate (B). Any number of attractive OPs may lie within or outside of the (A, B) segment of the strategy curve.

Under current acceptance policies, operating conditions and a known pool of applicants, data from the records of Bank Z show that

$$\omega_0 = 10.325, \quad 1 - F(s) = 0.720, \quad p_B(1 - F_B(s))/(1 - F(s)) = 0.026.$$

(Note that the fractions corresponding to the OP do not depend on a score cut-off; these data have been obtained from historical records of Bank Z.)

It follows that

$$p_G = 0.912, \ p_B = 0.088, \ p_B(1-F_B) = 0.0187, \ 1-F_G = 0.769, \ 1-F_B = 0.213.$$

Consider A on the strategy curve where the expected bad rate is maintained at the value of 1.87 per cent while the acceptance rate is increased from 72 to 78 per cent. The new OP is obtained at a score cut-off s_A where

$$\omega_A = 8.3, \ p_B(1 - F_B(s_A)) = 0.0187$$

$$1 - F_G(s_A) = 0.833, \ 1 - F_B(s_A) = 0.208$$

$$1 - F(s_A) = p_G(1 - F_G(s_A)) + p_B(1 - F_B(s_A)) = 0.778.$$

The slope of the strategy curve at A is proportional to the rate of bads relative to the rate of accepts, which includes goods and bads; it can be estimated in terms of fitted odds available from score tables (see Appendix):

$$\left.\frac{d\,p_B(1 - F_B(s))}{d(1 - F(s))}\right|_{s=s_A} = p_B \left.\frac{dF_B(s)}{dF(s)}\right|_{s=s_A} = \frac{1}{1 + \frac{p_G f_G(s_A)}{p_B f_B(s_A)}} = \frac{1}{1 + \omega_A}$$

$$= \frac{1}{1 + 8.3} = 0.108.$$

At A if we decrease the cut-off score to a small amount, we can expect to obtain 11 bads per 100 new accepts. At B, the marginal expected bad rate is $(1+\omega_B)^{-1} = (1+12.5)^{-1}$ or about 7 bads per 100 new accepts. The marginal tradeoff of other OPs can easily be evaluated.

As a practical matter, one does not need elaborate utility or preference models to study the effect of cut-off policies on statistical measures of Good/Bad outcomes and acceptance rates. One simply tries different OPs, compares the resulting bad and acceptance rates and, by trial and error, obtains a solution that tradesoff a portfolio manager's loss exposure with management demands for larger portfolio sizes. Although sensitivity analyses of marginal tradeoffs can be helpful in determining OPs, they still do not explicitly address issues associated with traditional business objectives such as portfolio profits, default losses, and market share.

8.4 Expected losses versus expected profits

As each Bad is assumed to result in a loss, one can easily plot expected losses versus the expected acceptance rate. It is clear that this would only involve a change in the scale of the vertical axis of Fig. 8.1; thus, the shape of a curve of expected losses

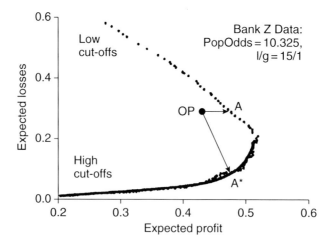

Fig. 8.2   Expected losses versus expected profits for different cut-offs, Bank Z.

versus acceptances is identical to the strategy curve. In the incoming stream of accepted accounts some will turn out to be Good and the rest Bad, which means that each accepted account will result in a random contribution to portfolio profit (positive or negative). Figure 8.2 is a plot of the expected losses versus the expected profits of a portfolio of accounts for Bank Z when the score or odds cut-off runs from very large to very small values. The origin corresponds to very large cut-offs and a negligible volume of business. As one moves counterclockwise along the curve away from the origin one uses smaller and smaller cut-offs. Even though the number of Bads is small the loss, l, associated with a default is 15 times as large as the gain, g, with a Good, eventually, all applicants are accepted and the expected default losses of the portfolio are so large that they dominate returns from Good accounts. Note that the slope of the top portion of the curve approaches -1 as the cut-off continues to decrease.

Recall that A coincides with the policy of maintaining the same bad rate as the current OP while increasing the acceptance rate. In Fig. 8.2 this means that A is not efficient in the sense that an OP with the same expected profit and smaller losses exists at Point A*, immediately below Point A, and lying on the shaded efficient frontier. Under the assumption that $l = 15$ and $g = 1$, it is easy to estimate the expected volume, losses, and profits with the current OP. With $1 - F_G = 0.769$, $1 - F_B = 0.213$ and $1 - F = 0.720$ we obtain

$$E[V_{OP}] = 0.720, \quad E[L_{OP}] = lp_B(1 - F_B) = 0.281, \quad E[P_{OP}] = 0.421.$$

One should multiply these results by 100 if $l = 1500$ and $g = 100$, which means that, although the scale of the axes will change, the shape of the curve in Fig. 8.2 remains unchanged.

Why would one ever use a low score or odds cut-off, such as A, that yields the same expected profit as a high score cut-off, such as A*, when the former exposes the lender to much greater expectation of large writeoffs and may require that costly reserves be set aside as insurance against these expected losses? This question has several answers but possibly the most important is that lower cut-offs lead to larger portfolios which, in turn, can lead to post-origination marketing opportunities among the accepted accounts. Although unquantified as to their effect on overall risk expos- ure, high-volume policies are often thought to be in the best overall interests of the firm because of the opportunities to cross-sell different financial products to existing cus- tomers. From a risk management perspective lower loss exposure is desirable but from a marketing perspective high volumes and large portfolio sizes are extremely attractive.

Can one quantify the economic value to be made up in operations not directly related to the origination decision, that is in operations such as cross-selling, loans, and other financial instruments that may be offered to the same applicant at a later point in time? In our example, the added value of such activities must be large enough to justify the large losses associated with A. At the operating point A

$$\omega_A = 8.3, 1 - F_G(s_A) = 0.833, 1 - F_B(s_A) = 0.208, 1 - F(s_A) = 0.778$$

$$E[L_A] = lp_B(1 - F_B(s_A) = 0.276,$$

$$E[P_A] = gp_G(1 - F_G(s_A)) - E[L_A] = 0.483$$

while at A* we obtain

$$\omega_{A^*} = 30.2, 1 - F_G(s_{A^*}) = 0.631, 1 - F_B(s_{A^*}) = 0.069, 1 - F(s_{A^*}) = 0.581$$

$$E[L_{A^*}] = lp_B(1 - F_B(s_{A^*}) = 0.0914,$$

$$E[P_{A^*}] = gp_G(1 - F_G(s_{A^*})) - E[L_{A^*}] = 0.483$$

This means that the difference in expected losses is equal to $E[L_A] - E[L_{A^*}] = 0.185$ per account when the l/g ratio equals 15/1. If the l/g ratio of 15:1 corresponds to an average loss of $1500 per Bad account and a gain of $100 per Good account, then the difference in expected loss exposure would be about $18.5 per account. In a portfolio of 1 million accounts this would be about $18.5 million and compares with an expected profit of about $48 million. This is about a threefold increase in exposure to expected losses for the same level of expected profits.

8.5   Plots of $E[V]$, $E[L]$, and $E[P]$

Whenever a cut-off policy is used to underwrite or originate loan accounts the result is, over time, an accumulation of accounts in a risky portfolio whose size (volume), losses, and profits are uncertain at the time the accept/reject policy is determined. In the

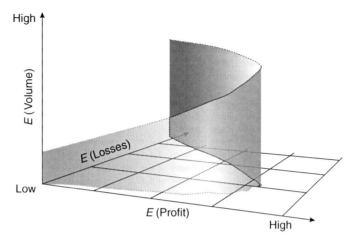

Fig. 8.3   Three-dimensional plot of $E[P]$, $E[L]$, and $E[V]$.

remainder of this chapter we examine some of the tradeoffs between these business objectives for a decision maker interested in the expectations of risk, volume, and profits. The effects of different cut-offs are plotted as a path in the three-dimensional graph of Fig. 8.3 which shows how portfolio performance varies in the L–P–V space. Figure 8.2 is a projection of this three-dimensional curve on the $E[P]$-$E[L]$ plane; later, we consider the $E[V]$-$E[P]$ plane.

If the underwriting policy is to accept applicants with a score greater than s_C, then the resulting measures of expected fractional volume, expected losses, and profit are proportional to

$$E[V(s_C)] = \int_{s_C}^{\infty} f(s)\,\mathrm{d}s = 1 - F(s_C)$$

$$E[L(s_C)] = \int_{s_C}^{\infty} lp(B|s)f(s)\,\mathrm{d}s = lp_B(1 - F_B(s_C))$$

$$E[P(s_C)] = \int_{s_C}^{\infty} (gp(G|s) - lp(B|s))f(s)\,\mathrm{d}s$$

$$= gp_G(1 - F_G(s_C)) - lp_B(1 - F_B(s_C))$$

Although we have not illustrated these effects, there are three-dimensional uncertainty bands around the path describing the volume–loss–profit expectations in Fig. 8.3. While there are some important exceptions, the general shape of the uncertainty bands around the cut-off path is not unlike the expanding funnel of a tornado tilted on its side with its apex at the origin of the graph. This increasing uncertainty is largely due to the uncertainties associated with riskier accounts obtained by lowering cut-offs.

Is there an 'optimal' score or odds cut-off? It should now be obvious that the answer to this question depends on the objectives of the institution and the tradeoffs of conflicting objectives, such as market share, default losses in the portfolio, profit to the institution, and others not considered here. Once the business objectives are well posed, cut-off policies represent a classic problem of decision making under uncertainty, that is, the cut-off must be chosen before the statistical or business performance is known.

8.6 Maximum expected profit objectives

Consider first the single objective of maximizing expected profits. The decision tree in Fig. 8.4 illustrates the accept/reject problem where an accepted Good results in a gain of g and an accepted Bad results in a loss of l (We appreciate that, in real world applications, l and g may be random variables that depend on risk score as well as other data.) Rejected accounts result in a payoff of 0. (The addition of a constant to all terminal branches (payoffs) in the tree of Fig. 8.4 does not change the optimal decision. Thus l and g can be interpreted as gains and losses net of the risk-free return.)

Although a careful analysis of optimal accept/reject policies would surely include the effects of the financial institution's aversion to risk, the determination of optimal accept/reject cut-offs appears to have been first described by Lewis (1992) as follows:

In theory, the setting of the optimum cutoff score is a simple matter. If the net profit from a Good account is known and the net loss from a Bad account is also known, then it is simple to calculate the number of Good accounts that are necessary to offset the loss from one Bad account. This quotient defines the odds at which the incremental gain is equal to the incremental loss, and the score associated with those odds is the appropriate cut-off score.

More recently, Marshall and Oliver (1995), Thomas (1998) and Hoadley and Oliver (1998) explore cut-off policies that maximize expected profit. The maximum unconstrained expected profit of all applicants with a single score cut-off s_C or odds

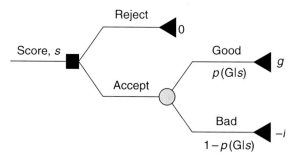

Fig. 8.4   Decision tree for accept or reject decision.

cut-offs $\omega_C = \omega(s_C)$ is given by

$$\bar{P} = E[P(\bar{s})] = \mathrm{Max}_{s_C} E[P(s_C)] = \mathrm{Max}_{s_C} \int_{s_C}^{\infty} (gp(G|s) - lp(B|s)) f(s) \, ds$$

$$= gp_G(1 - F_G(\bar{s})) - lp_B(1 - F_B(\bar{s})); \; \bar{s} = \ln(l/g)$$

where $f(s)$ is the density function of scores in the population of interest and subscript C refers to cut-off. In the second equation the terms within the large parentheses inside the integral can be rewritten as

$$(gp(G|s) - lp(B|s)) f(s) = gp(B|s)(\omega(s) - l/g) f(s).$$

Because g, $p(B|s)$ and $f(s)$ are always positive and both $p(B|s)$ and $f(s)$ are mono-tone in s, positivity in the right-hand expression is achieved by accepting those individuals whose odds of being good are greater than l/g; thus, the origins of sharp cut-off policies. The expected number of Goods required to offset the loss of one Bad is precisely the incremental (marginal) loss to gain ratio prescribed by Lewis. It is also the odds cut-off where one is indifferent to the risk-neutral reject or accept decision, that is a certain outcome of zero or a risky gamble with expected payoff equal to zero. Applicants with odds (of being a Good) greater than this ratio contribute positive expected profit and are accepted whereas applicants with lower odds are rejected. As odds is monotone in score, the set of accepts are the individuals whose posterior odds of being a Good lie in the interval $(\bar{\omega}, \infty)$ and whose scores lie in the interval $(\bar{s}, \infty)$.

Expected volumes and losses under the profit maximizing policy are therefore

$$\bar{V} = E[V(\bar{s})] = \int_{\bar{s}}^{\infty} f(s) \, ds = p_G(1 - F_G(\bar{s})) + p_B(1 - F_B(\bar{s}))$$

$$\bar{L} = E[L(\bar{s})] = \int_{\bar{s}}^{\infty} lp(B|s) f(s) \, ds = lp_B(1 - F_B(\bar{s}))$$

Hoadley and Oliver (1998) show that the expected profit for a cut-off of s with PopOdds ω_0 and any scoring technology, relative to the expected profit under perfect information, is

$$H(s) = H(s|\omega_0, \bar{\omega}) = (1 - F_G(s)) - \frac{\bar{\omega}}{\omega_0}(1 - F_B(s)).$$

We call this normalized version of the expected profit the HopScan function and note that the optimal expected profit can be written as $\bar{P} = gp_G H(\bar{s})$, where gp_G is the expected profit under perfect information.

As a practical matter the unconstrained profit-maximizing solution is seldom used. Estimates of l and g are difficult to assess and rarely independent of score, and risk-averse investors are unwilling to accept individual accounts with small expected profits if the potential loss exposure is very large. We therefore want to study the effect of more realistic business constraints on the cut-off policies.

Accept/reject cut-offs that maximize expected profit are similar to but not identical with classifications where the expected cost of misclassifications is minimized. In minimum cost classifications, model success is measured by being able to predict the number of 'Bad' accounts that turn out to be Good and vice versa. In our decision models the eventual Good/Bad status of rejected applicants can never be observed; hence, even though a misclassification model yields a similar mathematical structure for optimal policies, the solutions differ significantly from the ones we encounter in deciding whether to accept or reject an individual as a credit risk.

8.7   Expected profit and expected loss tradeoffs

In the previous section we reviewed the solution of the operating point cut-off associated with the problem of maximizing expected profit without constraints. In Fig. 8.2, for example, we saw that for any specified level of expected losses a businessman could seek an increase in expected profits by moving horizontally to the right. A businessman seeking a specified level of expected profit can minimize expected losses by moving in a downward direction. All points on the curve that are the result of minimizing expected losses for a given expected profit or maximizing expected profit for a given exposure to expected losses define an 'efficient frontier'. Its construction is easily stated in terms of a very simple non-linear optimization problem, which is to minimize expected losses with a lower bound on expected profits:

$$\text{Min}_s\, E[L] = \text{Min}_s\, lp_B(l - F_B(s))$$

subject to:

$$\lambda:\quad gp_G(1 - F_G(s)) - lp_B(1 - F_B(s)) \geq P_0,$$

where the non-negative shadow price is λ. We could, of course, include multiple constraints on expected profit and volume but, for the purpose of our discussion, a single constraint will suffice to illustrate efficient frontier tradeoffs.

The inequality on the lower bound for expected profits can also be written as $gp_G H(s) \geq P_0$. It is easy to show that the Kuhn–Tucker optimality conditions (see the references to non-linear programming by Whinston (1995) or Luenberger (1984) for the solution of this problem are

$$lp_B f_B(s) - \lambda(gp_G f_G(s) - lp_B f_B(s)) = 0$$
$$\lambda(gp_G(1 - F_G(s)) - lp_B(1 - F_B(s)) - P_0) = 0$$
$$\lambda \geq 0.$$

Solving the optimality equations yields the shadow price as a function of the profit constraint:

$$\lambda^* = \lambda^*(P_0) = \frac{lp_B f_B(s^*)}{gp_G f_G(s^*) - lp_B f_B(s^*)} = \frac{1}{(gp_G f_g(s^*)/lp_B f_B(s^*)) - 1}$$

$$= \frac{1}{(\omega^*/\bar{\omega}) - 1} \geq 0.$$

The optimal price has the economic interpretation that it equals the rate of change of minimum expected losses with respect to small changes in the expected profit constraint. It is unlikely that the shadow price would ever be zero except at the origin where expected losses and profits are zero. For this shadow price to be strictly positive the optimal cut-off odds for the constrained problem must be larger than the cut-off odds for the unconstrained solution discussed in the previous section, that is, $\lambda^* > 0 \Rightarrow \omega^* > \bar{\omega}$. In this case the expected profit constraint is a strict equality.

The optimal cut-off score is therefore the larger of the two arguments of the HopScan function that achieve the profit P_0 in units of the expected profit under perfect information:

$$s^* = s^*(P_0) = H^{-1}(P_0/gp_G).$$

If there is no solution to this equation then the profit constraint is infeasible. Expected losses and shadow price increase monotonically with P_0 along the efficient frontier shown in Fig. 8.5(a) which corresponds to a scorecard with $l/g = 15$ and $\omega_0 = 10.325$. The efficient frontier is the set of points between the origin and the maximum profit point with coordinates $(\bar{P}, \bar{L})$ coinciding with expected losses and expected profit smaller than these numbers and cut-off odds larger than $\bar{\omega}$. As one moves along the efficient frontier in a counterclockwise direction the increasing positive slope is given by $\lambda^* = \lambda^*(P_0)$ until it becomes infinite at the maximum profit point. Note that the shaded efficient frontier coincides with the region where the shadow price

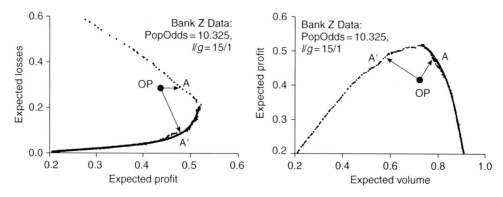

Fig. 8.5   Efficient frontiers for (a) $E[L] - E[P]$ and (b) $E[P] - E[V]$ objectives.

is positive. When cut-offs are smaller than co-expected profits decrease as expected losses increase; eventually the slope of the top portion of the curve approaches -1 as the expected losses dominate expected profits.

Consider the operating points A and A* described earlier with $\omega_A = 8.3$ and $\omega_{A*} = 30.2$. At A:

$$\frac{\omega_A}{\bar{\omega}} = \frac{8.3}{15} = 0.553 \quad \text{so that} \quad \left(\frac{\omega_A}{\bar{\omega}} - 1\right)^{-1} = \frac{1}{-0.447} = -2.37 < 0$$

whereas at A* on the efficient frontier we have

$$\frac{\omega_{A*}}{\bar{\omega}} = \frac{30.2}{15} = 2.013 \quad \text{so that} \quad \left(\frac{\omega_{A*}}{\bar{\omega}} - 1\right)^{-1} = 0.987 > 0.$$

At A we are not on the efficient frontier and expected losses increase at about twice the rate that expected profits decrease. At A* the reverse is true. Expected losses increase at a slightly slower positive rate than expected profits until we reach $\bar{P}$.

8.8 Expected volume and expected profit tradeoffs

In the previous section the efficient frontier might be characterized as a low-risk high-profit frontier. A very different efficient frontier with different implications for the decision-maker results if he or she is interested in finding the most efficient tradeoffs between profit foregone and increases in market share or expected volume of acquisitions. These new business objectives can be formulated as the mathematical problem of maximizing expected profit subject to a lower bound constraint on expected volume:

$$\text{Max}_s E[P(s)] = \text{Max}_s gp_G(1 - F_G(s)) - lp_B(1 - F_B(s))$$

$$\text{subject to } \mu : (1 - F(s)) \geq V_0$$

(Alternatively, one can maximize expected volume subject to a lower-bound constraint on expected profit. In this case the shadow price would be the reciprocal of the one computed above.)

If needed, multiple account and portfolio constraints can be included. The optimality conditions are now

$$(gp_G f_G(s_C) - lp_B f_B(s_C)) - \mu f(s_C) = 0$$

$$\mu((1 - F(s)) - V_0) = 0$$

$$\mu \leq 0,$$

which means that the equality on minimum expected volume holds whenever the optimal shadow price μ is strictly negative. The optimal solution of μ as a function of V_0 is therefore

$$\mu^* = \mu^*(V_0) = \frac{gp_G f_g(s^*) - lp_B f_B(s^*)}{f(s^*)} = \frac{l((\omega^*/\bar{\omega}) - 1)}{1 + \omega^*} \leq 0.$$

As long as cut-off score (odds) is less than the profit-maximizing score (odds) the tradeoff is negative and the optimal cut-off strictly satisfies the expected volume constraint:

$$s^* = s^*(V_0) = F^{-1}(1 - V_0).$$

On the other hand, if the desired expected volume is less than the expected volume achieved under the profit-maximizing policy then the optimal cut-off solution is

$$s^* = s \text{ with } V_0 < 1 - F(\bar{s}).$$

If one plots optimal expected profit as a function of expected volume the efficient frontier coincides with the shaded part of the curve in Fig. 8.5(b) where expected profit decreases with expected volume (thus the negative slope) and score or odds cut-offs are lower than the unconstrained profit-maximizing cut-off. The optimal policy for the volume-constrained profit objective can be summarized as

$$E[P(s^*)] = \begin{cases} g p_G H(\bar{s}) & \text{if } V_0 \leq 1 - F(\bar{s}) \\ g p_G H(s^*(V_0)) & \text{if } V_0 > 1 - F(\bar{s}) \end{cases}$$

where the optimal cut-off is determined by the fractional volume constraint, that is,

$$s^*(V_0) = F^{-1}(1 - V_0).$$

Let us now revisit the effect of the two cut-offs A and A^* in the $P-V$ plane. At A which is now an operating point on the new efficient frontier we have

$$\omega_A/\bar{\omega} = (8.3/15) = 0.553$$

so that

$$\frac{l((\omega_A/\bar{\omega}) - 1)}{1 + \omega_A} = \frac{l(-0.447)}{9.33} = -0.048l < 0$$

whereas at A^* (which is no longer on the efficient frontier) we have

$$\omega_A/\bar{\omega} = (30.2/15) = 2.013$$

so that

$$\frac{l((\omega_{A^*}/\bar{\omega}) - 1)}{1 + \omega_{A^*}} = \frac{l(29.2)}{31.2} = 0.936l > 0.$$

The A operating point gives up about 5 per cent in profit for every per cent increase in expected fractional volume whereas with low expected volumes at A^* expected profits increase in proportion to one. One can see that the roles of A and A^* are reversed in Fig. 8.5(a) and (b). A^* lies on the efficient frontier in the first case whereas A, not A*, lies on the efficient frontier when we are considering profit–volume tradeoffs.

These simple examples illustrate how optimal cut-off policies and tradeoffs differ significantly from the risk management policies studied earlier. If one focuses on traditional risk management the efficient frontier represents odds cut-offs that are higher than the profit-maximizing one and therefore lead to lower risk and lower volume portfolios. The efficient frontier in Fig. 8.5(a) acquires low risk individual accounts whereas the efficient frontier of Fig. 8.5(b) acquires riskier accounts in the hopes of increasing market share.

8.9   Summary

Calculations of risk, volume, and profit tradeoffs should be considered in credit-scoring to better understand the economic consequences of different objectives as well as the sensitivity to different PopOdds and loss/gain ratios. Because the motivation to build large portfolios and increase market share is so important in many business settings, portfolio managers have found it difficult to focus on risk management, that is, setting cut-offs that yield an acceptable number of defaults in a portfolio. Decision-makers primarily concerned with risk management usually tradeoff expected losses and number of acquisitions by examining desirable operating points on a strategy curve, the plot of expected Bad rate against the expected acquisition rate of new accounts. If one only considers Bad rates and acquisition rates, the effect of cut-off policies on profits and losses and their interaction with portfolio size may not be clearly understood. Fortunately, it is easy to model multiple business objectives within the decision problem and thereby estimate the tradeoffs between volume, losses, and profit. In considering efficient frontiers associated with different objectives, we found that the optimal policies in the expected profit-expected volume space are very different from those that consider the tradeoff's between expected losses and expected profit, the former yielding riskier portfolios than the latter.

We have shown by means of non-linear optimization models how efficient frontiers can be formulated with conflicting business objectives. Although we have not done so in this chapter it is straightforward to include additional account or portfolio constraints or more complicated objectives. Multiple profit, loss, and volume constraints can be simultaneously introduced; these lead to multiple shadow prices and slightly more complicated regions that describe the efficient frontiers but the theoretical techniques for solving such problems are well understood; reliable and efficient numerical procedures are widely available. We encourage their use.

Another important consideration is the effect of cut-off policies on relative uncertainty of the expected portfolio profits, losses, and volumes. There are uncertainties in all three dimensions and there are important correlations between these random variables. Although we have not given the derivations in this chapter the general shape of the uncertainty bands resembles the expanding funnel of a tornado tilted on its side with its apex at the origin representing very large cut-offs. The efficient frontiers obtained by considering tradeoffs between expected profit and the uncertainty or volatility of portfolio profits yield different cut-off policies and tradeoffs than the ones examined in this chapter.

A portfolio manager may also want to compare the economic impact of optimal policies on efficient frontiers that have been derived from the use of different scoring technologies; thus, one can estimate how the tradeoffs at efficient OPs differ as a result of the technology and whether there is an economic advantage to be derived from an investment in better scoring techniques or more informative databases. For all the reasons given above we emphasize that it is important to address different institutional objectives and identify, where possible, the dominant cut-off policies and tradeoffs that may result.

Appendix

Table 8.A1   Fitted odds and score distributions for Bank Z.

Fitted odds	$1 - F(s \mid G)$	$1 - F(s \mid B)$	$1 - F(s)$
7.000	0.852	0.239	0.798
7.200	0.848	0.232	0.794
7.500	0.844	0.224	0.789
7.800	0.841	0.218	0.786
8.000	0.837	0.215	0.782
8.300	0.833	0.208	0.778
8.600	0.830	0.200	0.774
8.900	0.827	0.193	0.771
9.300	0.821	0.183	0.765
9.600	0.818	0.181	0.762
9.900	0.816	0.178	0.760
10.300	0.813	0.173	0.757
10.600	0.806	0.168	0.750
11.000	0.803	0.166	0.747
11.400	0.800	0.157	0.743
11.800	0.788	0.151	0.732
12.200	0.782	0.146	0.726
12.700	0.774	0.141	0.718
13.100	0.765	0.140	0.710
13.600	0.762	0.138	0.707
14.100	0.757	0.133	0.702
14.500	0.751	0.129	0.696
15.100	0.746	0.126	0.691

Table 8.A1 *(Continued)*

Fitted odds	$1 - F(s \mid G)$	$1 - F(s \mid B)$	$1 - F(s)$
16.200	0.735	0.118	0.681
16.700	0.729	0.115	0.675
17.300	0.723	0.110	0.669
17.900	0.714	0.106	0.660
18.600	0.710	0.105	0.657
19.200	0.704	0.104	0.651
19.900	0.697	0.100	0.644
20.600	0.693	0.097	0.640
21.300	0.688	0.094	0.636
22.100	0.684	0.092	0.632
22.900	0.678	0.090	0.626
23.700	0.673	0.086	0.621
24.500	0.667	0.083	0.615
25.400	0.661	0.082	0.610
26.300	0.658	0.077	0.607
27.200	0.650	0.075	0.599
28.200	0.646	0.072	0.595
29.200	0.640	0.071	0.590
30.200	0.631	0.069	0.581
31.300	0.623	0.067	0.574
32.400	0.612	0.066	0.564

References

Capon, N. (1982) Credit scoring systems: a critical analysis. *Journal of Marketing*, 46, 82–91.

Hoadley, B. and Oliver, R. M. (1998) Business measures of score-card benefit. *IMA J Math Applied Business Industry*, 9, 55–64.

Keeney, R. L. and Raiffa, H. (1976) *Decisions with Multiple Objectives: Preferences and Value Tradeoffs*. Wiley, New York.

Lewis, E. M. (1992) *An Introduction to Credit Scoring*. Fair Isaac and Co. Inc.: San Rafael, CA, Chapter II. 3.2, p. 86.

Luenberger, D. (1984) *Linear and Nonlinear Programming*. Addison Wesley, New York.

Marshall, K. T. and Oliver, R. M. (1995) *Decision Making and Forecasting*. McGraw Hill, New York, Chapter 3.7, pp. 121–8.

Thomas, L. (1998) Methodologies for classifying applicants for credit. In *Statistics in Finance* (D. J. Hand, and S. D. Jacka, (eds). Arnold, London, Chapter 5, pp. 83–103.

Whinston, W. (1995) *Introduction to Mathematical Programming*. Duxbury Press, Wadsworth Publishing Co, Belmont CA, USA.

Part IV.   Features of Scoring

In Part IV we include chapters that explore certain features of credit scoring which are of generic interest to all scorecard builders. If there is a 'classic' chapter on reject inference it is surely that by Hand and Henley. While Hsai (1978) was the first to briefly describe the augmentation method, Hand and Henley were the first to publicly remove much of the mystique of reject inference by reviewing several techniques and proposing some new ones as well. Hand and Henley pointed out that when using extrapolation it is important to distinguish between the use of techniques which utilize the probability distributions of application characteristics, given performance, (such as discriminant analysis) and techniques which do not (such as logistic regression). If there is sparse sampling based on the applicants' characteristics alone then these probability distributions will no longer be normal and linear discriminant analysis will yield poor predictions. However this normality assumption is not made in logistic regression and so this technique would remain unaffected.

But the most significant contribution of the Hand and Henley chapter is to make the point that if an accept–reject model which is currently in use was parameterized using a set of variables X, and a new good–bad model is parameterized using a set of variables Y, where X is not a subset of Y, then the good–bad model will yield biased parameters. This argument builds on the theoretical missing data work of Little and Rubin (1987), with the situation described being an example of Little and Rubin's 'non-ignorably missing' case. Hand and Henley show that this criticism relates to the augmentation method of reject inference. They remind us that a key assumption of this technique is that the probability of being good, given the Y variables and a score for the rejects equals that for the accepts at the same score. But use of the Y variables for the new model, rather than the X variables, renders this assumption implausible. Hand and Henley then review other techniques including three which use supplementary information, for example, information on the performance of cases that would normally be rejected, possibly using information from other loans. Hand and Henley's chapter has stimulated a number of recent papers.

Of the many types of attempts to improve the accuracy of good/bad predictions, the inclusion of additional variables or even substantial changes in the regression coefficients when many variables are included, is unlikely to be very beneficial— according to Lovie and Lovie (1986). The second chapter in this part, by Overstreet and Bradley, explores the validity of this argument using data samples from US credit unions. Overstreet and Bradley estimate a logistic regression scoring model for each of 10 credit unions individually and then create a generic model by calculating a weighted average of the coefficients of the individual equations. While the predictive performance of the individual equations was superior to that of the generic model, they regarded the difference as being only marginal. The authors suggest that it may be worthwhile using generic models when the cost of building an individual model is large for a small organization. Alternatively, they may be used when an individual organization does not have a sufficiently large sample with which to build a scorecard. This chapter is one of the very few that examine the significance of the flat maximum effect in the credit scoring context and the methodology also gives insights into the possible significance of segmentation. The issue of segmentation is central to many developments in credit scoring.

Most scorecard developers would agree that the accuracy of a credit scoring model decreases over time. In the context of logistic regression we might think of the parameters changing over time as applicants with given characteristics change their repayment performance, and/or the appropriate cut-off (say to equalize the predicted and observed number of bads) changes. The third chapter in this part by Crook *et al.* explores the implications of classifying applicants according to scoring models which differ in the time period from which the sample was drawn. The characteristics of those who would be rejected on one model but accepted on another are identified for a bank credit card. Changes in the cut-offs alone and changes in the parameters alone, each had substantial effects on the proportion of cases accepted. For example, if the cut-offs were adjusted, so that the same predicted proportion of cases were rejected in 1989 and 1990, 7.4 per cent of cases would be rejected by one model but not the other. Thus, changing the cut-offs to maintain the same reject rate in the 2 years, would not yield the same decision for each applicant. The coefficients of the model had changed. Just how the state of the economy should be incorporated into scorecards is an ongoing research topic and several subsequent papers on how scorecards may be updated efficiently, have been written. Continuing the earlier theme, if parameters were stable for different states of the economy (albeit differing between states of the economy) one might see the issue as one of segmentation over time.

In the fourth chapter in this part Bennett *et al.* consider the joint problem of which existing customers to mail with information about a new product to both maximize the response while minimizing risk, and at the same time minimizing the number of responders who will be turned down. The latter is a genuine concern because current customers who are invited to apply for a credit product only to find they are then turned down, may take their custom elsewhere. Moreover this chapter is significant because it addresses questions that have been asked by rapidly increasing numbers of lenders. For example, in recent years the entry of new credit card issuers has led to massive increases in the amount of mail shots by many companies who will be especially interested in answering these questions.

Bennett *et al.* argue that there is a positive correlation between probability of response and probability of default and that traditional models do not identify the customers who are really wanted: those with low risk and a high chance of response. To do this a sample representative of the population of all applicants and of all of those who received a mail shot in the past was needed. As usual some, but not all past applicants, had been accepted using a previous scoring rule and so Bennett *et al.* decided that there was a need to employ reject inference to infer the performance of those who had been turned down. In addition some, but not their entire sample had been sent a direct mail shot in the past, again using a selection rule. So to derive a sample as close to the population as possible, there was a need to infer how those not previously mailed, would have responded if they had received a mail shot. Finally, they had to infer which of the inferred respondents to the mail shot would have been good or bad had they applied. Hence, the title of the chapter, 'inferring the inferred'. The high degree of success by the authors is demonstrated in their results.

References

Hsai, D. C. (1978) Credit scoring and the Equal Credit Opportunity Act. *Hastings Law Journal*, 30, 371–448.

Little, R. J. and Rubin, D. B. (1987) *Statistical Analysis with Missing Data*. Wiley, New York.

Lovie, A. D. and Lovie, P. (1986) The flat maximum effect and linear scoring models for prediction. *Journal of Forecasting*, 5, 159–86.

9.   Can reject inference ever work?

David J. Hand and William E. Henley

9.1   Introduction

When applicants apply for credit, they are assessed using a scoring instrument and either accepted or rejected. The accepted ones are followed up, and their true good or bad creditworthiness can be determined. However, the rejected ones are not followed up, so that their true status is unknown. 'Reject inference' is the process of attempting to infer the true creditworthiness status of the rejected applicants.

There are several reasons for being interested in this. A straightforward one is a wish to determine the number of good credit risks rejected by the scoring instrument. Another, more subtle, involves the effort to develop improved scoring instruments. In general, the only data available on which to develop new instruments will be: (a) the applicants' responses to the individual items comprising the scoring instrument (these will be available for both accepted and rejected applicants), and (b) the true good or bad status of those accepted (but not of those rejected). Unfortunately, as outlined below, instruments based solely on the accepted applicants could be biased. This observation has led to the idea that, if one can use reject inference to infer the status of those rejected, then perhaps this information could be combined with the known status of those accepted to reduce the bias in the new instrument. Reject inference has attracted a great deal of interest, and many methods have been proposed. Much of the work seems to have been based on a poor understanding of what can be achieved using the rejects. The aim of this chapter is to clarify this, and to describe some proposed methods of reject inference.

For simplicity, we shall discuss only the case of two classes: those with high probability of defaulting on the credit repayments (the 'bads') and those with a low probability (the 'goods'). In particular, we shall not consider a continuum of such probability

IMA Journal of Mathematics Applied in Business and Industry, 5, 45–55, 1993/4.

classification, and we shall not consider different kinds of defaulter. Nor, in this chapter, shall we discuss models based on changes of state between good and bad, as far as we are concerned, each credit applicant belongs to just one of the two classes and is fixed in that class. Thus, for the purposes of this chapter, each applicant may be regarded as having a true class.

9.2   Extrapolation from the accepts

Let χ be the set of characteristics measured for each applicant. This set could include such categories as age (perhaps grouped as <25, 25–29, 30–39, 40–49, 50–59, 60 or above), time at present address (<1 year, 1–5 years, >5 years), and type of accommodation (rented flat, owned flat, owned house). The possible responses to each such characteristic are termed *levels*—so that, for example, the characteristic 'accommodation' has three levels of response. The initial accept/reject decision is based on the pattern of these levels of response.

The probability that an applicant with a particular vector x of characteristic levels is good will been denoted by $P(g|x)$ and the probability density function of the good-risk applicants will be denoted by $p(x|g)$ (with corresponding notation for bad).

A fundamental approach to reject inference is straightforward extrapolation from the accept region of the χ space over the reject region. That is, using just the sample of 'accepts' (their known x vectors and their known true good/bad status) one constructs a model to predict the probability of being good in the accept region, and then extrapolates this over the reject region.

Of course, the extent of truncation (the size of the reject region) will determine how good a model can be fitted. A large reject region means there is little information on which to base the model. Moreover, problems will arise with any extrapolation method if the $P(g|\bullet)$ function differs in form between the accept and reject regions, or if the error variation is such that a highly accurate model cannot be constructed in the accept region. The latter would mean that the form of the model could not be accurately specified. For example, the accept data may not permit one to reject the hypothesis of a straight-line predictor in favour of a quadratic predictor. This being the case, extrapolating beyond the accept data into the reject region could well produce inaccurate results as the departure from linearity becomes more extreme.

As far as the extrapolation goes, one might base it on either of the two fundamental approaches to classifier design. In the first approach, of which logistic regression is an example, one estimates $P(g|\bullet)$ directly. In the second, illustrated by classical linear discriminant analysis, one estimates $p(\bullet|g)$ and $p(\bullet|b)$ and then derives $P(g|\bullet)$ using Bayes' theorem:

$$P(g|x) = \frac{p(x|g)P(g)}{p(x|g)P(g) + p(x|b)P(b)},$$

where $P(g)$ and $P(b)$ are the overall proportions of goods and bads in the population. The theory is standard and is explained in many places, for example, Hand (1981).

Now, for our purposes, there is a vital distinction between the two approaches (Dawid 1976). This is that a sampling fraction which varies arbitrarily across the χ space will lead to distortion of methods that estimate the probabilities via $p(\cdot|g)$ and $p(\cdot|b)$ but not of methods which directly estimate $P(g|\cdot)$.

For example, sparse sampling (based on x alone) from one side of a normal distribution will lead to an asymmetric distribution, and so methods that assume normality of the resulting $p(\cdot|g)$ and $p(\cdot|b)$ distributions will be biased. However, such sparse sampling will not influence $P(g|\cdot)$: the proportion of goods at any particular x will remain the same at that x whatever the sampling fraction, so that $P(g|x)$ will not be distorted.

In our situation, the distribution of known goods is truncated (containing only applicants from the accept region). The same applies to the distribution of bads. This truncation will bias any model-based estimate of $p(\cdot|g)$ and $p(\cdot|b)$ and, hence, of estimates of $P(g|\cdot)$ based on them. However, truncation will not bias methods based on estimating $P(g|\cdot)$ directly.

It would be possible to derive approaches based on $p(\cdot|g)$ and $p(\cdot|b)$ but modified to make allowance for the truncation; however, since these would depend on the validity of assuming, for example, multivariate normality under no truncation, it is unlikely that they would be very robust in practice.

The consequence of all this is that, if the accept/reject decision is based just on the scores in χ, then one might expect methods such as logistic regression to extrapolate reasonably well beyond the accepts, but methods such as classical discriminant analysis to perform badly. The latter would require extensive adjustment to account for the truncation resulting from the rejection. A number of empirical studies have demonstrated the truth of these observations: for example, Eisenbeis (1978) cites work by Avery showing how truncation of normal populations can cause bias in methods based on discriminant analysis. Of course, both approaches will be adversely influenced if an incorrect model form is adopted.

Extrapolation from a model built on the accept region and based on the $P(g|\cdot)$ is thus an appealing approach, and one which forms a natural baseline against which to assess the other methods outlined below.

9.3   Using the rejects

If one does not assume known distributional forms for the χ values of the goods and bads, $p(\cdot|g)$ and $p(\cdot|b)$, then it is simple enough to show that the χ values of the rejects (for whom the true good/bad status is unknown) do not contain information about the parameters of the $P(g|\bullet)$ function.

To see this, let S be a random variable taking values g and b and let X be the random vector of characteristics. Then the joint probability function of S and X is

$$P[(S, X) = P(s, x)] = P(s, x) = P(s|x; c)p(x; d),$$

where c and d are parameters for the indicated distributions. We wish to estimate $P(g|\bullet; c)$, (or equivalently $P(b|\bullet; c) = 1 - P(g|\bullet; c)$). If we do not assume a known form for $p(\bullet; d)$, then this does not contribute to the likelihood. That is, the χ values do not contain information about the parameters of $P(g|\bullet; c)$. This is true for both accepts and rejects; but in particular it means that using the rejects cannot lead to an improved scoring rule.

If, on the other hand, we do assume particular forms for the separate distributions of the χ values of the goods and bads, $p(\bullet|g)$ and $p(\bullet|b)$, over the entire space, then the parameters in $P(g|\bullet; c)$ intersect those in $p(\bullet|g)$ and $p(\bullet|b)$ so that the χ values, including those of the rejects, can be helpful. The parameters can then be calculated using mixture-decomposition methods (e.g. Everitt and Hand 1981). We shall discuss this possibility below.

Now suppose that some proportion of those applicants with response pattern x is accepted, where the accept/reject decision is based solely on x. Then the proportion of goods among the accepts at x must be equal to the proportion of goods among the rejects at x: no extra information on which the good/bad can be discriminated is being used.

However, if the accept/reject decision also uses extra information (such as, for example, extra characteristics not included in x), then the proportion of goods among the rejects will typically not equal that among the accepts at any particular point of χ. This means that a model based solely on the accepts will normally be biased.

From another perspective, if the accept/reject decision is made in the χ space and then a new scorecard is constructed using information in a set $\mathcal{Y}$ of characteristics, with $\mathcal{Y}$ a subset of χ, then a biased instrument will result. (Exactly the same applies if the new scorecard uses a set $\mathcal{Z}$ of characteristics where $\mathcal{Z}$ does not include all of χ.)

Moreover, the difference between the probability of being good among the accepts and the probability of being good among the rejects will normally vary between different points of $\mathcal{Y}$. Thus, to avoid bias when constructing a new instrument using an accept sample obtained from an earlier instrument, it is necessary to include all characteristics used by the earlier instrument. The fact that this is not always done may go some way towards explaining claims to have improved on the straightforward extrapolation method by using the rejects.

A simple example, in which the subset $\mathcal{Y}$ is a single characteristic, is as follows. Consider a characteristic such that low scores are associated with poor risks and high scores with good risks. Then it is likely that the scorecard will have rejected a high proportion of those with low scores. These rejections will not be based solely on the low scores on this characteristic alone, however, but on the overall score of the scorecard. Following the argument above, this implies that (conditional upon a particular level of this characteristic) the proportion of goods among the accepts will generally not equal the proportion of goods amongst the rejects. Moreover, if the instrument has any validity, one might reasonably expect that there will be a lower proportion of goods among the rejects than amongst the accepts. The consequence is that, looking at this characteristic alone, it would show apparent bias in its lower scores, in the sense that the accepts at these scores would underestimate the proportion of bads and overestimate the proportions of goods.

We explored this empirically as follows. A characteristic fulfilling the above criterion of low scores being associated with a risk of being bad is 'number of weeks since the last County Court judgement'. This had levels graded 1 (1–26 weeks), 2 (27–52 weeks), 3 (53–104 weeks), 4 (105–208 weeks), 5 (209–312 weeks), and 6 ($\geq$313 weeks, or no County Court judgement). As is outlined in the next section, we did have available a sample which covered the entire χ space. We built a scorecard and used this to divide the sample into accepts and rejects. This permitted us to compare the probabilities of being good at each level of this characteristic as calculated from the accept sample alone and as calculated from the entire sample.

The results are shown in Table 9.1. The first column gives the level. The next two give the proportions of goods in the full sample and accept sample, respectively. And the final column gives the ratio of these two 'proportions good'. It is quite striking that the ratio of the two proportions decreases as the level increases, that is, as the risk of being bad is expected to decrease (and indeed does, as is indicated by the trends in

Table 9.1 Ratio of the estimated probability of being good in the accept sample to the estimated probability of being good in the full sample, classified according to the number of weeks since the last County Court judgement.

Level (number of weeks)	Full sample: proportion good	Accept sample: proportion good	Accept/full ratio
1	0.227	0.446	1.964
2	0.304	0.469	1.542
3	0.314	0.492	1.567
4	0.378	0.552	1.460
5	0.426	0.631	1.481
6	0.556	0.692	1.245

the middle two columns). This is precisely what our model predicted. (And, since all the proportions are well away from unity, this is presumably not just a ceiling effect.) It follows from this that one might attain improved performance if one biased the scorecard based on the accepts to fit a lower proportion of goods than was available in the accept sample, for low levels of the characteristic.

This example has used a single characteristic as the $\mathcal{Y}$ subset, but the reasoning applies more generally. And, as noted above, it could explain claims of using the rejects to improve a scorecard. The mechanism is one of adjusting the estimated $P(g|\bullet)$ model towards one's beliefs about the proportions-basically, a Bayesian approach.

Of course, all of the above assumes that the full sample and accept samples are taken from the same populations. If this is not the case, then things become more complicated-and there are more possibilities for improving the scorecard. These are discussed below.

We shall finish this section with a brief discussion of three methods which have been proposed and which attempt to make use of the rejects. The first is the 'augmentation' method, which nicely illustrates some of the points made above. The second method is much more modest in the use it makes of the rejects, using them solely to obtain improved estimates of covariance matrices. And the third method is the mixture-decomposition approach mentioned above.

9.3.1   Method 1

Hsia (1978) describes the technique, which is widely used by developers of scoring systems in attempting to take advantage of the rejects' characteristic vectors. Implicit in it are assumptions that the accept/reject decision was made using a set χ of characteristics, and that the new scorecard is to be built using a set $\mathcal{Y}$ such that χ is not a subset of $\mathcal{Y}$. As we have seen above, this is likely to imply that the probability of being good among the accepts with any particular score on the new scorecard is not the same as the probability of being good among the rejects with that score.

The method begins by developing a new scorecard, using $\mathcal{Y}$, to discriminate between the accepts and rejects. Now, since $\mathcal{Y}$ does not include χ, there will be some elements of χ not in $\mathcal{Y}$. In general this will mean that each point in $\mathcal{Y}$ will be associated with some accepts and some rejects. The augmentation method then uses the accepts among these to estimate the conditional probabilities $P(g|\mathbf{y})$. The overall probabilities (of both accepts and rejects) $p(\mathbf{y})$ ($\mathbf{y} \in \mathcal{Y}$) then serve as a reweighting.

The reweighted data now provide nominal distributions of goods and bads through-out the $\mathcal{Y}$ space, so that standard methods of building classifiers can be applied. Of course, if an accurately specified model was being used, then the reweighting would have no effect on the estimated parameters.

The key assumption latent in this method is that the probabilities $P(g|y)$ for the accepts are the same as those for the rejects. This is unlikely to be the case in practice since the accept/reject decision, based on χ, which has information not included in $\mathcal{Y}$, is likely to serve to separate these two classes on the basis of the proportions of goods in them. In general, then, the augmentation method should not be expected to lead to valid estimates of good/bad probabilities.

9.3.2   Method 2

Reichert *et al.* (1983) compared a two-group (good accepts versus bad accepts) classical linear discriminant analysis with a three-group (good accepts, bad accepts, and rejects) classical linear discriminant analysis. They note that the inclusion of the rejects did not improve the discrimination between good and bad accepts. However, they observe that (p. 105): 'the key decision is whether to grant credit in the first place and not to identify good or bad borrowers once a loan has been granted. Thus a three-group model based on the entire population of applicants is conceptually more appropriate than a truncated two-group model'.

The first sentence here is obviously true. However, since the aim is to split the entire population into two groups, it is not clear that a three-group discriminant analysis is at all the appropriate thing to do. Constructing a model that specifically identifies characteristics of a third group which one can identify perfectly anyway, and which one would like to partition into good and bad, seems at best perverse. An extrapolation approach seems much more in tune with the objectives.

Be that as it may, classical linear discriminant analysis assumes a common covariance matrix for the three (or however many) groups in question. Thus this approach does try to make use of information in the rejects in devising the classification rules, in that the rejects are used to lead to more accurate estimates of this common covariance matrix. Having said that, it should be added that we do not believe that this will compensate for the other problems of this method outlined above.

9.3.3   Method 3

Classical linear discriminant analysis estimates $p(\cdot|g)$ and $p(\cdot|b)$ and then calculates

$$\frac{P(g|x)}{P(b|x)} = \frac{p(x|g)}{p(x|b)} \frac{P(g)}{P(b)} \tag{9.1}$$

If one assumes, as classical linear discriminant analysis does, that $p(\cdot|g)$ and $p(\cdot|b)$ belong to a particular family of distributions, then one can estimate the parameters using both the classified cases (the accepts) and the unclassified cases (the rejects) using the EM algorithm. (The EM algorithm is an algorithm for finding maximum-likelihood solutions when there are missing data. The true good/bad status of the rejects may be regarded as missing data Dempster *et al.* 1977.) This is an example of making the truncation explicit, noted above. Indeed, one can go even further, and use the EM approach in a mixture decomposition on entirely unclassified cases. That is, one can estimate $p(\cdot|g)$ and $p(\cdot|b)$ from rejects alone, requiring no accepts whatsoever, and then use (9.1) to estimate $P(g|\cdot)$ throughout the whole space.

To see how this is done, define $p(\cdot)$ as the overall distribution of applicants (regardless of whether their good/bad classification is known). Now

$$p(x) = p(x|g)P(g) + p(x|b)P(b) \tag{9.2}$$

The left-hand side can be estimated from the overall distribution of the sample. For particular assumed values of $P(g)$, $P(b)$, and the parameters of $p(\cdot|g)$ and $p(\cdot|b)$, the right-hand side gives a completely specified distribution. Then we choose the set of parameters that leads to the smallest difference between the two sides.

This is straightforward enough, and is illustrated in a slightly different context, in Hand and Fitzmaurice (1987). And it seems like magic: even without knowledge of the good/bad classification of any accepts, we seem to have produced a reasonable estimate of the good/bad classification throughout the entire space. Predictably enough, this power has been gained at the cost of an assumption. We assumed that the distributions belonged to some parameterized family. A common assumption is that of classical linear discriminant analysis, based on multivariate normality. Unfortunately, in the credit-scoring context, with many categorical variables and markedly non-normal marginal distributions, assuming normality is unrealistic, and there does not seem to be any obvious parametric alternative. Nevertheless, this approach does seem to offer a genuine way in which advantage might be taken of the rejects, and might be worth pursuing.

9.4   Methods with supplementary information

As noted above, the difficulties arise because there are regions of χ on which no good/bad information at all is available (the reject region). It is clear that the most straightforward way of obtaining valid reject inferences would be to obtain some information about these regions. The easiest way to do this would be to take a subsample of the cases, which lie in these regions.

Naturally cost considerations enter here. Every accepted bad applicant represents a financial loss, so that somehow the information gained in terms of increased accuracy of the subsequent scorecard has to be balanced against this loss.

In this section, we assume that some such supplementary information is available. In what follows, we shall call it the 'calibration sample'. Given that such information is available, the next question to be addressed is how best to make use of it.

If we knew that the calibration sample had been randomly chosen from the population of interest (or even by some arbitrary sampling mechanism dependent solely on the characteristics spanning χ) then we could simply combine the accepts and the calibration samples and use a statistical technique based on the posterior probabilities $P(g|x)$ of being a good risk, such as logistic regression. (But not, note, a technique based on the class-conditional distributions $p(\cdot|g)$ and $p(\cdot|b)$, such as classical linear discriminant analysis, for the reasons described in detail above.) In such a case, the accept sample may add little information to that already contained in the calibration sample. On the other hand, if we are unsure about this, then either we have to compare the two samples (the accepts and the component of the calibration sample lying in the accept region) or we have to consider what aspects of the calibration sample we can reasonably expect to hold also for the new population, and see if use can be made of these. Three methods aimed at doing that are now presented.

9.4.1   Method 4

We first outline the idea behind this method, which we believe to be original, and then present a simple (and simplistic) example. The method assumes that several calibration samples are available. These samples are partitioned, using whatever method was used to partition the original sample, into accepts and rejects. For each calibration sample, the distribution of the probability of being good over the reject region is known (this is the definition of a calibration sample). The same is true, of course, over the accept region. Thus one can identify characterizing features of the distributions in each of the two regions for each calibration sample. Moreover, by studying the whole set of calibration samples, and the values that the characterizing features take over this set, one can estimate the relationship between the values of the features in the two regions. Finally, these relationships allow one to map from the values of the characterizing features taken on the accepts of the new sample to the values of the characterizing features of the rejects of the new sample and hence to the form of $P(g|\cdot)$ over the reject region.

The following example is absurdly oversimplified for reasons of exposition. Suppose the scorecard consists of just one characteristic with three levels. Also suppose that one of these levels represents the reject region—all applicants who respond at this level are rejected—and that the other two represent the accept region. Now suppose that we have ten calibration samples. These may be obtained from different time periods, from different geographical locations, or from loans on different products, for example.

One feature is sufficient to characterize the population of rejects: this is the proportion of goods in the single level that constitutes the reject region. Similarly, two are sufficient to characterize the accept region: the proportions of goods in each level comprising the accept region. This means that each of the ten calibration samples is described by just three numbers.

We can now use these ten samples to build a simple regression model showing the relationship between the two accept proportions and the single reject proportion. Then, for any pair of proportions, representing a population's scores in the accept region, we can predict, from the regression model, that population's score in the reject region. That is, we can predict that population's proportion good in the reject level of the characteristic.

Of course, to make this realistic, it must be extended substantially in a number of directions. First, the cross-classification of a number of characteristics must be considered. Typically this will also mean that there will be multiple cells in the reject region. Moreover it will normally mean that there will be far too many cells, in both reject and accept regions, for the characterizing features to be merely the proportions in the cells. Some more subtle summarizing statistics will be needed. Obvious suitable examples are low-order log-linear models or perhaps regression models with cells replaced by scores derived using correspondence analysis. Note also that a multivariate multiple regression or canonical correlation analysis will be needed to relate the two sets of characterizing variables together. This, in turn, implies that the number of calibration samples must be large enough to span the space of the combined set of variables (those used to describe the accept proportions and those used to describe the reject proportions) effectively, and permit sufficiently accurate estimation of the model coefficients.

This means that the calibration samples should come from different sources, such as times, locations, and products, as noted above. To some extent one can achieve this by partitioning any available calibration sample; but, of course, a tradeoff is necessary between the number of such subsamples produced and the size of each one: each one must yield sufficiently accurate estimates of its characterizing feature values.

9.4.2   Method 5

This method, which we also believe to be original, requires a single calibration sample.

In the above, we have described extrapolation methods. These are based on building a model on the accept region and extrapolating it over the reject region. The assumption is that the model will extrapolate validly. This assumption, of course, is risky since it is a classic example of extrapolating beyond the data. Indeed, the reject region has been so designated precisely because it differs in an important way from the accept region. Thus the assumption that the model may legitimately be extrapolated over this region might be regarded as shaky. This is the sort of argument which motivated the idea that things could be improved by utilizing subjective information about the shape of the function in the reject region.

In method 5, we try to use objective information provided by the calibration sample. We begin by constructing a scorecard using the accepts who comprise the new sample. Then using the calibration sample we construct two scorecards. The first uses the entire calibration sample, including applicants in both accept and reject regions. The second scorecard constructed from the calibration sample uses only those applicants lying in the accept region. To the extent that the extrapolation method will perform poorly, this will differ from the complete calibration sample scorecard. This difference is then used as an adjustment to the scorecard built using the accepts comprising our new sample.

As an example, suppose that linear regression is used to build the scorecards. Suppose that the vector of regression coefficients for the new sample (accepts) is $a = (a_1, \ldots, a_n)$, and likewise $b = (b_1, \ldots, b_n)$ for the validation-sample accepts and $c = (c_1, \ldots, c_n)$ for the entire validation sample. Then a simple way of describing the relationship between b and c would be via a diagonal matrix M, the elements of which are simply the ratios of the components of c to those of b. That is, the ith diagonal element M is c_i / b_i. Using this matrix, an estimate of the regression coefficients for the entire new population would be Ma.

Many other adjustment schemes are possible, and the identification of those which are most effective is a topic needing further work.

9.4.3 Method 6

In Section 9.3.3 above, we described how a mixture decomposition approach could be used to estimate the parameters of $p(\cdot|g)$ and $p(\cdot|b)$ by comparing the mixture of these distributions with the empirical distribution of $p(\cdot)$. If information about the true good/bad classes of some of the applicants is known, then this can be used to improve the estimate, but this was not necessary. What was necessary was that some parameterized form for the component distributions could be assumed.

Now we are assuming that there is some information about the true good/bad classes of some of the applicants—available from the calibration sample and hence available through χ (and not restricted just to the accept region). Such information could be used to choose families for the distributions of the $p(\cdot|g)$ and $p(\cdot|b)$ distributions. As before, once the families have been chosen, estimates of the parameters can be obtained using both classified applicants and unclassified applicants via (9.2). Again, as far as we know, this approach has not been tried in practice.

9.5 Conclusion

Reject inference is the process of inferring the good/bad credit risk status of applicants who have been rejected. Approaches to such inference have been reviewed, dividing them into three classes: straightforward extrapolation methods, methods that attempt to utilize information in the distribution of the rejects, and methods based on supplementary information.

We have shown that it is important to distinguish between two broad classes of classification methods for use in reject inference: methods based on direct estimation of the probabilities of being good and methods based on indirect estimation via the class-conditional distributions. Of these, the latter is particularly susceptible to bias induced by the truncation implicit in the accept/reject decision.

We also pointed out the necessity of using all the characteristics used in the original accept/reject decision when attempting to build an improved classifier. Again, without this, a biased result is likely.

Much effort has been expended on trying to utilize information in the distribution of the rejects. We pointed out that such information can, in general, only do this if additional assumptions are made.

Sometimes a calibration sample is available, giving some information on the true good/bad class of applicants throughout the characteristic space, though often these samples are not from precisely the same sample as that to which one wishes to apply reject inference. Three original methods for using such samples have been described.

Our overall conclusion is that reliable reject inference is impossible. In particular, claims that such improvements have been achieved by reject inference are based on the following circumstances.

- *Chance.* The new rule is better than the old one by luck.
- *The use of additional information*, such as approximately correct assumed distributional forms in a mixture decomposition method, or an extra 'calibration' sample, or expert skill and knowledge of the area. The latter may, of course, be subconscious.
- *Ad hoc adjustment of the rules* in a direction likely to lead to reduced bias. For example, in the augmentation method, one might reasonably assume that the rejects with a particular x vector had a lower probability of being good than the accepts with that vector.

Acknowledgement

W. E. Henley was supported in this work by a Research Studentship awarded by Littlewoods plc.

References

Dawid, A. P. (1976) Properties of diagnostic data distributions. *Biometrics*, 32, 647–58.

Dempster, A. P., Laird, N. M., and Rubin, D. B. (1977) Maximum likelihood from incomplete data. *Journal of the Royal Statistical Society*, B, 39, 1–38.

Eisenbeis, R. A. (1978) Problems in applying discriminant analysis in credit scoring models. *Journal of Banking and Finance*, 2, 205–19.

Everitt, B. S. and Hand, D. I. (1981) *Finite Mixture Distributions*. London, Chapman and Hall.

Hand, D. J. (1981) *Discrimination and Classification*. Chichester, Wiley.

Hand, D. J. and Fitzmaurice, G. M. (1987) Error rate estimation by mixture decomposition. *Computers and Mathematics with Applications*, 14, 573–8.

Hsia, D. C. (1978) Credit scoring and the equal credit opportunity act. *The Hastings Law Journal*, 30, 371–405.

Reichert, A. K., Cho, C.-C., and Wagner, G. M. (1983) An examination of the conceptual issues involved in developing credit-scoring models. *Journal of Business and Economic Statistics*, I, 101–14.

10. The flat-maximum effect and generic linear scoring models: a test

George A. Overstreet, Jr., Edwin L. Bradley, Jr., and Robert S. Kemp, Jr.

10.1 Introduction

Predicting human behaviour patterns with linear correlation models has challenged researchers for the past five decades.[1] Although most observers generally concede that humans are inferior to such models in combining information, linear scoring models are, unfortunately, plagued by the flat-maximum effect, or the 'curse of insensitivity'.[2] As Lovie and Lovie (1986) observe, 'the predictive ability of linear models is insensitive to large variation in the size of regression weights and to the number of predictors'.[3] Even more intriguingly, regression weights can be approximated by simpler systems, such as unit or equal weights, with minimal reduction in predictive accuracy.[4] In essence, seemingly different linear scoring models tend to produce indistinguishable predictive outcomes.

Since its demonstration by Dawes and Corrigan (1974), the flat maximum has been viewed in a decidedly negative light. Lovie and Lovie (1986) offer a provocatively contrarian view, noting: 'for applied areas such as forecasting and prediction ... the

---

[1] For a representative sampling, see Wilks (1938), Myers and Forgy (1961), Dawes and Corrigan (1974), Einhorn and Hogarth (1975), Wainer (1976, 1978), Laughlin (1978), Dawes (1979), and Lovie and Lovie (1986).

[2] See Rapoport (1975), Von Winterfeldt and Edwards (1982), and Wainer's (1976) particularly lucid summary (p. 213).

[3] Lovie and Lovie (1986: 160).

[4] Lovie and Lovie (1986), citing Dawes and Corrigan (1974), Wainer (1976, 1978), and Laughlin (1978). The magnitude of loss in predictive accuracy (no more than $k/48$ where k is the number of predictor variables) reflects Laughlin's comment on Wainer (1976).

IMA Journal of Mathematics Applied in Business and Industry, 4, 97–109, 1992.

insensitivity can be less of a problem in forecasting and prediction. Indeed, . . . the presence of a flat maximum is positively advantageous, since it offers practitioners a freedom of choice denied them when the response variable . . . peaks sharply round a particular value'.[5]

Our chapter is an outgrowth of this thesis. More specifically, we examine the predictive power of a generic credit-scoring model versus individual empirically derived systems. If, as Wainer (1976) noted in regard to the flat maximum, 'it don't make no nevermind',[6] generic credit-scoring models could provide cheaper alternatives to company-specific empirically derived models. Such models would find ready use in auditing consumer loan portfolios for institutions without individually derived models. Moreover, small cooperative credit grantors such as the numerous US credit unions with assets under $5 million would be potential users.

10.2   Method

From 1984 to 1988, a series of individual linear credit-scoring models was developed for ten US credit unions, nine in the Southeast and one in the Washington DC metropolitan area. For each credit union, stepwise multiple regression was employed to select a subset of explanatory variables to be used in a discriminant analysis.[7] The two classifications on which the discriminant analyses were based were 'good' (paid as expected over at least an 18-month period) and 'bad' (charged-off, including bankruptcies). A credit-scoring equation was then developed from the resulting discriminant analysis. The credit score Z is given by a logistic function of the form

$$Z = 1000/[1 + \exp(-B_o - B_1 X_1, \ldots, -B_n X_n)],$$

where $X_1, \ldots, X_n$ are predictor variables, B_0 is a constant, and $B_1, \ldots, B_n$ are regression coefficients. Separate equations were formulated for each of the ten credit unions.

The types, coefficients, and number of variables for the ten equations are illustrated in Tables 10.1 and 10.2. It is not possible to define the variables, for proprietary reasons.[8] Variable selection was conservative in terms of complying with Regulation B

---

[5] Lovie and Lovie (1986: 161).

[6] Wainer (1976: 213) citing H. F. Kaiser (1970: A second generation little jiffy. *Psychometrika* 35, 401–15). Kaiser's comment was in regard to a similar problem in factor analysis (p. 403); it may be paraphrased as 'it is of little concern'.

[7] See Draper and Smith (1981: 294–313) and Anderson (1984: 195–217).

[8] The equations are owned by the credit unions represented anonymously in Table 10.1. Among the predictor variables common to these equations were the following: various debt-ratio and other cash-flow-oriented surrogates, employment time, home ownership, major credit-card ownership, and representations of past payment history. For a detailed equation not in this group, see Overstreet and Kemp (1986: table 2, 83). For the only other consumer-credit-scoring equation explicitly illustrated in the literature, see Crook *et al.* (1991).

Table 10.1 Development sample equations and generic equation calculation.

Coefficient	Variable type	Individual credit union equations					Weighted average coefficient
		A	B	C	D	E	
B_0		−2.4200	−2.8105	−2.1071	−2.7956	−2.0384	−2.4483
B_1	A	0.0005	0.0000	0.0000		0.0005	0.0001
B_2	A		−1.0440		−3.4313		−0.7929
B_3	A	−0.1630				−0.1832	−0.0549
B_4	A			−0.0461			−0.0105
B_5	B			0.0001		0.0001	0.0000
B_6	B					0.0304	0.0061
B_7	B	0.1088		0.0615	0.0273	0.0532	0.0403
B_8	B	0.5632	0.6456		0.8223	0.8448	0.5520
B_9	B		0.8668	1.6066		1.2076	0.8968
B_{10}	B	0.0252	0.0405				0.0160
B_{11}	B		1.0329	0.5455	2.6573		0.8127
B_{12}	C				2.7719	−1.6563	0.0291
B_{13}	C	0.7056	0.7044		2.7719		0.6721
B_{14}	C		−1.0948	−0.9240		−3.2158	−1.2213
B_{15}	C					−0.2614	−0.0529
Sample		356	1067	747	428	659	

Note: A, Cash-flow variables; B, Stability variables; C, Payment-history variables.

of the Equal Credit Opportunity Act. Care was taken to avoid nonintuitive relationships between predictor variables.[9] The credit-scoring models are arrayed by age, with A the most recent and H the oldest. Equation J, which was developed in 1988, is the same age as equation A, the most recent in the group.

The five most recent equations (A–E) were used to develop the generic equation shown in Table 10.1. It deserves noting that equations A–E were clearly not the most predictive equations in the 10 sample set. Generic coefficients were obtained by taking a weighted average of the coefficients for each variable represented in the five equations. Certain equations contained some variables not found in other individual equations. In the cases where a variable was not present in an equation, the corresponding coefficient was set equal to zero before averaging occurred. The weights were based on sample sizes used to create the discriminant equation for each system. This weighting system ensures that the influence of each system is directly proportional to the amount of data used in modelling its discriminant equation. This method thus yielded stratified sampling estimates for the generic-equation coefficients.[10] It would have been possible to have pooled the data and reformulated a new discriminant

---

[9] Overstreet and Kemp (1986: 80) citing Capon's (1982) criticism or credit-scoring systems.
[10] See Cochran (1977: 89–103).

Table 10.2   Validation sample equations.

Coefficient	Variable type	Individual credit union equation				
		F	G	H	I	J
B_0		1.2924	-1.5079	-2.1458	-0.7235	-5.6324
B_1	A		0.0001	0.0002	0.0002	0.0029
B_2	A	-2.5720	1.4790	-0.2700		-3.8179
B_3	A	-0.1542	0.2000	-0.1166		
B_4	A	-0.0791				
B_5	B			0.0003	0.0011	
B_6	B	0.0365				0.0293
B_7	B	0.0594		0.0367		0.0655
B_8	B	0.5183	1.4220	0.5425	1.5685	
B_9	B			1.0744		
B_{10}	B		0.0357			0.0456
B_{11}	B		1.0250	0.7277	1.1972	0.8641
B_{12}	C					
B_{13}	C	2.2196	1.3591	1.0318		1.5097
B_{14}	C	-3.4881	-1.1010	-1.4191		-1.3064
B_{15}	C				-0.0898	
Additional variables not present in development equations						
B_{16}	A		-1.4529			
B_{17}	A			-2.1737	-3.6588	
B_{18}	A			-0.8476	1.3190	
B_{19}	A				0.9456	
B_{20}	A				-0.0595	
B_{21}	B	-3.7464	-1.3590			
B_{22}	B					0.1467
B_{23}	C	-2.6050	-0.4953			
B_{24}	C		-0.3409			
Sample		426	875	845	474	476

Note: A, cash-flow variables; B, stability variables; C, payment-history variables.

equation, but averaging appealed to the flat-maximum effect. Numerous methods of creating such equations, including equal coefficients, are possible and deserve testing. Our purpose here was to test a generic equation created with a minimum of effort demonstrating the flat maximum's positive potential.

The generic equation is thus an empirically derived model based on over 3150 accepted (good plus bad) credit applications and 370 rejected applications. An initial and uncontrolled evaluation was made, by comparing cumulative distributions for the goods and bads for the generic equation versus the cumulative results of the individual empirically derived equations from which the generic equation was derived (equations A–E). This comparison is illustrated in Table 10.3.

Table 10.3 Relative performance of generic and individually derived equations for development samples.

Credit union	Rating[a]	Sample	200 Generic	200 Individ	300 Generic	300 Individ	400 Generic	400 Individ	500 Generic	500 Individ	700 Generic	700 Individ	900 Generic	900 Individ
A	G	239	9.20%	4.20%	23.40%	15.50%	36.00%	25.90%	51.00%	34.70%	79.90%	55.20%	100.00%	88.30%
	B	117	19.70%	10.30%	53.80%	42.70%	75.20%	66.70%	82.10%	84.60%	95.70%	93.20%	100.00%	99.10%
	B/G		2.14	2.45	2.30	2.75	2.09	2.58	1.61	2.44	1.20	1.69	1.00	1.12
B	G	771	3.10%	2.20%	11.00%	8.60%	17.80%	14.80%	27.40%	22.60%	58.60%	51.50%	95.50%	94.00%
	B	296	16.90%	15.20%	40.90%	35.80%	56.40%	49.30%	67.20%	62.20%	86.50%	83.40%	99.70%	99.30%
	B/G		5.45	6.91	3.72	4.16	3.17	3.33	2.45	2.75	1.48	1.62	1.04	1.06
C	G	547	5.10%	2.00%	10.20%	4.40%	19.20%	18.20%	29.80%	34.40%	55.00%	71.70%	88.30%	98.50%
	B	204	18.60%	12.50%	33.80%	21.20%	51.00%	46.20%	59.80%	68.10%	78.90%	93.80%	97.50%	100.00%
	B/G		3.65	6.25	3.31	4.82	2.66	2.54	2.01	1.98	1.43	1.31	1.10	1.02
D	G	282	3.20%	7.20%	5.70%	10.10%	12.10%	15.30%	19.10%	20.80%	38.30%	31.80%	77.70%	41.90%
	B	146	28.80%	64.30%	52.70%	71.30%	69.20%	77.80%	80.10%	88.30%	94.50%	93.00%	99.30%	97.10%
	B/G		9.0	8.93	9.25	7.06	5.72	5.08	4.19	4.25	2.47	2.92	1.28	2.32
E	G	361	3.00%	2.80%	11.90%	4.70%	23.30%	10.10%	38.00%	21.80%	78.10%	58.70%	97.50%	91.90%
	B	198	22.20%	27.30%	36.90%	36.10%	59.60%	51.50%	71.20%	62.90%	93.40%	93.80%	100.00%	100.00%
	B/G		7.40	9.75	3.10	7.68	2.56	5.10	1.87	2.89	1.20	1.60	1.03	1.09
Total	G	2200	4.30%	3.11%	11.60%	7.86%	20.30%	16.14%	31.20%	26.49%	60.60%	55.58%	92.20%	87.48%
	B	961	20.50%	23.98%	41.90%	39.00%	60.10%	55.54%	70.20%	70.29%	88.70%	90.40%	99.30%	99.23%
	B/G		4.77	7.72	3.61	4.96	2.96	3.44	2.25	2.65	1.46	1.63	1.08	1.13

[a] G, a loan that paid out as expected over at least an 18 month period; B, a loan that did not pay as expected (i.e. bankrupts and charge-offs).

10.2.1   Developmental results

In testing the generic equation against its parts, the presence of sample bias clearly favours the individual equations. In essence, each sample set serves as a holdout sample for the generic model, which in turn is compared against its own development sample.

The cumulative percentages of 'good' and 'bad' samples for the generic equation and each of its five separate developmental samples are arrayed in Table 10.3. The ratio of 'bads' to 'goods' ('kill' ratio) is calculated from the respective cumulative percentages at varying interval ranges across the 1,000-point scale on which each equation was based.

Since the optimal cut-off score differs for each individual equation as well as for the generic equation, determination of the relative performance of the generic versus its individual components is not clear cut.[11] The most appropriate point of comparison in the 1,000-point range differs for each comparative evaluation. The analyst must consider the comparative level of bads eliminated versus incorrectly identified goods for the generic equation versus its individually derived counterpart at different points in the 1,000-point range on which each equation was based. As expected, the individual equations outperformed the generic model across most of the range. With the exception of equation D, the individual equations clearly outperformed the generic model. Even with D, most analysts would prefer the individual model which identifies 71.3 per cent of the bads versus 10.1 per cent of the goods at the 300 level. In comparison, the generic equation identifies 52.7 per cent of the bads versus 5.7 per cent goods at the same level. It never quite reaches the same high level of discrimination, but it comes close at the 400 level (69.2 per cent versus 12.1 per cent, Table 10.3).

More formally, the Kolmogorov–Smirnov test for equality of distributions was used to evaluate statistically the difference between the two sets of results. As one would expect from causal observation, the results in each case were statistically significant-in fact, at a probability level of 0.0001. Still, the generic equation must be judged to have performed relatively well.

---

[11] It would have been possible to have measured the predictive power or each credit-scoring equation by the Kolmogorov–Smirnov (K–S) statistic. This statistic measures the ability of a formula to separate the two types of creditworthiness. Moreover, the equations could have been compared on a percentage basis with the highest K–S denoted as 100 per cent and the others indexed to that amount. We felt more comfortable in arraying the cumulative percentages for the creditworthy and non-creditworthy, letting the reader consider the gross predictive results. The optimal cut-off score is marginally defined as the point where marginal benefits equal marginal costs. With 400–500 basis-point difference in consumer loan versus investment yields, it takes 10–20 good loans to equal a single bad loan. Cut-off scores were set in practice at relatively low levels (i.e. below the optimal cut-off score), thereby favouring the applicant-member.

10.2.2   Validation

As noted, neither of the preceeding analyses was intended as a test of the generic model's relative predictive power. Four Southeastern samples (F–I) and one recent northern Virginia sample (J) illustrated in Table 10.2 were used to test the generic model's performance formally. A fortuitous aspect of using a sample of credit unions is their closed or narrow fields of membership, generally related to employment. Given the large number of members in the generic equation, it should represent the average Southeastern credit-union consumer. Individual credit-union samples tend to differ markedly from the average demographic profile of individual credit-union member-ships. Only credit union H represented a statewide sample. Employee groups such as county employees, national guardsmen, teachers, and paper-manufacturing employees are represented in the Southeastern holdout samples. Credit union J's membership of specialized federal-government employees living in the affluent northern Virginia area presents an even more challenging predictive task for the generic model.[12] Clearly, the generic equation would not be expected to perform on a par with such narrowly defined groups and their respective equations, much less government employees in a much more affluent setting. Unless, of course, 'it (really) don't make no nevermind'.[6]

Like the earlier analysis, the presence of sample bias again affects the more con-trolled holdout test. Equations F–J (Table 10.4) serve individually and cumulatively as a holdout sample for the generic equation. In contrast, individual equation performance was based on each equation's development sample. Limited sample sizes precluded the use of individually drawn holdout samples. Clearly, both the sample's bias and its demographic makeup favour individual equation performance over the generic model. Table 10.4 presents the comparative results for the generic equation and each of the five holdout sample equations. As in the preceding discussion, cumulative percentages of goods and bads are arrayed at varying points on the 1,000-point scale. In studying the comparative results, the analyst is immediately struck by the fact that both the generic and individual equations performed better than the developmental equations (equations A–E) from which the generic equation was developed (see Table 10.3). Both the generic and individual equations exhibited excellent discriminatory power.

The historical performance of the individual equations underscores this important aspect of test validity. All the individual equations represented in Table 10.4 contrib-uted to dramatically lower charge-off rates (to average loans) with no appreciable loss in loan volume. For example, credit union J's 1988 charge-off ratio of 0.7 per cent,

---

[12] Family members and employees no longer working at the credit union's sponsor are also eligible for membership. For the credit unions in the sample, these factors have not contributed to more diversified groups. Nor have they taken select employee groups into their fields. The 'common bond' of employment thus provides us with a natural form of control, further enhancing the holdout sample test of the generic equation.

Table 10.4 Relative performance of generic and individually derived equations for validation samples.

Credit union	Rating[a]	Sample	200 Generic	200 Individ	300 Generic	300 Individ	400 Generic	400 Individ	500 Generic	500 Individ	700 Generic	700 Individ	900 Generic	900 Individ
F	G	294	0.30%	6.50%	1.40%	8.50%	2.00%	10.50%	4.80%	10.50%	19.40%	15.00%	74.10%	25.50%
	B	132	18.20%	67.40%	28.00%	73.50%	40.20%	82.60%	59.80%	82.60%	78.80%	90.20%	97.00%	94.70%
	B/G		60.67	10.37	20.00	8.65	20.10	7.87	12.46	7.87	4.06	6.01	1.31	3.71
G	G	585	2.40%	5.80%	6.00%	9.60%	10.10%	17.40%	17.30%	17.40%	36.20%	28.70%	86.00%	55.20%
	B	290	21.70%	56.20%	40.30%	65.90%	56.20%	79.70%	68.60%	79.70%	87.90%	87.60%	99.00%	96.20%
	B/G		9.04	9.69	6.72	6.86	5.56	4.58	3.97	4.58	2.43	3.05	1.15	1.74
H	G	856	5.00%	4.30%	11.90%	11.80%	19.90%	19.90%	22.20%	22.20%	58.20%	50.60%	94.20%	92.50%
	B	402	28.90%	30.60%	46.00%	48.90%	62.20%	69.70%	74.40%	69.70%	91.30%	98.10%	99.80%	100.00%
	B/G		5.78	7.12	3.87	4.14	3.13	3.14	2.50	3.14	1.57	1.76	1.06	1.08
I	G	330	0.30%	5.80%	4.20%	7.90%	10.60%	10.60%	29.40%	16.70%	67.00%	34.20%	98.80%	66.10%
	B	146	7.50%	52.10%	32.20%	67.10%	61.00%	77.40%	80.80%	85.60%	96.60%	92.50%	100.00%	99.30%
	B/G		25.00	8.98	7.67	8.49	5.75	7.30	2.75	5.13	1.44	2.70	1.01	1.50
J	G	265	3.80%	0.80%	7.90%	3.4%	15.80%	6.80%	25.70%	13.20%	35.10%	35.10%	67.90%	82.60%
	B	84	48.80%	20.20%	64.30%	36.90%	83.30%	50.00%	85.70%	66.70%	91.70%	85.70%	100.00%	98.80%
	B/G		12.84	2.525	8.14	10.85	5.27	7.35	3.33	5.05	2.61	2.44	1.47	1.20
Total	G	2330	2.95%	4.77%	7.55%	9.32%	13.40%	16.12%	22.98%	17.72%	46.40%	36.52%	87.27%	69.82%
	B	1054	24.20%	44.40%	41.72%	58.22%	59.31%	73.56%	72.76%	76.03%	89.57%	89.03%	99.27%	98.10%
	B/G		8.20	9.31	5.53	6.24	4.43	4.56	3.17	4.29	1.93	2.44	1.14	1.41

[a] G, a loan that paid out as expected over at least an 18-month period; B, a loan that did not pay as expected (i.e. bankrupts and charge-offs).

approximately the level of its peer institutions, dropped to 0.2 per cent for 1991, which was well below the average of its peers. During the same period, loan volume increased significantly, with credit union J's loan-to-deposit ratio rising from 50 to 70 per cent approximately. In the cases represented in Table 10.4, the respective credit-union experience represents a benefit–cost ratio in the range 12–15 approximately. The generic model's performance should be considered within the context of this rather impressive record for the individually developed credit-scoring models.

Interestingly, the generic equation performed better on the validation or holdout sample than for the developmental sample on which it was derived (Tables 10.3 and 10.4). Comparing the cumulative per cent of bads versus goods at 200, 300, and 400 (generic equation results for all systems, Tables 10.3 and 10.4), the more accurate discriminatory power of the generic equation on the holdout sample is readily apparent. At a 300 level in the validation sample, for example, the generic equation correctly identified 41.7 per cent of the bads while falsely labelling 7.5 per cent of the goods. In comparison, the generic equation's relative identification rates of bads versus false goods for its developmental sample was 41.9 per cent and 11.6 per cent at the 300 level (all systems, Table 10.3). At other points in the scoring range for the two samples, the generic equation consistently did better on the holdout or validation sample. Although the generic equation should have performed better on its developmental sample due to sample bias, it would appear that 'it (really) don't make no nevermind'.[6] Perhaps this can be attributed to the robust nature of a more complete set of predictor variables than that offered by individually derived equations.[13] Certainly, this would tend to be the general case associated with a larger sample size such as that associated with the generic equation.

As illustrated in Table 10.4, the individual equations outperformed the generic model on a combined basis and, with perhaps the exception of credit union F, on an individual basis. Grouping the generic and individual combined results based on their respective identification of bads, it becomes obvious that the individual equations had a slight edge in predictive power. For example, at 300 level, the generic model identified 41.7 per cent bads with a corresponding misclassification of goods of 7.6 per cent. By comparison, the individual combined results were 44.4 per cent bads with a comparatively lower loss of 4.8 per cent goods (200 level, individual results, Table 10.4). Results are similar if the same procedure is followed at other levels of bad loans, for example, 58.2 per cent bads and 9.3 per cent goods (individual results at 300) versus 59.1 per cent bads and 13.4 per cent goods (generic results at 400).

---

[13] As Dawes and Corrigan (1974: 105) note, 'the whole trick is to decide what variables to look at and then know how to add'.

In short, the individual equations were favoured due to sample bias and, in fact, demonstrated slightly better results. Once again, however, 'it (really) don't make no nevermind'.[6] Both systems perform relatively well.

10.2.3   Further results

Following a suggestion by Lovie and Lovie (1986), an additional exercise was designed for the generic equation and a holdout sample. Among various future research paths, Lovie and Lovie point to the need to assess the effects of employing alternative regression estimators such as ridge regression and using more than two outcomes on the performance of scoring models.[14] It was decided to develop an alternative regression model from which to test the predictive power of the discriminant models presented in Tables 10.3 and 10.4. The generic model's results would be arrayed against both. Additional categorizations of creditworthiness would be tested as well, including 'slow' payers and 'poor' payers. The former classification was defined as having not more than two payments 30 days overdue, and the latter as having more than two 30-day payments overdue but not more than one 60-day payment overdue. Goods and bads were categorized, respectively, as having paid as specified for at least 18 months, with no more than one 30-day overdue, and all charge-offs, including bankruptcies. Let us emphasize that we did not re-estimate the model to reflect four possible outcomes (i.e. good, slow, poor, and bad); instead we scored the two intermediate categories with two-class good/bad) regression models.

Biased estimation in data analysis and model building has been shown to predict and extrapolate better when predictor variables are highly correlated, a problem common to credit-scoring data sets.[15] It is desirable to have more variables in the discriminant function than just those selected stepwise, or by any other single variable selection method, for the following reasons. Loan officers applying the resulting equation have difficulty understanding, for example, why 'income' is included as a predictor variable and 'net worth' is not included. That is, the equation should include, where possible, those variables that the user believes to be predictive. The more variables there are in the equation, the less likely it is that one variable will dominate the results.[15]

Biased regression techniques, such as the technique of principal-components regression that we chose, offer other potential benefits. The regression parameter estimates obtained from principal-components regression offer one of the best opportunities for a large reduction in mean square error.[16] Marquardt and Snee (1975) note that

In achieving optimum fit to the estimation data, least squares often destroys good prediction of new data (possibly outside the region covered by the estimation data . . .). Variable selection

---

[14] Lovie and Lovie (1986: 166).   [15] Kleinbaum et al. (1988: 560–94).
[16] Gunst and Mason (1977).

Table 10.5   Relative performance of generic and individually derived equations for credit union J.

Estimation method	Rating[a]	Selected credit-score intervals					
		200	300	400	500	700	900
Stepwise-discriminant	G 265	3.8	7.9	15.8	25.7	35.1	67.9
analysis	S 49	6.1	14.3	18.4	26.5	44.9	87.8
	P 25	12.0	24.0	56.0	76.0	84.0	88.0
	B 84	48.8	64.3	83.3	85.7	91.7	100.0
	R 95	21.1	28.4	42.1	52.6	70.5	87.4
Principal-components	G 265	4.5	9.4	12.8	19.6	38.9	74.3
analysis	S 49	6.1	14.3	20.4	24.5	51.0	87.8
	P 25	24.0	32.0	40.0	56.0	84.0	88.0
	B 84	51.2	64.3	73.8	83.3	92.9	100.0
	R 94	22.1	37.9	41.1	54.7	74.7	91.6
Generic equation	G 265	0.8	3.4	6.8	13.2	35.1	82.6
	S 49	6.1	12.2	14.3	28.6	55.1	85.7
	P 25	0.0	4.0	16.0	32.0	68.0	100.0
	B 84	20.2	36.9	50.0	66.7	85.7	98.8
	R 95	16.8	26.3	38.9	52.6	82.1	98.9

[a] G (goods) paid as expected over at least an 18-month period with no more than one 30-day overdue; S (slows) two 30-day payments overdue; P (poors) more than two 30-day overdues; and B (bads) charge-offs, including bankruptcies; R, rejects in the original sample, which are scored for comparative purposes.

implies a simplistic two-valued classification logic wherein any predictor variable must either be important or unimportant. Large prediction biases can result from elimination of 'non-significant' predictors. It is better to use a little bit of all the variables than all of some of the variables and none of the remaining ones ... Biased estimators can alleviate both of these limitations.[17]

Table 10.5 presents the results of this latter analysis. It was conducted on credit union J's sample, because it offered the greatest demographic difference to the generic sample. In addition, J's individual equation was completed in 1988, eliminating potential bias in regard to time. The greater predictive power and sample bias favouring the individual discriminant equation have already been discussed.

Comparing the good–bad percentage mix for the stepwise discriminant versus the generic equation at various levels confirms this overall assessment of the results. At the 200 level, the discriminant equation identified 49 per cent of the bads while misclassifying 4 per cent of the goods. At the 400 level, the generic equation performs

[17] Marquardt and Snee (1975: 4).

almost as well, with 50 per cent of the bads and 7 per cent of the goods misclassified. Certainly, the generic equation's predictive power is respectable. This is particularly good in light of the sample bias inherent in the analysis and the impressive historical performance of credit union J's scoring model. The biased regression equation performs approximately as well as its discriminant counterpart (see Table 10.4).

As expected from the estimation procedure, which excluded the slow and poor classifications, none of the models displayed outstanding abilities in identifying the incremental classifications. None of the equations did well in classifying correctly the 'slows'. However, it could be argued that the generic equation was the winner in this regard. If a cut-off score of 500 were chosen for the generic model, it would have identified almost 30 per cent of this group. Given a similar level of performance, the two individually developed models correctly identified approximately 20 per cent of the 'slows' (see Table 10.5 at the 300 level for the discriminant model and 400 level for the principal-components model). However, the 'kill ratio' or discrimination of bads to goods was not as robust for the generic model as for the individually developed regression models. Nor can it be claimed that the principal-components equation is an improvement over the discriminant model in this particular case.

The most obvious conclusion from this secondary analysis is the rather solid performance of all equations, particularly the generic example. Once again, it must be observed, 'it (simply) don't make no nevermind'.[6]

10.3   Conclusions

Our findings support Lovie and Lovie's (1986) challenge to the conventional wisdom that the flat maximum casts a pall on the successful modelling of judgement processes. Theoretically, the flat maximum implies a positive role for simpler and hence cheaper generic models. Our tests of such a model confirm this hypothesis empirically. Additionally research needs to be conducted regarding the optimal structure of such models. If it is the variables that matter in credit scoring, it should be possible to develop hybrid models with generic cores that perform as well as empirically derived linear models. Achieving more accurate and humane assessment of creditworthiness is an important social goal. The use of generic models can hopefully 'make some nevermind'.

References

Anderson, T. W. (1984) *An Introduction to Multivariate Statistical Analysis*, 2nd edn. Wiley, New York, pp. 195–217.

Capon, N. (1982) Credit scoring systems: a critical analysis. *Journal of Marketing*, 46, 82–91.

Chandler, C. G. *et al.* (1979) A comparative analysis of empirical vs. judgmental credit evaluation. *Journal of Retail Banking*, I, 15–26.

Cochran, W. G. (1977) *Sampling Techniques*, 3rd edn. Wiley, New York, pp. 89–103.

Crook, J. N., Hamilton, R., and Thomas, L. C. (1991) A comparison of discriminators under alternative definitions of default. In *Credit Scoring and Credit Control* (eds. L. C. Thomas, J. N. Crook, and D. Edelman). Oxford University Press, Oxford.

Dawes, R. M. (1979) The robust beauty of improper linear models. *American Psychologist*, 34, 571–82.

Dawes, R. M. and Corrigan, B. (1974) Linear models in decision-making. *Psychological Bulletin*, 81, 95–106.

Draper, N. R. and Smith, H. (1981) *Applied Regression Analysis*, 2nd edn. Wiley, New York, pp. 294–313.

Einhorn, H. J. and Hogarth, R. M. (1975) United weighting schemes for decision making. *Organizational Behavior and Human Performance*, 13, 171–92.

Gunst, R. F. and Mason, R. L. (1977) Biased estimation in regression: an evaluation using mean squared error. *Journal of American Statistical Association*, 71, 616–28.

Haggstrom, G. W. (1983) Logistic regression and discriminant analysis by ordinary least squares. *Journal of Business and Economic Statistics*, 1, 229–37.

Hooarth, R. M. (1980) *Judgement and Choice*. Wiley, New York.

Hollander, M. and Wolfe, D. A. (1973) *Nonparametric Statistical Methods*. Wiley, New York, pp. 219–28.

Kleinbaum, D. B., Kupper, L. L., and Muller, K. W. (1988) *Applied Research Analysis and Other Multivariable Methods*, 2nd edn. PWS-Kent, Boston. pp. 560–94.

Laughlin, J. E. (1978) Comment on estimating coefficient in linear models: it don't.make no nevermind. *Psychological Bulletin*, 85, 247–53.

Lovie, A. D. and Lovie, P. (1986) The flat maximum effect and linear scoring models for prediction. *Journal of Forecasting*, 5, 159–68.

Marquardt, D. W. and Snee, R. D. (1975) Ridge regression in practice. *American Statistician*, 29, 3–20.

Meehl, P. E. (1954) *Clinical versus Statistical Predicion: A Theoretical Analysis and a Review of the Evidence*. University of Minnesota Press, Minneapolis.

Myers, J. H. and Porgy, E. W. (1963) The development of numerical credit evaluation systems. *Journal of American Statistics*, 58, 799–806.

Overstreet, G. A. and Kemp, R. S. (1986) Managerial control implications of empirically derived credit scoring systems: a case analysis. *Journal of Retail Banking*, 8, 79–86.

Rapoport, A. (1975) Research paradigms for studying dynamic decision behavior. In *Utility, Probability, and Human Decision Making* (eds. D. Wendt and C. A. J. Ylek). Reidel, Dordrecht.

Von Winterfeldt, D. and Edwards, W. (1982) Cost and payoffs in perceptual research. *Psychological Bulletin*, 91, 609–22.

Walner, H. (1976) Estimating coefficients in linear models: it don't make no nevermind. *Psychological Bulletin*, 83, 213–7.

Wainer, H. (1976) On the sensitivity of regression and regressors. *Psychological Bulletin*, 85, 267–73.

Wilks, S. S. (1938) Weighting systems for linear functions of correlated variables when there is no dependent variable. *Psychometrika*, 3, 23–40.

11. The degradation of the scorecard over the business cycle

Jonathan N. Crook, Lyn C. Thomas, and Robert Hamilton

The published literature on credit scoring has neither compared the characteristics of those who default nor the discriminating power of individual variables used to predict default, under different economic conditions. Similarly, scorecards constructed by credit-scoring agencies are estimated from data relating to two or three consecutive years for applications over 3–5 years before. The aim of this chapter is to explore the effects of changes in a scoring function over time on the classification of applicants into those likely to default and those not likely to default.

Linear discriminant analysis is applied to a training sample of 26,043 applicants for a bank credit card to estimate empirically a model of their repayment behaviour in 1989 and 1990. The variables that have additional statistically significant discriminating power over others are broadly similar between the 2 years, although some differences exist. Using a holdout sample of 17,084 cases, which is thought to be representative of a profile of applications to the data-supplying organization, we cross-tabulate the number who would be accepted and rejected using the 1989 model with the corresponding predictions using the 1990 model. The characteristics of those who would be accepted using the 1989 model but rejected using the 1990 model are identified. Differences in the predicted classification of a case may be due to differences between the 2 years in the functions estimated and/or to differences in the prior probabilities of default. We consider the proportion of applicants who would be accepted in a year but not in the other if the prior probabilities were adjusted to give the same rejection rate in both years, and discuss their characteristics.

In *Credit Scoring and Credit Control*, (eds. Thomas, Crook, and Edelman), pp. 111–23. OUP, Oxford 2002.

11.1   Introduction

The literature on credit-scoring systems has concentrated on two issues. One is the pre-dictive performance of different statistical techniques that may be used to distinguish between defaulters and non-defaulters (Myers and Forgy 1963; Wiginton 1980; Boyle *et al.* 1991). The other issue is how to predict whether a person who has missed a given number of consecutive payments will subsequently miss more (Chandler and Coffman 1983–4; Bierman and Hausman 1970; Crook *et al.* 1992a). However, the following questions have not been addressed: how do changes over time in default rates affect the ability of certain variables to predict default, and what are the characteristics of people who are predicted to be good in 1 year but bad in the other? The aim of this chapter is to shed some light on these questions.

The proportion of credit-card holders who default varies considerably over time, as does the importance of different characteristics of individuals that are used to predict defaulters and non-defaulters in a scoring rule. This means that an applicant for credit may be accepted (rejected) if (s)he is scored on a rule developed from payment performance in, say, an economic depression but rejected (accepted) if (s)he is scored on a rule developed from performances during an economic boom.

Credit grantors may react in a number of ways. One option is to develop a scoring rule over a number of years that includes a complete cycle of economic activity. A difficulty with this option is that it may involve so long a time period that the model is no longer accurate for the future period for which it is required to predict. There may be changes in culture, attitudes, and other factors that can affect repayment behaviour but which are often not included in scorecards. Another option is to develop and use a different scoring rule in different time periods, for example, a scoring rule may be developed and used for periods of economic depression only, and another scoring rule developed and used in periods of economic prosperity. Since the state of the economy varies continuously, this policy may involve updating a scoring rule annually. A third option is to develop a scoring rule in a period of depression or prosperity, and vary the cut-off score to maintain the same reject rate.

In this chapter, we estimate a scoring model in each of 2 years separately. The default rate differs between the 2 years. We consider how the discriminating power of different variables differs between the 2 years, and the characteristics of those who would be rejected using a model estimated for 1 year but accepted on the basis of a model estimated for a different year. We also consider the characteristics of those who may be affected by a change in the cut-off score from that indicated by the default rate in the observation period.

Following an explanation of our methodology in Section 11.2, Section 11.3 con-siders the relative discriminating power of each variable in the 2 years. Section 11.4 considers the effects of changes in the cut-off scores, Section 11.5 discusses the implications of the results for credit grantors in their policy decisions, and Section 11.6 concludes.

11.2   Methodology

11.2.1   The data

Data were acquired for two recent years, which differed in terms of the state of the national economy. The years chosen were 1989 and 1990. Table 11.1 shows values of the Coincident Indicator of the state of the UK economy calculated from those published by the Central Statistical Office. It shows that the level of economic activity was clearly lower in 1990 than in 1989.

The initial sample consists of 37,213 individuals who held a bank credit card and who had used it since it was issued, and 6,444 individuals whose application for a card was rejected. Seventy per cent of the accepted applications were randomly selected as a training sample. The remaining 30 per cent were combined with an appropriate number of rejects to form a holdout sample such that the rejects made up 35 per cent of the total holdout. This was the proportion that industry sources suggested were typically rejected. The holdout was therefore representative of a typical batch of applications to a bank credit-card issuer. Applicants aged under 18 in 1989 were deleted from the sample.

Many alternative definitions of 'default' by an individual could be adopted. In this chapter we define *default* as the missing of three consecutive payments due on their

Table 11.1   Values of the coincident indicator for the UK economy.[a]

1989		1990	
Q1	107.1	Q1	103.9
Q2	105.2	Q2	103.0
Q3	104.5	Q3	98.5
Q4	104.2	Q4	93.8

Long-term trend = 100

[a] Calculated from 'Cyclical Indicators for the UK', Economic Trends, No. 454, August 1991, Page 72, Table A.
Notes: The Coincident Indicator is a weighted average of the following series: GDP(A) at factor cost, constant prices, 1985 = 100; Output of the production industries, 1985 = 100; CBI Quarterly Survey: below-capacity utilization (%); Index of volume of retail sales, 1985 = 100; CBI Quarterly Survey: change in stocks of raw material (% balance).

Table 11.2　The samples.

	1989		1990	
	Training sample	Holdout sample	Training sample	Holdout sample
Non-defaulters	25,070	10,744	24,135	10,381
Defaulters	973	420	1,908	783
Rejects	0	5,920	0	5,920
Total	26,043	17,084	26,043	17,084

credit-card debt outstanding. This definition was chosen because it is consistent with that used by the industry. Table 11.2 shows the division of the training and holdout samples into defaulters, non-defaulters, and rejected applications.

Data were available on 24 socio-demographic and economic variables that have been used in previous discriminant analysis scoring models (see Capon 1982) or for which an a priori reason why they may act as effective discriminators could be made. The 24 variables are shown in Table 11.A1 of the Appendix. All data, excluding repayment history data, were taken from each applicant's application form.

11.2.2　Estimation

The methodology follows that of Crook *et al.* (1992*b*). Briefly, many of the variables were measured at nominal level, whereas the estimation method used—linear discriminant analysis—requires data to be measured at least at interval level (see Klecka 1980). Additional information was used to derive interval-level data by ascribing to each predictor the values

$$X_j = \ln(g_k/b_k) + \ln(B_T/G_T) \tag{11.1}$$

where X_j = value of predictor for case j, g_k = number of good payers in nominal category k, the category of which j was a member, b_k = number of poor payers in nominal category k, the category of which j was a member, G_T = number of good payers in the sample, B_T = number of poor payers in the sample.

The use of the X_j transformation means that X_j may not be monotone in the values of the original variable. High degrees of collinearity between predictor variables were removed by deleting cases where such collinearity had been detected in a different sample of 1001 cases who applied for a card around 1 year earlier than the cases in this study.[1]

---

[1]　Let A denote the earlier sample, and B the sample used for this study. Sample A contained data on exactly the same variables from the same bank as was used in sample B. To determine which variables to delete in sample B, it was assumed that the degree of collinearity detected in sample A applied to sample B also. Sample A consisted of 1001 cases, with data relating to applications in the period September 1986 to December 1987. To detect such collinearity, the tolerances were calculated for each variable, and the matrix of linear correlation coefficients was examined.

We were interested in variables that individually contributed additional statistically significant discriminatory power beyond that contributed by other variables. Therefore, in each discriminant analysis, predictors were selected for inclusion in the empirical function by a stepwise procedure.[2]

11.3   Changes in discriminating functions

Separate discriminant analyses were performed for 1989 and 1990, using the values of X_j for each respective year and the repayment behaviour of each individual in the relevant year. For both functions, the group centroids (goods and bads) are statistically different using a Chi-square test of the significance of Wilk's lambda. The classification matrices are shown in Table 11.3. These relate to the holdout sample. In each matrix the prior probability of group membership, that is, the probability that a case is a member of a particular group when no information about it is available, was calculated by treating the rejected cases (34.65 per cent of the total holdout) as defaulters as well as the actual defaulters. That is

$$P_b = (B + R)/(G + B + R) \qquad P_g = G/(G + B + R), \qquad (11.2)$$

where P_b = prior probability that a case is a bad, that is defaults, P_g = prior probability that a case is a good, that is does not default, G = number of goods, B = number of bads, R = number of rejects.

Table 11.3 clearly shows that the empirical scoring systems predict group membership better than chance.

Table 11.4 shows the standardized canonical discriminant-function coefficients, which indicate the relative additional discriminatory power that each variable has, given the other variables in the function. Only those variables that have a significant amount of discriminatory power are included. While the discriminatory power of many variables was similar in both years, the relative discriminatory power of certain predictors was markedly different. First, 'number of children', 'major credit card', and 'deposit account' had relatively higher discriminatory power compared with the other included variables in 1989 (the year with the greater default rate) than in 1990, while outgoings had relatively greater discriminatory power in 1990 than in 1989. In 1990, 'residential status', 'charge card', and 'mortgage balance outstanding' had statistically significant additional discriminatory power over that of other included

---

[2] At each step, the variable that resulted in the greatest squared Mahalanobis distance D^2 was added. The significance of a change in D^2 when a variable was included was tested using a partial-F statistic. The probability that the F-to-enter value was significant was set equal to 5%, regardless of the change in the degrees of freedom that occurred with the change in the number of included predictor variables. The same probability was adopted for the F-to-remove.

Table 11.3 Classification matrices.

	Predicted group					
	1989			1990		
	Goods	Bads	Total	Goods	Bads	Total
Actual						
Good	9,543	1,201	10,744	8,744	1,637	10,381
Bad	319	101	420	535	248	783
Reject	4,401	1,521	5,922	3,463	2,457	5,920
Total	14,253	2,823	17,086	12,742	4342	17,084
% correct		65.35			67.02	
$C_{prop} = 100(P_b^2 + P_g^2)(\%)$		53.32			52.32	

Table 11.4 Standardized canonical discriminant function coefficients.

1989			1990		
	Value	Rank		Value	Rank
Years at bank	0.45	1	Years at bank	0.43	1
Cheque card	0.33	2	Cheque card	0.32	2
Number of children	0.33	3	Outgoings	0.31	3
Applicants employment status	0.27	4	Applicants employment status	0.25	4
Outgoings	0.25	5	Number of children	0.21	5
Years at present employment	0.21	6	Phone	0.20	6
Major credit card	0.20	7	Residential status	0.19	7
Phone	0.19	8	Years at present employment	0.19	8
Deposit account	0.11	9	Charge card	0.13	9
Store card	0.11	10	Store card	0.10	10
			Major credit card	0.09	11
			Mortgage balance outstanding	0.09	12
			Deposit account	0.08	13

variables, which they did not have in 1989, and so were not included in the estimated function for the latter year by the stepwise routine.

11.4   Effects of changes in cut-off scores

Our data suggest that the behaviour of some individuals differed between the 2 years. First, the overall default rate differs between the 2 years. This implies a difference in the prior probabilities of membership of a specific group. Second, the default rates for each value of each predictor variable differ between the 2 years. Therefore the X_j value for each group of values for a given variable differs between the 2 years.

Table 11.5 Total effect cross-tabulation.

	Actual 1989 priors and function		
	Good	Bad	Total
Actual 1990 priors and function			
Good	12,506 (73.2)	236 (1.4)	12,742
Bad	1,755 (10.3)	2,587 (15.1)	4,342
Total	14,261	2,823	17,084 (100)

Figures in parentheses are the number of cases in the cell as a percentage of the number of cases in the total holdout sample.

The second difference results in different standardized and unstandardized canonical discriminant-function coefficients between the 2 years, and in differences in the degree of separation between the two groups. This implies that there may be a difference between the 2 years in the conditional probability $P(S/G_i)$ that a case gains a score S, given that it is a member of group i (see the Appendix). A case is classified into the group in which the probability of its membership, given its score, is greater. That is

$$P(G_i/S) = P(S/G_i)P(G_i i) \bigg/ \sum_{i=1}^{n} P(S/G_i)P(G_i i) \qquad (11.3)$$

where $P(G_i/S)$ is the posterior probability that a case with score S is classified into group i, and $P(G_i)$ is the prior probability that a case is a member of group i. Therefore the difference in both the prior and conditional probabilities between 2 years implies that a case may be classified as a good (bad) in 1 year and a bad (good) in the other.

We now examine the effects that both the different empirical models and the different prior probabilities ('priors') together have on predicted applicant performance. Specifically we ask what the characteristics are of those who would be accepted in 1989 using the 1989 canonical function coefficients and priors but rejected in 1990 using the 1990 canonical function coefficients and priors.[3] Table 11.5 shows the number of people affected. While the same decision would have been given to 88.3 per cent of the holdout cases if either function and priors were used, the decision would have been different in 11.7 per cent of cases. Approximately 10 per cent of the holdout would have been accepted if the 1989 function and priors were used, but rejected if the 1990 function and priors were used instead, and 1.4 per cent of cases would have been accepted if the 1990 function and priors were used but rejected using the 1989 model.

---

[3] In the interests of brevity, the term 'differences in the canonical coefficients between the 2 years' will be taken to include differences between the 2 years in the variables included in the predictive models by the stepwise routines.

Table 11.6   Modal groups: total effects.

	The holdout sample in aggregate		Those predicted to be good on the 1989 function with 1989 priors but bad on the 1990 function with 1990 priors	
	Modal group	% of cases	Modal group	% of cases
Number of children	0, 6, 7, 8	69	0, 6, 7, 8	76
Number of dependants	0, 3, 4, 5, 24	98	0, 3, 4, 5, 24	98
Applicant's employment status	Private sector	65	Private sector	66
Deposit account	No	64	No	65
Loan account	No	95	No	96
Cheque card account	No	75	No	79
Current account	Yes	67	Yes	67
Major credit card	No	60	No	68
Charge card	No	76	No	86
Store card	No	78	Yes	78
Applicant's employment category	Services—Office, sales, labourer, executive, trades, others	46	Services—Office, sales, labourer, executive, trades, others	52
Age in 1990	18–24 years	27	25–30 years	31
Building society card	No	92	No	91
Phone	No	83	No	70
Spouse's income	£0	78	£0	82
Years at present employment	0, 1 years	28	0, 1 years	39
Years at same bank	0, 1 years	28	0, 1 years	35
Value of home	£0	64	£0	79
Applicant's income	£0–6000	24	£0–6000	26
Mortgage balance outstanding	£0	68	£0	92
Outgoings	£0	24	£1–99	30
Residential status	Owner	38	Tenant furnished	33
Spouse's employment category	No response	68	No response	74
Years at present address	0, 1 years	28	0, 1 years	38
Sample size	17,084		1755	

Table 11.6 compares the characteristics of those who would be accepted on the 1989 model but rejected using the 1990 model[4] with those of the holdout sample in aggregate. The table suggests that those for whom a different decision would be made depending on the year to which the model related are very similar to the holdout sample as a whole. The modal groups for both cells are the same for 20 characteristics. The differences in modal groups are whether or not a store card is possessed ('yes' for the

---

[4] We could examine the characteristics of those in any of the cells in Table 11.5. To save space, we consider only the one referred to.

1990 rejects, 'no' for the holdout), age in 1990 (25–30 years for the 1990 rejects, 18–24 years for the holdout), outgoings (£1–99 for the 1990 rejects, £0 for the holdout), and residential status (tenant (furnished) for the 1990 rejects, owner for the holdout).

We now ask a second question. Suppose that we keep the proportion of cases who are predicted to be good (bad) the same in two years, years t and n. That is, we alter the priors in year n such that, when used with n's canonical function coefficients, the same proportion of cases is rejected (i.e. predicted to be bad) as in year t. What, then, are the characteristics of those who would be predicted to be *bad* (good) by year t's model (year t's canonical function coefficients and actual priors) but who are predicted to be *good* (bad) using the model of a year n (year n's canonical function coefficients, hypothetical priors)? Notice that the hypothetical priors applied in year n are not the priors used in year t's classification matrix (Table 11.3). Instead they are the priors which, with year n's canonical function coefficients would give the same proportion of cases predicted to be bad as predicted for year t. That is, they represent the 'cut-off score' that a credit-granting agency would impose if they wished to use the current year's (n's) function, but also wished the proportion of cases that are rejected to be the same as in another year (t).

This issue has been explored by performing two cross-tabulations. In both cases, we adjust the priors of 1990 so as to predict the same proportion of bads as were predicted for 1989. First, we cross-tabulate the *numbers predicted to be good (bad) in 1990* with the numbers predicted to be good (bad) in 1990 had the priors been set so as to predict the same proportion of bads as predicted for 1989. Second, we cross-tabulate the *numbers predicted to be good (bad) in 1989* with those predicted to be good (bad) in 1990 again with the priors set to give the same proportion of bads as in 1989. The results are shown in Table 11.7.

Table 11.7 Two cross-tabulations for 1990 priors set to give same predicted proportion of bads as predicted in 1989, 1990 function.

	Goods	Bads	Total
Actual 1989 priors, 1989 function			
Good	13,629 (79.8)	640 (3.7)	14,269
Bad	632 (3.7)	2,183 (12.8)	2,815
Total	14,261	2,823	17,084 (100)
Actual 1990 priors, 1990 function			
Good	12,742 (74.6)	1,527 (8.9)	14,269
Bad	0 (0.0)	2,815 (16.5)	2,815
Total	12,742	4,342	17,084 (100)

Figures in parentheses are the number of cases in the cell as a percentage of the number of cases in the total holdout sample.

Table 11.8 Modal groups: total effects.

	The holdout sample in aggregate		Those members of the holdout sample predicted to be			
			Good on 1989 function but bad on 1990 function with adjusted priors		Bad on the 1990 function but good on adjusted 1990 function	
	Modal group	% of cases	Modal group	% of cases	Modal group	% of cases
Number of children	0, 6, 7, 8	69	0, 6, 7, 8	69	0, 6, 7, 8	74
Number of dependants	0, 3, 4, 5, 24	98	0, 3, 4, 5, 24	98	0, 3, 4, 5, 24	98
Applicant's employment status	Private sector	65	Private sector	65	Private sector	65
Deposit account	No	64	No	64	No	66
Loan account	No	95	No	95	No	97
Cheque card account	No	75	No	75	No	84
Current account	Yes	67	Yes	67	Yes	68
Major credit card	No	60	No	60	No	78
Charge card	No	76	No	76	No	94
Store card	No	78	No	78	No	79
Applicant's employment category	Services—Office, sales, labourer, executive, trades, others	46	Services—Office, sales, labourer, executive, trades, others	46	Services—Office, sales, labourer, executive, trades, others	55
Age in 1990	18–24 years	27	25–30 years	32	18–24 years	34

Building society card	No	92	No	91	No	92
Phone	No	83	No	56	No	77
Spouse's income	£0	78	£0	80	£0	83
Years at present employment	0, 1 years	28	0, 1 years	34	0, 1 years	41
Years at same bank	0, 1 years	28	0, 1 years	37	0, 1 years	41
Value of home	£0	64	£0	93	£0	81
Applicant's income	£0–6,000	24	£13,000+	29	£0–6,000	29
Mortgage balance outstanding	£0	68	£0	94	£0	83
Outgoings	£0	24	£299+	28	£99–199	35
Residential status	Owner	38	Tenant (unfurnished)	43	With parents	31
Spouse's employment category	No response	68	No response	68	No response	75
Years at present address	0, 1 years	28	0, 1 years	44	0, 1 years	34
Sample size	17,084		632		1,527	

Table 11.7 shows that, if the priors of 1990 are adjusted to give the same reject rate in 1990 as in 1989, then 3.7 per cent of 17,084 cases in the holdout sample would have been rejected using the 1990 rule, but accepted using the 1989 rule and cut-offs. On the other hand, 8.9 per cent of cases would have been accepted using the 1990 system and adjusted cut-offs, but rejected if the 1990 function and cut-offs were used.

Table 11.8 summarizes the characteristics of these two groups, and compares them with the characteristics of the total holdout sample. First we compare the holdout with those accepted using the 1989 function and priors but rejected using the 1990 function with adjusted priors. The persons accepted on the 1989 model but rejected on the adjusted 1990 model are similar to the holdout in all respects except the following. They are older than the holdout (modal age group 25–30 years versus 18–24 years), they have a higher income (modal income range £13,000+ versus £0–6,000), they have greater outgoings (modal range £299 plus per month versus £0) and they typically have a different residential status (modal group 'tenant unfurnished' versus 'owner').

We now turn to those cases that would be rejected on the 1990 function but would be accepted if the priors were adjusted to give the same reject rate as the 1989 model. These persons have the same modal values for characteristics as the holdout, except that they have greater outgoings (£99–199 versus £0) and they typically live with their parents as opposed to being owners.

11.5   Discussion

The hold-out sample was constructed to have the same proportion of cases that were accepted and rejected by the organization supplying the data. Therefore, since the cases were also randomly selected by the organization for our sample, we believe that our holdout sample is representative of the applications that the organization would typically receive. We will interpret our results having made this assumption.

Table 11.5 shows that, even between the two adjacent years, changes in cut-off scores and canonical function coefficients can make a noticeable difference in the rejection rates yielded by a scoring model: 16.5 per cent using the 1989 model against 25.4 per cent using the 1990 model. A much greater proportion of applicants would have been rejected using the 1990 model but accepted on the 1989 model than vice versa: 10.3 per cent compared with 1.4 per cent. Since the prior probability of default in 1990 was much greater than in 1989, the cut-off score appears to have an effect on the classification of a case.

When we removed the effects of changes in the cut-offs, by adjusting them to give the same predicted proportion of cases rejected (when combined with the 1990 coefficients) in 1990 as was predicted using the 1989 priors and coefficients (Table 11.7), we found that 12.8 per cent of cases would be rejected by both models, but 7.4 per cent would be rejected by only one of the models. This gives some indication as to the effects of changes in the coefficients between the 2 years, since the priors—the other possible cause of a different classification—have been adjusted to give the same rejection rate in both years. Furthermore, of the 10.3 per cent of cases accepted using the 1989 model and rejected using the 1990 model (Table 11.5), 3.7 percentage points would still be rejected if the 1990 cut-off scores were adjusted (Table 11.7). Therefore, adjusting the cut-offs to maintain the same predicted rejection rate will not lead to the predicted group being invariant with respect to the year to which the data for the model relates. The different coefficients will result in some cases being classified differently between the 2 years.

If we change the 1990 cut-offs to give the same reject rate as in 1989 (Table 11.7), we would accept 83.5 per cent of cases rather than 74.6 per cent without cut-off adjust-ment (Table 11.5). Of the 83.5 per cent of cases, we would have rejected 8.9 percentage points (83.5 per cent less 74.6 per cent) of cases if the unadjusted 1990 model were used (Table 11.7). Whether the 3.7 per cent of cases that would be rejected in 1990 but accepted in 1989 (using the same proportion of rejects) should concern the credit grantor depends on the profit that these cases would have generated if they had been accepted. We have not built a profit model, but Table 11.6 shows the characteristics of such applicants. The same argument applies if the 1990 model was used, with 8.9 per cent of cases rejected if the cut-offs indicated by 1990 behaviour were retained rather than the adjusted ones being used.

11.6   Conclusion

Our results suggest that changes in cut-off scores and in canonical function coefficients do result in sizeable differences in the proportion of applicants who would be rejected if the scoring model were based on a linear discriminant analysis estimated using data for 1 year rather than another, even if the years are adjacent to each other. Furthermore, changing the cut-off scores to maintain the same reject rate will not restore the same decision for each applicant. This suggests that credit grantors who build scoring models must be especially careful when choosing the years for which the data used in their model relates. They should attempt to estimate the profit that may be forgone by rejecting applicants on one model when another suggests acceptance, and to estimate the increased loss that may result from accepting an applicant on one model when another suggests rejection. Only when the grantor has an accurate estimate of the financial cost of the errors involved in using one decision strategy rather than another will (s)he be able to evaluate different strategies accurately.

Appendix

A case is classified into the group for which $P(G_i/x)$ is greatest, where

$$P(G_i/x) = P_i D_i^* \bigg/ \sum_{i=1}^{n} P_i D_i^*;$$

here n is the number of groups, P_i is the prior probability that a case is a member of group i,

$$D_i^* = (\det D_i)^{-1/2} \exp\left(-1/2\chi_i^2\right),$$

and D_i is the covariance matrix of the canonical discriminant functions for group i, with

$$\chi_i^2 = (f - f_i)^T D_i^{-1}(f - f_i), \quad \text{and} \quad f = Bx + a,$$

where x = a $z \times 1$ vector of discriminant variables for a case, B = the $m \times z$ matrix of un-standardized canonical discriminant function coefficients, f = the $m \times 1$ vector of canonical discriminant function values, f_i = the group centroid vector, a = a vector of constants.

Table 11.A1   The sociodemograhic variables.

Number of children	Building society card (yes/no)
Number of dependants	Phone (yes/no)
Applicant's employment status	Spouse's income
Deposit account (yes/no)	Years at present employment
Loan account (yes/no)	Years at same bank
Cheque guarantee card (yes/no)	Value of home
Current account (yes/no)	Applicant's income
Major credit card (yes/no)	Mortgage balance outstanding
Charge card (yes/no)	Outgoings
Store card (yes/no)	Residential status
Applicant's employment category	Spouse's employment category
Age in 1990	Years at present address

References

Bierman, H. and Hausman, W. H. (1970) The credit granting decision. *Management Science* B, 16, 519–32.

Boyle, M., Crook, J. N., Hamilton, R., and Thomas, L. C. (1992) Methods of credit scoring applied to slow payers. In *Credit Scoring and Credit Control* (eds. L. C. Thomas, J. N. Crook, and D. B. Edelman). Oxford University Press, Oxford.

Capon, N. (1982) Credit scoring systems: a critical analysis. *Journal of Marketing*, 46, 82–91.

Chandler, G. C. and Coffman, J. Y. (1983–4) Applications of performance scoring to accounts receivable management in consumer credit. *Journal of Retail Banking*, 5, 1–10.

Crook, J. N., Hamilton, R., and Thomas, L. C. (1992*a*) A comparison of a credit scoring model with a credit performance model. *The Service Industries Journal*, 12, 558–79.

Crook, J. N., Hamilton, R., and Thomas, L. C. (1992*b*) A comparison of discriminators under alternative definitions of default. In *Credit Scoring and Credit Control* (eds. L. C. Thomas, J. N. Crook, and D. B. Edelman). Oxford University Press, Oxford.

Eisenbeis, R. A. (1977) Pitfalls in the application of discriminant analysis in business, finance and economics. *Journal of Finance*, 32, 875–900.

Eisenbeis, R. A. (1978) Problems in applying discriminant analysis in credit scoring models. *Journal of Banking and Finance*, 2, 205–19.

Hair, J. F., Anderson, R. E., and Tatham, R. L. (1987) *Multivariate Data Analysis*. Collier Macmillan, New York.

Klecka, W. R. (1980) *Discriminant Analysis*. Sage, Beverley Hills, CA.

Kshirsagar, A. M. (1972) *Multivariate Analysis,* Vol. 2. Marcel Dekker, New York.

Lindley, J. T., Rudolph, P., and Selby, E. B. (1989) Credit card possession and use: changes over time. *Journal of Economic and Business*, 41, 127–42.

Morrison, D. G. (1969) On the interpretation of discriminant analysis. *Journal of Marketing Research*, 4, 156–63.

Myers, J. H. and Forgy, E. W. (1963) The development of numerical credit evaluation systems. *Journal of the American Statistical Association*, 58, 799–806.

SPSSX INC (1983) *SPSSX Statistical Algorithms*. SPSS Inc, Chicago.

Thomas, L. C. (1988) Behavioural scoring. Department of Business Studies, University of Edinburgh, Working Paper, 88/32.

Wiginton, J. C. (1980) A note on the comparison of logit and discriminant models of consumer credit behaviour. *Journal of Finance and Quantitative Analysis*, 15, 757–70.

12. Inferring the inferred

Gaynor Bennett, Graham Platts, and Jane Crossley

Reject inference has an established role in the development of scorecards for credit applications. The performance of the rejects, had they been accepted, is inferred to be good or bad in order to obtain a complete picture of the population applying for credit. Once this is done, the scorecard to assess this population can then be developed. But consider the following problem. A company mails its customer base with an offer of additional finance facilities. The problem is: who should it mail to maximize response while minimizing risk, while also minimizing the number of responders who are rejected at application time to avoid jeopardizing the existing customer relationship?

This problem has three inferences required to tackle it completely. First, there is the classic inference at the point of application to infer which rejects, had they been accepted, would have been good (or bad). Second, there is the inference at the point of mailing to infer which customers, had they been previously mailed, would have responded—a response inference. But third, and most interesting, is the double inference of inferring which of the inferred responders would have subsequently been good, bad, or rejected—an inference on an inference!

This chapter discusses the problem and the solution adopted, and gives figures from the analysis (rescaled to protect commercial confidentiality). Marks and Spencer Financial Services cover some of the issues regarding implementation of the Scorex solution within Fair Isaac's Triad, utilizing both CCN and Equifax bureau data—a unique combination of multiple suppliers' products. Further, the results of a mailing campaign are analysed and compared with the predictions.

IMA Journal of Mathematics Applied in Business and Industry, 7, 327–38, 1996.

12.1   Introduction

Any organization looking to exploit its customer database to cross-sell financial services through direct marketing is presented with a problem: How can the number of customers who respond to a new product offer be maximized, while minimizing the credit risk associated with these responders? The nub of the problem is that those customers who are most likely to respond to a direct marketing offer also tend to be a high credit risk. Therefore, the use of traditional response-scoring techniques often means that a significant number of responders are rejected when they apply for the product. Not only can this cause costly wastage, but also a rejected application can jeopardize the relationship with a loyal customer.

Marks & Spencer Financial Services appointed Scorex to tackle precisely this problem. With a retail-card portfolio of nearly 4 million cardholders, M&S have an excellent opportunity to cross-sell a range of financial services. In order to achieve the objectives, it was apparent that a totally new approach to scorecards for mailing-list selection was required. This introduced the 'double reject inference' approach—leading to the development of integrated models to assess the likelihood of response and risk at the point of mailing and subsequent risk at the point of application.

12.2   The classic problem

The classic scenario is as follows. When through-the-door population applies for credit, they are either accepted or rejected. Given time, the 'accepts' can be classified as either good or bad and, based on these, a model can then be built, which will be successful at separating previous accepts. However, unless the previous decision process was random, the model will not be totally effective in the assessment of the overall through-the-door population. Therefore, the overall population of 'goods' and 'bads' needs to be re-created, via the process of reject inference, combining art (experience!) and science to determine the performance of the rejects, had they been accepted (Hoyland 1994). This produces a 'swap set', whereby previous accepts who turned out to be bad can be exchanged for those rejects who would have been an acceptable risk, thus improving the decision process. Having recreated the overall population, a scorecard can then be developed on all applicants. Applied to the through-the-door population, this may then be used to answer the question: which applicants should I accept and which should I reject?

12.3   The new problem

But consider the new problem. A company has a large base of customers to whom they wish to offer an additional facility. The question is now: Who should I mail who will respond to the offer at an acceptable risk, such that I will not have to reject them on the basis of their application details?

Maximizing response rates while controlling risk are obviously desired conditions for the success of the business. However, these cannot be considered in isolation, as it is just as important not to jeopardize existing customer relationships by rejecting those who have been invited to apply.

12.4   The historical solution

The historical solution would have been to develop a response scorecard, based upon the mailed customers, and a risk scorecard for the responders, based upon the information available at the time of mailing. Then the application risk model would use only the details relating to the application, to decide whether to accept or reject. While these scorecards were capable of discriminating between response and non-response, and between good and bad, they failed to address the relationships between response and mailing risk, and more obviously between mailing and application risk.

When selecting customers to mail, the aim is to identify low-risk responders. Unfortunately, low-risk responders are few and far between: The relationship of response and risk tends to be that those customers who are most likely to respond are the most risky. This relationship was highlighted when the eligible customers were scored through the two traditional point-of-mailing scorecards and a matrix of scores produced. The diagonal area on Fig. 12.1 shows that the scorecards were very successful in identifying low risk with low response and high risk with high response, but could not

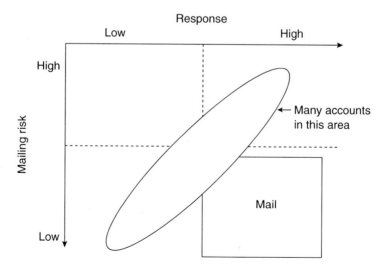

Fig. 12.1   The historical solution.

satisfactorily identify the precise pocket of customers required. This drawback was highlighted further at the time of application. Many of those customers who appeared to be an acceptable risk based on the point-of-mailing scorecard, were in fact considered to be too high a risk when assessed using the application-risk scorecard. Thus, having been invited to apply, many applicants were turned away, jeopardizing the existing customer relationship.

12.5   The proposed solution

In order to take account of the relationships between response and risk, it was clear that the development of the scorecards had to be integrated. The first process was to re-create the M&S customer 'universe', classifying everyone as either responder or non-responder and then further classifying the responders as either good or bad. Figure 12.2 shows that there were many customers within the sample for whom this classification was unknown. Therefore, this problem has three inferences required to tackle it completely. First there is the classic inference at the point of application to infer the rejects: to determine whether they would have been good or bad had they been accepted. Second, there is the response inference at the point of mailing to infer which of the customers, had they been previously mailed, would have responded. But third, and most interesting, is the double inference of inferring which of the inferred

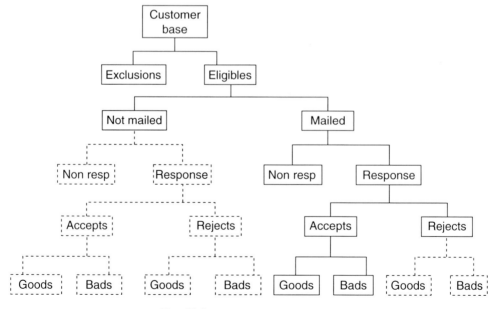

Fig. 12.2 Population flow diagram.

responders would have subsequently been good, bad, or rejected—an inference on an inference!

There are various complications associated with reject inference (Hand and Henley 1993). To ensure confidence in a single reject inference requires thorough examination of the results. When an inference on an inference is necessary, data and results must be scrutinized in depth.

Once the M&S 'universe' had been re-created scorecard development could begin.

12.6   Integrated models

Three scorecards were required to provide the complete solution. As data for the whole population were now available for examination, an integrated approach to the development of the scorecards was possible. This meant that all criteria could be cross-referenced in terms of their ability to predict response or risk. Those which were opposed in predictive nature were excluded in order to concentrate on those which would identify the pocket of customers with high response rates and low risk.

The mailing models utilized previous customer account performance, prior customer demographics, and Equifax bureau data. The application-risk model built upon the mailing-risk model, utilizing additional application-time information regarding customer demographics and CCN bureau data.

12.7   Complications

Although the project approach seemed straightforward enough on paper, there were actually several obstacles to overcome.

First, the creation of the initial database, from the vast amount of data files held by M&S FS was no trivial task. The quality of the data and successful matching processes had to be ensured if a meaningful sample was to result. All potential scorecard characteristics had to be identified, and hundreds more invented, to provide enough information to select low-risk responders successfully.

Second, due to the low previous mailing and response rates, the development sample contained a high proportion of unmailed and unresponsive customers. Therefore, the problems associated with the inference of a large proportion of accounts, based on a low proportion of accounts with known performance, had to be dealt with (Hoyland 1994). Again, experience of similar projects proved invaluable.

Third, this was the debut of 'double inference', and the software to perform this task did not exist. Pooling the ideas of experienced analysts and technical consultants led to the successful adaptation of Scorex's software.

Another limitation was the non-existence of customer application details for the inferred responders (since they were not mailed and hence did not have the chance to apply!). Although the only solution to this problem was to assume that these characteristics would be similar to those for the genuine applicants, bureau data at the time of application were available for all customers to refine the decision process.

Finally, the expected results for acceptance and bad rates had to be based on an imitation of the mailing selection. Producing the statistics based on the entire sample would not have been appropriate, since the application-time distribution depends upon the subset of customers who were mailed.

12.8   Implementation

Figure 12.3 provides an overview of the systems used at M&S FS.

New applications are processed using CCN's Autoscore system. All characteristics relating to the customer and the loan at the time of application are fed into the system. Those criteria which are utilized by the Scorex application scorecard are extracted and scored accordingly, resulting in an accept/reject decision. The account-management package is Cardpac, which is run on the M&S plc mainframe at Stockley Park. This holds details regarding monthly transactions for the accepted accounts. The decision-management system is Fair Isaac's Triad system which sits alongside Cardpac retrieving account behavioural data and feeding back decisions in relation to authorizations, collections, credit limit setting, re-issue, and marketing

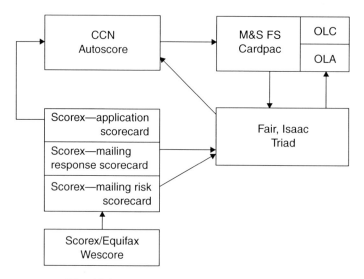

Fig. 12.3   Overview of main M&S FS systems.

communications. The two Scorex models used at the point of mailing, the risk and response scorecards, sit within the Triad communications area. Within the risk model, the generic bureau score 'Wescore' is used, which is currently fed in from a file supplied by Equifax Europe.

12.9   Mailing response/risk matrix

All customers eligible to be mailed (after standard exclusions) are scored on both the risk and response scorecards. A matrix approach allows customers to be segmented into various cells, depending on their likelihood to respond and the risk group that they fall into; see Table 12.1. In the table, the figures for each score listed are the cumulative counts (in terms of the total mailing volumes), the cumulative response rate, and the predicted bad rate (based on a 100 per cent acceptance rate).

Previous mailing volumes have been around 700,000–800,000. For this mailing, the Marketing Department wanted to increase volumes to 1.3 million. The question raised earlier comes up again:

Which customers should be mailed to maximize the response rates but minimize decline rates and subsequent bad rates?

The boxed entries in Table 12.1 indicate where the actual cut-offs were set. It is evident from the figures for the uppermost left score group in the box that this would provide the required maximum mailing volume of 1.37 million customers with an anticipated overall response rate of 0.49 per cent. This expected response rate may appear to be low; however, bearing in mind the significant volumes being mailed, such a response would be satisfactory. The figures also show that, if every application made were accepted, then the expected overall bad rate, after a maturity period of 27 months, would be 5 per cent.

The selected mailing population was then split into 20 distinct categories (Table 12.2) with like predicted response rates and bad rates.

Within the overall mailing, the 'offer' made to the customer may be varied dependent upon the level of risk. The maximum loan amount can be varied as £5,000, £7,500, £10,000, and—for the very low risk bands—£15,000. This approach also enables a more direct comparison to be made between the predicted (and subsequently the actual) results from this mailing with previous mailings. In addition, the Marketing Department wished to test three different 'creatives'. These consisted of two fairly plain 'austere' packs and, the third pack, photographs of M&S customers with 'miniatures'. This meant that each mailing cell then had to be split randomly to test the different response rates within the different creatives as well. Reference codes were assigned at the level of each creative within each category, so that the response could be accurately tracked.

Table 12.1 Mailing response—risk matrix.

Response score (cumulative values)

Risk score		Total	155	163	175	182	185	200	205	225
Total	Counts	2,206,831	1,962,056	1,733,266	1,298,083	1,102,394	933,007	572,643	491,277	241,407
	Response rate	0.46	0.49	0.54	0.67	0.76	0.86	1.17	1.26	1.60
	Bad rate	10.4	10.5	10.6	10.9	11.1	11.2	12.0	12.2	12.6
150	Counts	1,972,020	1,733,445	1,512,742	1,098,146	915,584	759,038	435,722	366,425	164,152
	Response rate	0.43	0.46	0.51	0.63	0.72	0.82	1.13	1.24	1.58
	Bad rate	6.3	6.4	6.5	6.6	6.7	7.1	7.2	7.6	12.6
165	Counts	1,814,842	1,582,808	1,369,885	974,073	803,057	657,488	362,440	300,942	126,301
	Response rate	0.41	0.44	0.49	0.61	0.70	0.80	1.12	1.22	1.56
	Bad rate	5.0	5.0	5.0	5.1	5.2	5.2	5.6	5.6	5.9
175	Counts	1,655,298	1,432,841	1,230,358	858,024	700,110	566,577	300,877	246,711	97,362
	Response rate	0.39	0.42	0.47	0.60	0.68	0.78	1.09	1.19	1.54
	Bad rate	4.2	4.2	4.2	4.3	4.4	4.5	4.8	4.9	5.4
195	Counts	1,206,337	1,022,693	860,127	570,719	452,822	355,232	170,081	134,271	44,221
	Response rate	0.35	0.38	0.43	0.55	0.62	0.71	1.03	1.12	1.58
	Bad rate	2.5	2.5	2.5	2.6	2.7	2.7	2.9	3.0	3.3
210	Counts	794,736	664,047	549,809	350,646	271,733	206,598	87,253	64,845	17,859
	Response rate	0.32	0.35	0.40	0.51	0.58	0.65	0.95	1.06	1.49
	Bad rate	1.7	1.6	1.6	1.7	1.6	1.8	1.9	1.9	2.2
230	Counts	293,275	245,469	200,633	123,011	92,502	67,384	22,931	15,851	3,041
	Response rate	0.28	0.30	0.33	0.42	0.47	0.51	0.71	0.79	1.50
	Bad rate	0.9	0.9	1.0	1.3	0.7	1.0	2.3	—	—

Table 12.2   Mailing results.

Risk category		Ex. Low	V. low	Low	Med	High	Total	
	Response category							
High	{	16,000	11,216	10,770	27,339	56,827	122,152	Mail volume
	{	32	103	84	149	168	157	Decline rate
	{	55	73	62	127	335	203	Gross response
Medium	{	77,220	36,484	33,591	76,324	123,184	346,803	Mail volume
	{	71	62	118	106	121	478	Decline rate
	{	41	50	64	104	255	134	Gross response
Low	{	86,415	37,052	31,049	63,227	79,204	296,947	Mail volume
	{	113	65	61	65	99	89	Decline rate
	{	32	53	59	86	205	95	Gross response
V. low	{	194,666	76,830	63,532	116,484	84,621	536,133	Mail volume
	{	46	38	31	39	55	46	Decline rate
	{	31	38	42	62	140	57	Gross response
Total	{	374,301	161,582	138,942	283,374	343,836	1,302,035	Mail volume
	{	66	58	69	83	118	100	Decline rate
	{	34	47	53	85	228	100	Gross response

A mailing file containing the names, addresses, and chargecard account numbers of all those customers mailed was loaded onto Autoscore. This ensured that, when an application was received, by keying the customer's chargecard account number into Autoscore, their name and address and the reference code could be correctly retrieved. This ensured the accurate tracking of the volume of responders in each of the separate mailing categories. In addition, the risk score, calculated at the time of mailing, was held on the mailing file and used as part of the application model.

CCN bureau data was accessed at the time of application, both in the scorecard and through a series of policy rules. As part of the development, a comparison was made of CCN and Equifax bureau data. The models were developed so as to result in the strongest possible combination of Equifax data at the time of mailing and CCN data at the time of application. The overall combination was possible due to the flexibility of the systems involved to hold independent scorecards.

12.10   Results

Table 12.2 shows the results from the mailing sent out to customers during May 1995, allowing approximately 2 months to respond.

The actual response rates and decline rates have been replaced with an index to disguise the true results. A score of 100 is used to measure the overall response rate and the overall decline percentage. By comparing the index in each cell with the overall total, it is clear that the distribution is very different across the categories. Extremely low responders with very low risk, situated at the bottom left, achieved a response rate of 31 and a decline proportion of 46. This steadily increases across the matrix, peaking at the top right-hand corner, as expected, with an index of 335 for response and 168 for the decline rate.

Any apparent misalignments in risk and response rates across the categories are likely to be due to a combination of factors. These include the compilation of results after the short exposure period of 2 months, the different marketing strategies in terms of the various creatives, and staggered loan amounts offered across the different risk bands. Fluctuations due to low counts should also be considered, especially in the categories of high risk with low response rates.

In summary, the response rates within each response-risk category were higher than predicted, resulting in a significantly higher overall response rate. Not only were M&S delighted with the high response rate, but also with the subsequent percentage of applicants who were declined, which was much lower than previously. While double reject inference would have been the major factor in this improvement, it is also likely that external forces, such as increased consumer optimism, would have played a part.

12.11   Conclusion

The initial objectives for the Scorecard development were to improve the response rate and reduce the decline rate significantly while maintaining the current quality. M&S FS have seen a dramatic uplift in response together with a significant reduction in the decline rate, providing improved customer relations. It is much too early to measure delinquency, but the predicted bad rate also indicates an improvement.

References

Hand, D. J. and Henley, W. E. (1993) Can reject inference ever work? *IMA Journal of Mathematics Applied in Business and Industry*, 5, 45–55.

Hoyland, C. (1994) *Data-driven Decisions for Consumer Lending: Credit Scoring Techniques for Risk Management*. Lafferty Publications, London. Chapter 3, pp. 53–5.

Part V. Other Applications of Scoring in Credit Risk

In this fifth part we have chosen chapters that have explored novel applications of credit scoring in credit risk. Every credit grantor suffers losses from fraud. Leonard's chapter was one of the first to outline how credit card accounts which are subject to fraud could be identified before the fraud activity has been reported to the lender. This is especially important because where the cardholder is unaware of fraud (e.g. counterfeit cards) the loss to the lender is usually greater than when, for example, a card is lost or stolen and discovered by the borrower more quickly. Leonard shows that the use of a rules based expert system applied every hour to each credit card account of a Canadian bank detected one fraud for every 2.23 non-fraud customers contacted, with 65.9 per cent of frauds detected. Prediction of fraud is naturally a confidential process and so little has been published on it. Leonard's chapter is significant because it is not only the first to give a public indication of the success of using an expert system applied to credit, but also because it is the first to publicly describe fraud detection. Many fraud detection systems in use today use expert systems and/or neural networks to make their predictions.

The second chapter in this part is of profound importance because it anticipates future developments in the European credit market. Specifically, Platts and Howe ask whether data predicts differently across Europe and whether the performance of a generic scorecard that has been estimated using data pooled from different countries would give acceptably accurate results. With many European countries using the same currency, exchange rate risk is removed for countries that use it. A borrower living and working in France may have a card from a bank in Germany and use it to buy a meal in Italy. Before these countries adopted the Euro, exchange rate movements

Since the chapters were written the affiliation of some of the authors has changed. The changes the editors are aware of are: D. J. Hand is now Professor of Statistics at Imperial College, University of London. L. C. Thomas is now Professor of Management Science at the University of Southampton. K. Leonard is now Associate Professor at the University of Tornoto. A. Lucas is now one of the principals of Rhinorisk.

would reduce the attractiveness of the borrower applying for a credit card in a different country. This is no longer so. But how should a lender respond, given applications from many countries? Should it build a scorecard for each country or use a generic one?

Platts and Howe give an indication of the differences in performance between a country specific and a generic scorecard. They consider data for five European countries. They find that for the United Kingdom the percentage improvement in bad debt compared with a generic European scorecard was around 12 per cent but only around 4 per cent for the other countries. The authors conclude that the generic scorecard is sufficiently inferior to country specific scorecards, so that the latter should be the aim of lenders. This objective presents lenders with some difficult challenges, not the least of which is how to obtain, initially, a large enough sample. These issues have recently become a major line of research.

Constructing scorecards when the sample is small is the issue addressed in the third chapter in this part. This may be useful when, for example, launching new products, or moving into new niches in a market. Lucas and Powell describe a methodology for deriving a scorecard using only 120 cases. Since the number of variables available was too large to gain reliable estimates, the variable list was reduced using a sequential process involving correlation, expert opinion, and graphical models. With low multi-collinearity, the scorecard consisted of the sum of weights of evidence for the attributes of a particular applicant. To reduce the variation in the data, caused by the small sample size, Lucas and Powell calculated weights of evidence using a weighted average of the bad rate for an individual attribute and the overall mean bad rate for the characteristic. The attribute, bad rate, was combined with that estimated by an expert, using a Bayesian technique. The bad rates for each attribute were then combined to give that for the characteristic and converted into a weight of evidence.

The broad range of circumstances when only small samples exist are often the circumstances when the benefits of an accurate model are especially great. It is therefore especially useful to have a technique like that presented in this chapter in such circumstances. As the authors say, this chapter should stimulate much future research, and in the most recent 2003 conference there was an interesting paper suggesting what methods to use for different sizes of sample available.

13. Detecting credit card fraud using expert systems

Kevin J. Leonard

13.1 Introduction

The incidence of consumer credit card fraud has been on the increase worldwide over the past 2 years. In Canada alone, the cost of credit card fraud totalled (for Visa and Mastercard) more than 46 million Canadian dollars for 1991. This number compares to totals of about $29 million for 1990 and only $19 million for 1989 (Appleby 1992). The two predominant growth areas are that of counterfeit fraud (where an unauthorized duplicate of the card exists in circulation) and that of non-receipt fraud (where a re-issued card is intercepted by a third party). In both instances, the cardholder is unaware that a copy of his or her card is in the hands of criminals and hence, the fraud is not reported. Consequently, the amount of financial exposure for the financial institution is substantially higher than that for a lost or stolen card, for example, where the cardholder is aware almost immediately. The lost or stolen card is usually reported within the first day to the issuing company and a block is placed on that account, thereby limiting spending.

The objective of this chapter is to construct and implement a rule-based, expert system model to detect the fraudulent usage of credit before the fraud activity has been reported by the cardholder. If this can be accomplished, the credit granting institution will NOT have to rely on the cardholder to report the fraudulent activity. In the case of counterfeit fraud, for example, this can take a substantial number of days—on average, 8–10 days according to bank statistics. The methodology is as follows. Suspicious activity can be detected from deviations from 'normal' spending patterns through the use of expert systems. As a result, the customer can be contacted and the account blocked (if so warranted)—all within the first few hours of the fraud

Computers and Industrial Engineering, 25 (1–4), 103–6, 1993.

activity. This would then reduce the 'run' on the fraud accounts from a number of days down to some time within a day. Although no confirmed figures are currently available, this should provide a substantial dollar saving.

In this study, data from one specific Canadian bank were analysed. Due to reasons of confidentiality, the actual name of the bank and the details of the model developed were not permitted to be disclosed.

13.2   Current fraud monitoring

At present, the bank generates a number of standard reports after account processing each night. These reports are passed to managers the following morning who then peruse the reports and flag suspicious accounts. These cardholders are then contacted and appropriate action is taken. This is a very time-consuming and labour-intensive task, which can be simplified greatly though automation and a rule-based structure. These reports consist of accounts which fail certain criteria:

- too many high value items
- too many frequent purchases
- too many consecutive authorizations at a specific merchant.

There are four different 'levels' of models that can be applied. They are briefly listed here:

(1) Off-line; batch mode; end of day summary reports;
(2) Off-line; individual accounts; analysis during course of day;
(3) On-line; real-time—update for next purchase;
(4) On-line; real-time—analysis at time of transaction.

As stated above, at present, the bank is working with 'level one' models. Reports are generated off-line, end-of-day and analysis takes place subsequently off-line as well. The model that is presented in this chapter is intended to be of the 'level two' type. Accounts will be analysed on an individual basis multiple times throughout the day (still off-line) with action being available within the same day. Specifically, after every hour, the authorization information will be downloaded to a personal computer. Authorization data for all active accounts will be updated and the fraud model will be then executed for each active account. Those accounts which fail the fraud test will be written to a report that will be sent to the fraud and security department of the bank. Inspectors will then attempt to contact the customer to ascertain whether the recent activity is legitimate or not. Blocking of the account can take place almost instantly.

Primarily, there are two possible courses of action that can be taken once an account has been identified as suspected fraud—call the customer and inquire as to the recent activity (validation) OR block the account from any activity and then contact the customer. Blocking the account immediately limits the financial institution's risk exposure, however, it has tremendous customer service ramifications when incorrectly applied. It was decided by the management of the bank that, as a first course, contacting the customer would be the best approach. The cardholder's account could then be subsequently blocked if the customer acknowledges that fraud has indeed occurred.

13.3   The analysis

Although the models cannot be given explicitly for proprietary reasons, the development process can be summarized. The models' performances were measured based on classification accuracy and based on the cost of misclassification. For the purposes of generating a cost of misclassification, the middle managers were canvassed. Since very little information existed as to actual costs, these had to be estimated. It was assumed that the cost of one fraud would be approximately equal to the cost of disturbing 20 good customers. Additionally, a key assumption was that the cost of disruption was the same regardless of the number of times the same account had been disturbed.

In the real bank data analysed, there were 12,132 non-fraud accounts and 578 fraud accounts. Using a purely naïve system of classifying all accounts as either fraud or non-fraud, the data allows for 95.45 per cent classification accuracy (when all accounts are classified as non-fraud). The cost of misclassification, however, is equal to the cost of disturbing 11,560 good accounts (578 fraud accounts missed times 20). (A dollar value for disturbing one good account was not determined. Instead all misclassification costs are translated into units of 'good accounts disturbed'. This then allows a broad basis for comparison across different institutions and different time frames.) Contrarily, all the accounts could have been classified as fraud whereby the cost would be 12,132A (12,132 good accounts disturbed).

The Expert System model classifies at a lower accuracy level overall (91.78 per cent) however, the model classifies 65.92 per cent correct (381/578) within the fraud category. Therefore, even though the accuracy level is lower, the cost of misclassification is lower for this model at 4,788A. This is calculated from 197 missed frauds ($197 \times 20 = 3,940$) and from 848 missed classified non-frauds giving a total of an equivalent 4,788 good accounts disturbed. In other words, 381 frauds can be identified by disturbing only 848 good accounts—which equates to approximately 2.23 to 1 (848/381) good accounts to frauds.

The Expert System model was also tested on a holdout sample. The Classification accuracy level is fairly stable at 91.35 per cent and the fraud classification has also improved slightly to 70.76 per cent (951/1,344). However, due to the change in sample and the fraud rate, the cost of misclassification is much higher at 8850A.

The good accounts disturbed per fraud identified ratio is relatively constant at 2.52 to 1 (990/393).

One final measure of the success of this expert system (at least, as defined on the sample database), was the estimate of cost saving. To arrive at this calculation, the most conservative position was taken throughout (presented in Table 13.1). Only counterfeit fraud was considered (incidence of 50 per cent) and we assumed that the exposure for all accounts was equal to that of the classic accounts (which is significantly less than exposure for premier accounts). Even with a conservative approach, a cost saving directly from the expert system fraud model was determined to be approximately $245,000 per month. This cost saving estimate, based on accuracy rates described herein, has motivated the management of this bank to continue to investigate better and more efficient models that can be implemented to predict and identify occurrences of credit card fraud. It should be noted that the cost saving total only reflects the explicit cost of dollars currently lost to fraud.

Table 13.1   Estimate of fraud savings using reduced model.

Number of fraud accounts	1000 per month
Percentage incidence of counterfeit fraud	50 %
Total number of counterfeit accounts	500 per month

Assume model can detect fraud with 70.76% accuracy after the first day. Further, the counterfeit often runs as long as 10 days (or costs about $77 per day for the Classic accounts). Therefore this model will be able to block the account before the last 9 days of fraud has taken place.

Cost saving: $500 \times (77 \times 9) \times 0.7076 = \$245, 183.00$ per month.

13.4   Conclusion

One primary assumption is that current fraud patterns continue to exist. Second, cost of good accounts disturbed is not factored in. This is primarily due to the fact that this is an implicit cost and proper marketing of the effectiveness of the fraud model for all parties (reduce customer inconvenience and interest rates) may be able to drive down this portion of the overall cost substantially.

References

Appleby, T. (1992) Credit card fraud rising. *The Globe and Mail Newspaper*, Toronto, Ontario, Wednesday, March 18, 1992, p A1–A2.

Biggs, D., De Ville, B., and Suen, E. (1991) A method of choosing multiway partitions for classification and decision trees. *Journal of Applied Statistics*, 18(1), 49–62.

Kidd, A. L. (1987) *Knowledge Acquisition for Expert Systems.* Plenum Press, New York.

Laudon, K. C. and Laudon, J. P. (1991) *Management Information Systems: A Contemporary Perspective*, 2nd edn. MacMillan Publishing, New York.

Liang, T. P. (1991) A composite approach to inducing knowledge for expert systems design. *Management Science*, 38(1), 1–17.

Nikbakht, E. and Tafti, M. H. A. (1989) Application of expert systems in evaluation of credit card borrowers. *Management Finance*, 15(5), 19–27.

14. A single European scorecard? Does data predict differently across Europe: An Experian Scorex investigation

Graham Platts and Ian Howe

14.1 The background

The direction of Europe and the pace and extent of integration across the European countries is the political debate of the decade.

Trade barriers and borders are coming down and Europe is moving towards a single European currency as the economies of Europe harmonize. But the question for our industry is whether credit granting in different countries is fundamentally different. Does data predict differently across Europe or is it similar? Could a scorecard built in one country work well in another country? Could there be a single European scorecard?

This chapter sets out to try and answer these questions. It explores how data predicts at the point of application across the countries of Europe. It looks for similarities as well as differences and scores up similar portfolios with scorecards built in different countries.

We have different customs, different histories, and different attitudes but deep down are we all the same credit risks?

14.2 The challenges

When we started to think about how we were going to answer the questions we had set ourselves we began to realize the enormity of the task.

Proceedings of Credit Scoring and Credit Control V, Credit Research Centre, University of Edinburgh, 1997.

Credit covers a whole range of industries as well as different products within industry. Should we be looking at

Banking
Finance houses
Retail credit
Credit cards
Mail order
Utilities
Mobile telephony

Within that should we consider

Cheque accounts
Overdrafts
Personal loans
Gold cards
Classic cards
Mail order accounts
Gas and electricity bills
Telephone accounts

Should we consider all the countries of Europe or should we try and home in on countries that are representative of their region.

And having decided on all this the next level of challenge emerged:

- Should we pick several portfolios in each area to limit the possibility of a rogue portfolio distorting results
- What should we do about the different good/bad definitions and exposure periods from country to country and portfolio to portfolio
- Should we compare before or after inference

And this was before we began to consider the work!

Every portfolio has a different database content. Characteristics are not common and different codes are used within characteristics. The more portfolios we considered the more laborious data conversions we would have to undertake. This was big and we were doing it in our spare time!

So the ultimate question we asked ourselves was: should we give in!

14.3   The approach

Given the potential dimensions of the project and our limited resource we started to scale down the work. We restricted the number of countries to five to represent regions of Europe

UK   United Kingdom
Germany   Northern Europe
Greece   Emerging markets
Belgium   France/Belgium
Italy   Southern/Latin Europe

We then decided to restrict ourselves to one area of credit. We chose retail credit. We then pooled the retail credit databases we had at our disposal from Experian and Scorex in each of the countries.

The results we show are therefore associated with retail credit across some of the countries of Europe. It is for the reader to decide if more general conclusions can be drawn.

First we looked and compared the profile of the applicants for credit. We looked at the proportions of each characteristic by each attribute and compared the predictiveness by looking at the weights of evidence for each attribute. This comparison for five of the key characteristics is shown in Section 14.4.1. Then we started to consider building scorecards.

In developing a pan European scorecard the first question we asked was what criteria should we consider. If the scorecard was to be truly European then it was important to select only those variables that were common to all regions of Europe. Hence variables such as UK post code statistics, whilst predictive, were not relevant to the rest of Europe.

With all country and portfolio specific criteria eliminated we were left with around 20 global variables. These were extracted from each database and transformed into a common format for analysis.

Having selected the potential variables the next step was the classification of each criterion. For simple discrete variables such as home phone this proved straightforward. With only two attributes (Yes or No) the classification was the same for all countries.

For continuous variables and complex discrete variables the classification proved more challenging.

- The applicant profile varies from one country to another.
- The predictive patterns in the data are different with each country.

The differences in applicant profile and predictive content necessitate different classification. The classification of Age of Applicant in Germany, for instance, may not be appropriate in Greece.

The global grouping of criteria represents the collective view of Europe and hence waters down to a certain extent the subtle patterns seen for each country. However, for a single European scorecard we must use a single classification and therefore we have looked to select the grouping which maximizes the predictive power of the criterion.

With all criteria classified we were ready for the next phase, the modelling phase. A new phase meant a new challenge:

- What modelling strategy should we adopt?
- Should we maximize the contribution of bureau data?
- Should we minimize bureau data?

Clearly each country will have its own modelling strategy. However, in developing a single European scorecard we have used the strategy appropriate for the database.

Comparing the Europe scorecard with the regional portfolio scorecard is perhaps a little unfair. In the original development database there are additional regional and client specific criteria that are not available in the Euro database.

To achieve a fairer comparison five additional models were developed, one for each region of Europe, by re-classifying and re-weighting the variables to reflect each country. By using only the same criteria we are in a better position to measure the performance of a single European scorecard.

14.4   The results

14.4.1   Applicant profile

The applicant profile was compared by looking at the proportions of applicants with various attributes. A small selection is shown in Figs 14.1–14.5.

The United Kingdom has a lot more homeowners who are generally on the telephone. Credit card penetration is the highest and the level of negative bureau data is about average. The distribution of number of dependants is around the average.

Germany is characterized by very low home ownership and a high level of tenancy. Home telephone is less than average but credit card penetration is the second highest. Although not shown the average age was a little younger in Germany.

The Greeks have an average level of home ownership. Home telephone is the lowest of the five and credit card penetration is very low.

The Belgians are around the average for home-ownership, home telephones, credit card ownership, and number of dependents.

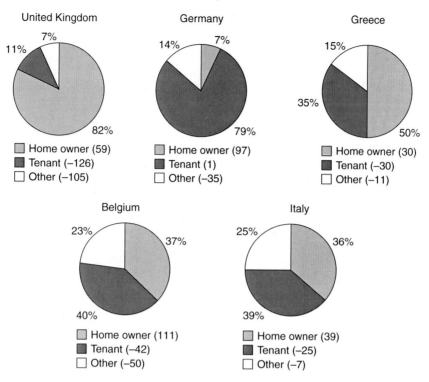

Fig. 14.1 Residential status.

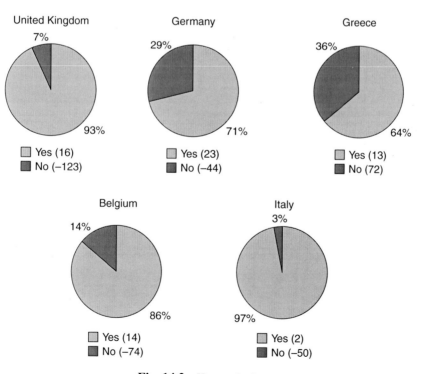

Fig. 14.2 Home telephone.

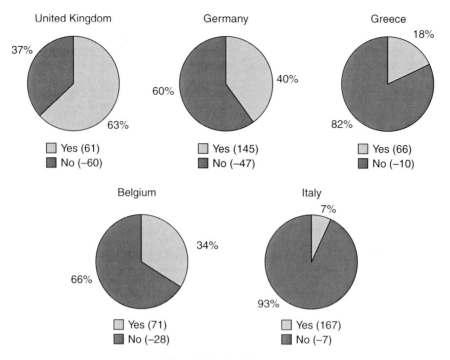

Fig. 14.3 Credit card.

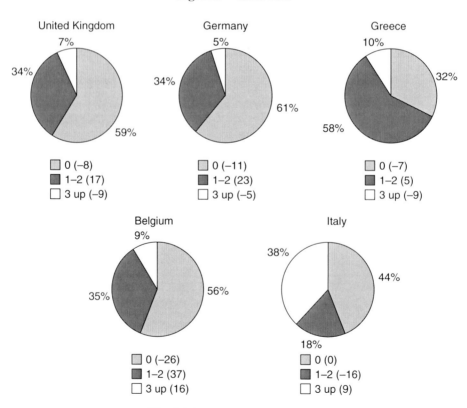

Fig. 14.4 Number of dependants.

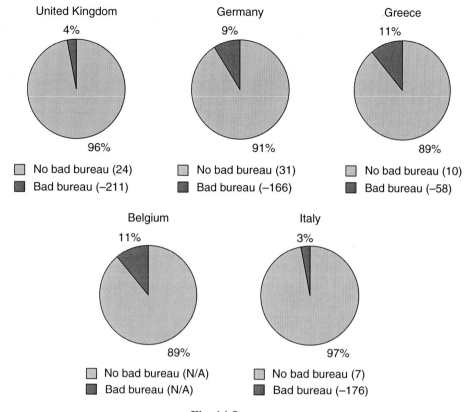

Fig. 14.5 Bureau.

The Italians have average levels of home-ownership but have more dependants than the other countries. There is a very high ownership of telephones! Credit card ownership is very low.

For each of the five characteristics the weight of evidence is shown in brackets. This clearly shows that certain attributes are far more predictive in certain countries than in others. However, the relative significance of these differences can only really be measured after models have been built.

14.4.2   Models

Armed with a single European scorecard, five country scorecards and five portfolio scorecards we were ready to measure the results. The development of each type of scorecard is summarized below:

- European scorecard: Developed by creating a single European database with common variables

- Country scorecard: Developed using the same criteria as the Euro scorecard but with classification and attribute weights appropriate for each of the regions of Europe
- Portfolio scorecard: Developed by considering all characteristics available in the portfolio country specific variables

There are a number of ways in which we can look at the performance of a scorecard:

- The information value
- The gini coefficient
- The percentage improvement in bad debt at the previous acceptance rate
- The percentage improvement in acceptance rate at the previous bad rate.

We have chosen to look at the performance of the scorecards from a business perspective. How will they perform when applied to real portfolios? Often the area of most interest to credit managers is what will happen to the bad debt if we look to maintain the current portfolio acceptance rate. By analyzing the percentage improvement in bad debt at the same portfolio acceptance rate we measure the effect on the business of introducing the three types of scorecards. Figure 14.6 illustrates this.

The results show that for all countries there is a marked difference in the improvements made by the country scorecard compared to the Euro scorecard. This suggests that regrouping and re-weighting the same criteria in order to reflect the country will have a large impact on bad debt.

This is most evident in the United Kingdom where introducing the Euro scorecard would actually increase the bad debt by 9.09 per cent. Using the country scorecard would reduce the bad debt by 4.55 per cent. The dramatic improvement in the bad

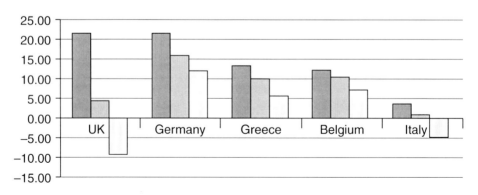

Fig. 14.6   Percentage improvement in bad debt.

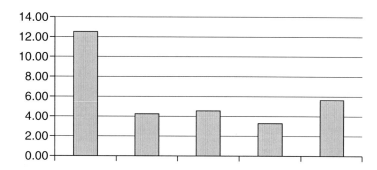

Fig. 14.7   Percentage improvement in bad debt given by country model compared to the Euro model.

debt using the portfolio scorecard may be attributed to the wealth of predictive bureau characteristics available in the United Kingdom.

In Belgium the Euro scorecard comes closest to the individual country scorecard in terms of improvement in bad debt followed by Greece, Germany, and then Italy. Italy also shows an increase in bad debt from introducing the Euro scorecard.

Whilst this can be used as a measure of the business impact of introducing new scorecards it is dependent on the previous decision-making process. Hence in countries where scoring is already a significant part of the decision making introducing a new powerful scorecard will not necessarily give good improvements in bad debt.

A comparison of the Euro scorecard with the portfolio scorecard is not comparing like with like as they did not have the same criteria available for the modelling.

Perhaps a more interesting comparison is the percentage improvement in debt given by the country scorecard over and above that of the Euro scorecard. Again the cut-off chosen was the previous portfolio acceptance rate.

Figure 14.7 illustrates by how much the country scorecard will improve the bad debt compared to the Euro scorecard.

The country scorecard gives respectable improvements over and above the Euro scorecard for all countries. In the United Kingdom the difference is most marked where re-classifying the criteria and re-weighting gives a 12.5 per cent improvement compared to the Euro scorecard. Even in Belgium where the country model is closest to the Euro model a respectable 3.38 per cent improvement is achieved.

14.5   Conclusions

The Euro and country scorecards were developed using the same criteria. However, the latter were shaped to reflect the individual country by re-classifying and re-weighting the attributes. The improvements in bad debt made from using the country scorecard over and above that of the Euro scorecard leads us to conclude the following. Whilst we all consider ourselves European there are differences from one country to the next and the data will necessarily reflect the intrinsic economic and social diversity of each region of Europe and reflecting those differences in the modelling will impact on the level of bad debt.

Perhaps the results are not as strong as one might intuitively expect and so one day with further European integration and a single European currency, it will be possible to score up more Europeans with a single scorecard. However, for the present, in the Authors' opinion, we must accept our differences and therefore the need to be scored differently.

15. Small sample scoring

Alan Lucas and Joanna Powell

Barclaycard's principal tools for controlling credit risk are 'Credit Scorecards' and 'Behaviour Scorecards'. These are linear models which predict the chance that a customer will continue to make regular repayments within, say, the next year. Usually these scorecards are built using large samples (e.g. 10,000 accounts).

In today's highly competitive marketplace, situations are arising more and more often where it is necessary to build scorecards on much smaller sample sizes. For example:

- when undertaking experiments on new applications forms
- when launching new products
- when moving into new markets
- when examining atypical niches within existing markets.

This chapter details an approach to building a scorecard on an extremely small sample for self-employed applicants using data from a trial questionnaire. The methodology used encompasses Bayesian techniques to incorporate prior opinions from in-house experts. The resultant scorecard was implemented with a new style application form reflecting the relevant features of the self-employed applicants.

Alongside the Bayesian approach other recondite techniques were used to overcome sample size problems. This chapter explains the problems encountered and their practical resolution. The authors welcome comments and advice from the academic establishment, particularly on the foundations of the approach. It is hoped that the work undertaken by the authors will spur similar attempts by other financial institutions.

Proceedings of Credit Scoring and Credit Control V, Credit Research Centre, University of Edinburgh, 1997.

The authors feel that with the intensification of niche marketing and product differentiation, more formal methods for combining data and expertise must quickly become part of a credit manager's arsenal.

15.1   Introduction and background

Barclaycard accepts self-employed applicants for its Classic Visa and Mastercard credit cards. Historically, the acceptance rate for such applicants has been below average. While this was acceptable to management throughout the recession, when the proportion of those self-employed who defaulted rose considerably, management felt that a less restrictive policy towards such applicants was more appropriate after the recession.

It was difficult to see how the acceptance rate could be improved without asking further or different questions of the applicant as, given the data that was already available, the existing credit scorecards were performing effectively. A decision was thus made to send a questionnaire to 1,000 existing self-employed customers to determine what questions were easy to complete. The questions asked were principally about the applicant's business and were arrived at after an internal brainstorm session. Extra points on the 'Profiles' rewards scheme was offered as an incentive for completion and return of the questionnaire.

From the mailing 120 useful replies were received. The disappointing response rate was thought to be owing to the fact that the number of Profile points on offer was insufficient as an incentive.

Having been involved in the questionnaire brainstorm the 'Predictive Modelling' section within Barclaycard was asked to comment on the responses. After some reflection we decided that an opportunity had presented itself to create and test out a scorecard building methodology for small samples. This was particularly relevant as Barclaycard was implementing a new computer system that would enable new products to be easily launched to segments of customers. These niche products would need scorecards created using data (if any at all existed) that was not directly relevant to the product in question. It was felt that the methodology for the self-employed would be allied to such niche product scorecards.

The opportunities that would be created by putting together a small sample decision making methodology were sufficiently attractive to set in motion a semi-research project on the self-employed applicants. This article details the result of this project.

15.2   The specific problem

The project had become one of utilizing the data from the sample of self-employed responses to build a scorecard.

Generic scorecards for particular types of credit and for particular markets are offered by the scoring consultancies. Indeed, when one of the authors was working with such a consultancy he put together a methodology for a *four* stage process of updating such a scorecard as soon as data became available, basing it initially on correlations in the data and subsequently on early delinquency measurements. Such scorecards do not, however, take account of any data that is already available. The self-employed applicants who had been mailed had had their Barclaycards for around 9 months. Each account had a *behaviour score* attached reflecting the subsequent probability of the customer defaulting on his payments. After 9 months there was sufficient information for the behaviour score to be effective. This behaviour score was thus a potential surrogate for an outcome variable, as there were obviously not enough bad accounts for a scorecard build.

15.3   Issues

Based on this approach some of the issues raised were:

- What should the outcome variable be? Options were:

  (i) Behaviour Score or some function of it
  (ii) A function of generic credit bureau score, behaviour score, and bank current account score

- Using the behaviour score as an outcome required that each of the nine behaviour scorecards be a 'statistically sufficient' predictor of risk. Was this the case?
- No rejects were included within the sample. How should reject inference be done?
- There was potential bias because the applicants who had responded may not be representative. How should this be detected and resolved?
- The potential characteristic set was too large and needed to be reduced—how should this be done?
- How should the correlations between characteristics be handled, given that the data size was rather small for measuring the correlations?
- It was obvious that the data needed to be augmented with expert opinion. This raised its own problems such as:

  (i) who to use as experts
  (ii) how to elicit the information
  (iii) how to determine how confident that one should be with the experts' opinions
  (iv) how many experts to use

- To incorporate the expert opinion a Bayesian approach seemed sensible, but none of the predictive modelling team had direct experience of building such models. What was the best approach?
- Some expert knowledge maybe difficult to incorporate in a Bayesian fashion— for example, the expert might believe that the bad rate for attributes within a characteristic are in a particular order, although he may be far less sure about their actual values. How should this be resolved?
- What software did we need to undertake the analysis and how should we procure it?
- How should the scorecard be implemented once built?
- How could a methodology be incorporated so that when actual account delinquency came through the scorecard could adapt itself by accounting for this extra information?

15.4   Operational considerations

Implementation of any new approach is the first problem that needs to be considered, as there is no point in allocating resources to produce a predictive model that cannot be implemented.

Given that the project was more revolutionary than usual and given that the success of the scorecard would not be apparent for some time, it was decided at the outset on a safe implementation method that would involve the minimum of IT resource.

The existing credit decision mechanism was at the time based on a mainframe application processing system, with a subsidiary 'Appeals' system for handling the applications within a grey-band below the scorecard cutoffs. Applications that failed credit scoring, but were close to the cut-off were given a reason for the decision (in accordance with Office of Fair Trading recommendations) and a chance to appeal if they supplied extra information. The initial implementation route chosen for the self-employed was to feed them through the appeals process. Each applicant with an application that had failed credit scoring but was within a preset region below the cut-off would be sent a form to fill in with the questions that were to be determined by this project. These questions would then be scored and, depending on the result, the original credit decision could be overturned.

15.5   The data

Eighty four characteristics were formed from the questionnaire data and from the original application data (for confidentiality reasons these cannot be disclosed). They were divided into the categories shown in Table 15.1.

Table 15.1 Characteristics formed from
the questionnaire.

Characteristic category	Number of characteristics
Personal	10
Financial—Company	9
Financial—Personal	15
Cards	21
Bank	7
Business	22
Total	84

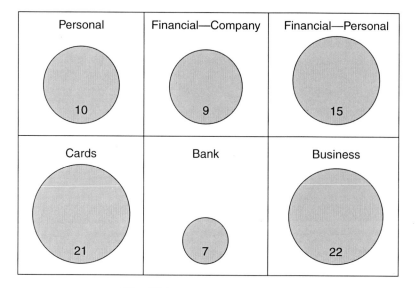

Fig. 15.1 Original characteristics.

Figure 15.1 shows this in pie-chart form.

The first stage of the modelling was to ignore from further analysis those characteristics that had had low responses from the questionnaire. After this process only 58 characteristics remained as shown in Fig. 15.2. These characteristics were those chosen for the modelling process. The original application credit score and its component scores (a credit bureau generic score, a bank current account score, and a post-code grade) were not included in the modelling but were put aside for comparison purposes.

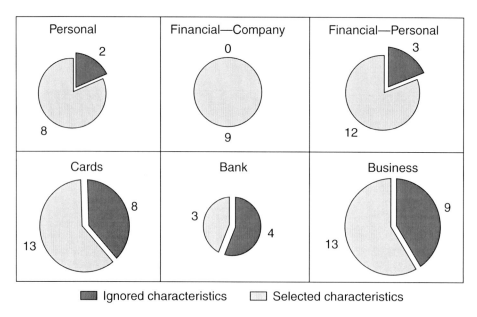

Ignored characteristics　　Selected characteristics

Fig. 15.2　Initial cut—low responses, irrelevant data.

15.6　Predictive modelling

15.6.1　Sampling considerations

Some initial work was undertaken to examine the bias in the sample. The distribution of behaviour score of the 120 responses was compared to that of those of the original 1,000 sample who had not responded. Unsurprisingly, it was found that those applicants who responded were, in general, higher scoring than those who did not respond. Figure 15.3 displays the distributions [20 additional points on the behaviour score corresponds to doubling the good/bad odds]. Although it can be seen that bias exists, it was felt not to be severe enough to warrant correction.

　　More seriously, the sample was for accepted accounts (above cut-off) only, whereas the intended implementation was for accounts below cut-off. Owing to the small sample size and the experimental nature of the work it was felt that the bias caused by this was too difficult to correct and should be ignored. Extra impetus for this decision came at the end of the project when examining the final scorecard—each variable in the scorecard was one that had not previously been considered—hence a model built on accepts alone would be much more likely to be applicable to rejects, as there would be no hard and fast cut-off rules.

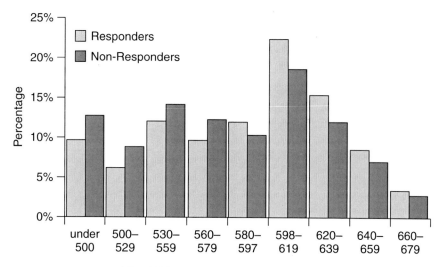

Fig. 15.3 Behaviour score distribution.

15.6.2 The outcome definition

Within the sample there were too few bad accounts for a reasonable analysis. However, every established Barclaycard account has a behaviour score calculated by one or other of nine behaviour scorecards. These scorecards predict the probability of not reaching 3-cycles delinquent within the subsequent 9 months. It was decided to use the behaviour score alone as an outcome variable in the analysis. Other scores were ignored, as it was felt that the behaviour score would be the most powerful predictor on the account in question. For simplicity, where the customer had been allocated a Visa card and a Mastercard, only the Visa behaviour score was used. This decision was based on the knowledge that bad customers tended to default on both their cards, with the Visa credit card defaulting first.

Despite degradation with time, the behaviour scorecards were still nearly '(statistically) sufficient' predictors of risk, given available data, and thus should have given reasonably good results as outcome indicators. Also, there was no overlap between the characteristics in the behaviour scorecards and those in the credit scorecards as the behaviour scorecards were built using account performance information alone.

It is generally accepted practice within the Scoring Industry that when building scorecards accounts are classified into two categories—those reaching a specific delinquency threshold, denoted Bads, and those not reaching the threshold, denoted Goods. The reason for this is easy interpretation of the data. Within this project we decided to adopt the same practice for some of the analysis, but for a different reason connected to the inclusion of expert data. Basically, the mathematical analysis of the statistics

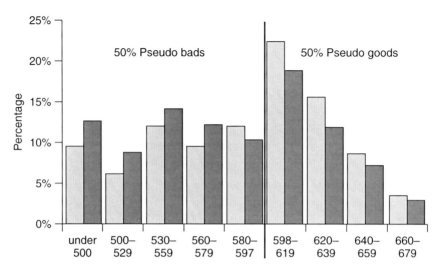

Fig. 15.4   Good/bad definition based on behaviour score distribution.

behind the approach seemed much simpler for the discrete outcome scenario and so, first time around, it seemed better to keep to a simple approach rather than a complex one, even at the expense of losing some scorecard power. Accounts were thus divided into two categories according to whether they lay below or above the median behaviour score (597):

Category 1   'Pseudo-Bads'
Category 2   'Pseudo-Goods'

The division can be seen in Fig. 15.4.

Henceforward, Pseudo-Bads will be called Bads and Pseudo-Goods will be called Goods.

15.6.3   Selection of characteristics

The values of each of the characteristics mentioned in Section 15.5 were classed, based upon a mixture of what the data revealed and pre-conceptions. This was not as subjective as might be thought as, in common with other credit-scoring developments, most characteristics are already discrete with only a few possible attainable values.

The attributes of each characteristic were then ranked according to either a natural ordering (e.g. ranking in 'time' order for the 'years business has been operational' characteristic) or a logical ordering—again subjective. The characteristics were then correlated with behaviour score using Spearman's rank correlation coefficient, and then divided into four 'predictive power' categories:

Category	Data Predictiveness
O	Not predictive
L	Low Predictiveness
M	Medium Predictiveness
H	High Predictiveness

On calculation, it was recognized that the confidence intervals on the correlation coefficients were large [surprisingly so] but no characteristics were excluded at this stage solely based on lack of predictiveness.

It is a general rule of thumb that the number of characteristics should not exceed 15 per cent of the number of data records. In this situation the 15 per cent limit had been exceeded by a long way and so some rational way had to be devised to reduce the number of characteristics. The chosen methods for doing this are explained below.

First, the opinions of two experts were elicited. David was included as a 'scoring' expert who had seen various sources of scorecard development data and Sarah was selected as an expert on self-employed consumers. Each was asked to provide an opinion about the predictive power of each of the 58 characteristics (plus various component sub-scores of the credit score), categorizing their responses into the O, L, M, and H categories above. Table 15.2 displays the distribution of agreement/disagreement between the two experts.

The percentages within each category were similar, as can be seen by comparing the marginal totals. Exact agreement was at 36 per cent, but 85 per cent of the time the experts were within one category of each other in their assessment.

Based on the expert views a joint view was obtained. Sarah was judged to have more knowledge of self-employed consumers specifically, and so the joint view was weighted in her direction. Table 15.3 shows this joint expert view.

The next step was to combine the predictiveness shown by the data with the joint expert view. A symmetrical table was used as shown in Table 15.4. The key facet

Table 15.2 Characteristics power cross table.

David's view	Sarah's view				
	O	L	M	H	Total
O	0	0	2	1	3
L	2	9	5	6	22
M	1	6	4	8	19
H	0	0	11	11	22
Total	3	15	22	26	66

Table 15.3 Joint expert view on characteristic power.

David's view	Sarah's view			
	O	L	M	H
O	O	L	L	M
L	O	L	M	M
M	L	L	M	H
H	M	M	H	H

Table 15.4 Predictiveness of final characteristics.

Data view	Joint expert view			
	O	L	M	H
O	O	O	M	H
L	O	O	M	H
M	M	M	M	H
H	H	H	H	H

of this table is that it separates those characteristics that are judged to be medium or highly predictive by either the data or the experts from the characteristics that are judged to be non or low predictive by both the data and the experts. This was to ensure that characteristics were only excluded if they showed no signs at all of usefulness. All characteristics with a joint expert/data predictiveness of zero were excluded from further analyses.

Figure 15.5 shows the characteristics that remained after this exercise.

The final stage in the preliminary characteristic reduction was to consider the correlations between the characteristics. This was examined in two ways.

1. First, a cross correlation matrix was drawn up between each and every characteristic. This was then examined to get an initial idea of characteristic duplications. Table 15.5 highlights a subset of the correlations. Care has to be taken in the interpretation of this table because of the large confidence intervals (caused by the small sample size).
2. Second, Graphical Models were built on the various characteristic categories— one model for each category mentioned in Section 15.5. The models were built by assuming that there were no interactions in the data other than first order ones and hence the links were obtained by regressing each variable on every other. The variables used for the regression were rank orderings, where the rank

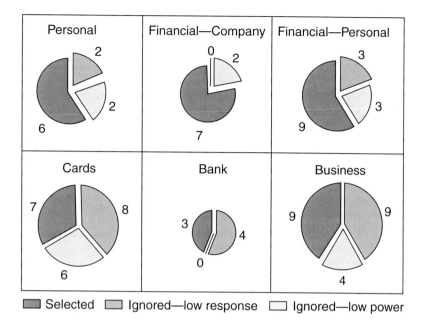

Fig. 15.5 Characteristics left.

Table 15.5 Correlations.

%	Emp	Isyourbs	Ymbusadd	Ymbusop
Emp	100.0	**36.1**	**−6.7**	**5.1**
Isyourbs	**36.1**	100.0	**−1.4**	**12.9**
Ymbusadd	**−6.7**	**−1.4**	100.0	**57.2**
Ymbusop	**5.1**	**12.9**	**57.2**	100.0

was assigned according to the bad rate of the attribute. An example of one of the models is shown in Fig. 15.6. Its interpretation is that each characteristic is independent of the characteristics not connected to it given the ones that are connected to it.

By examination of both the correlation table and the graphical models and by using common sense [i.e. knowledge of what the charactersitics mean] a number of characteristics were selected for exclusion from further analysis. Figure 15.7 shows the characteristics remaining after this process. No characteristics in the personal category remain because of the correlations with the credit score.

The final result of the characteristics reduction process had been to reduce the number of characteristics from the original 84 to a manageable 13.

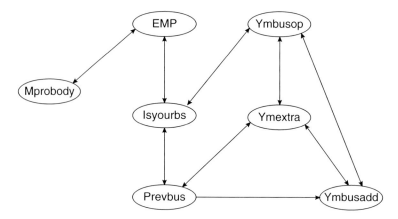

Fig. 15.6   Characteristic graphical model.

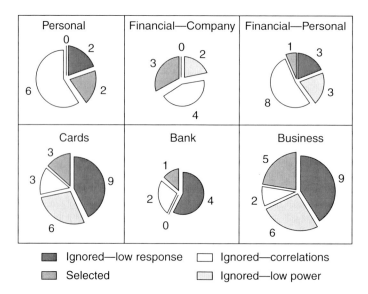

Fig. 15.7   Characteristics left.

15.6.4   Model structure

Because characteristic correlations had been roughly accounted for, the correlations amongst the 13 remaining characteristics were not too high. It was thus decided to build a scorecard by assuming independence of each characteristic with the others (given the outcome variable). The implication of this is that each of the characteristics can be treated in isolation when combining data with expert opinion. A justification for this approach is that previous research by one of the authors had suggested that the independence models work surprisingly well for credit scorecards where the number of records is small. In fact if there are less than 200 records (with equal numbers of goods and bads) one is unlikely to be able to improve on the independence model.

In an 'independence' scorecard the points values are calculated by calculating the 'weights of evidence' of the individual attribute bad rates (see Appendix 15.C for an example calculation). Thus getting from characteristics to scorecard can be done with a pencil and paper.

15.6.5   The model building approach

15.6.5.1   Shrinkage & James–Stein Estimators. It was obvious, even before the data was examined, that much of the variation in the data was caused by the small sample size rather than the data predictiveness. The authors were aware of a method to cater for this, as some many years ago an article had appeared in *Scientific American* on James–Stein Estimators, which purported to be able to use these estimators to adjust individual means (averages) towards a grand mean. An example was given whereby the results for an individual baseball player in last year's baseball season were not the 'best' estimator of his results for this season. Instead, a 'better' estimator could be obtained by averaging (using a weighted average) the player's results with the team's average results. 'Best' in this case was defined by the smallest difference in squared error between this year's result and the estimate. The weight was referred to as a 'lambda value'.

After some thought it was decided that the approach could be applied to individual bad rates for each attribute of a characteristic. For example, consider a characteristic with two attributes (note, records with missing values are excluded) as shown in Table 15.6.

The grand average bad rate is 48.1 per cent and the bad rate for Partnerships is only 17.4 per cent. However, the numbers are small and a better estimate of the Partnership bad rate is given by the weighted average:

$$17.4 \times \lambda + 48.1 \times (1 - \lambda) \qquad \text{[for some } \lambda \text{ (lambda) to be determined]}.$$

The obvious question is 'how to determine λ?', as it should depend on both the sample size and the relative bad rates between the grand mean and the attribute.

Table 15.6   Calculation of bad rates.

Characteristic	Business type	Bads	Total	Bad rate %
Attribute 1	Partnership	4	23	17.4
Attribute 2	Sole trader	46	81	56.8
Total		50	104	48.1

In fact, the authors had available to them the original work by James and Stein—unfortunately the maths was too involved to be unravelled in a short space of time. A simple approach that was decided upon was to write a simulation programme to determine the best set of λ values [one for each attribute of each characteristic] and then to subsequently refactor the results so that the new estimated bad rates referred to the same attribute totals (i.e. 23 and 81 in the example above). It was recognized that treating each attribute separately and refactoring would introduce bias, but it seemed a simple approach.

The authors did in fact write a simulation programme, but subsequent thought revealed that an exact solution was possible. The maths of this solution are detailed in Appendix 15.A (l represents the λ value).

Although the solution was neat, neither of the authors was overly happy with this approach as there was some uneasiness about what to plug in for the 'true' attribute bad rate in the formula. The figure chosen by the authors was the actual value from the sample [i.e. for attribute 2, q_a was set to be 17.4 per cent and m was set to be 48.1 per cent]. For attribute 1 this gives a λ value of 0.94. Selecting such a q_a places too much emphasis on the data as opposed to the grand mean. Another lesser problem with the approach was that the true grand mean itself had to be approximated by 48.1 per cent.

Despite the conceptual problems the authors decided to continue with the James–Stein approach because, if anything, the approach taken was conservative, it seemed a simple way of starting the analysis and, as will be seen, it fitted very well with the subsequent Bayesian approach.

15.6.5.2 The Bayesian Method. The most crucial step in the process is detailed in this section. One expert on self-employed bad rates was chosen to supply the expert data for the analysis. Each characteristic was dealt with separately in the analysis. The following was applied to each of the characteristics that were still under consideration.

For each attribute the shrunken bad rate (from the Section 15.6.5.1) and the number of customers with the attribute were available. If these are multiplied we have 'number of bads' and 'total' for the attribute, say 'b' and 't'. Assume that an expert's view is taken into account and that the expert has based his view on another sample, which contained B bads out of a total T. Then Appendix 15.B shows that, under suitable assumptions, the data view and the expert view can be combined using a Bayesian approach to give a joint 'data and expert view' bad rate of:

$$\frac{b + B}{t + T} \tag{15.1}$$

Thus to get the joint data and expert view one just adds the bads, adds the totals, and divides.

This can also be represented as

$$\kappa\frac{b}{t} + (1 - \kappa)\frac{B}{T} \tag{15.2}$$

where $\kappa = t/(t + T)$, which can be seen to be a weighted average of the sample bad rate with the expert's bad rate, with the weight being linked to sample size.

The above simple method is at the heart of the approach taken by the authors. The assumptions within it are:

(a) the binomial distribution can be approximated by the normal distribution;
(b) the expert's view on bad rates can be linked to a binomial view (and hence a normal view);
(c) bad rates per attribute can be viewed independently.

Although (a) does not in general hold for small numbers, a computer simulation convinced us that the approximation was sufficiently valid to be workable. Condition (b) is equivalent to a standard Bayesian practice of choosing a so-called 'conjugate' distribution for the prior, essentially, choosing a distribution that simplifies the mathematics. Condition (c) obviously does not hold, but the refined details below explain how this was handled.

Given that the distributional form governing the expert's opinion has been agreed to be binomial/normal, there are two parameters to estimate, vis the mean bad rate and its variance.

15.6.5.3   Eliciting the expert's mean bad rate. The main problems that arise in estimating the expert's view of a bad rate (i.e. B/T in formula (15.2) above) are that:

(a) the development sample has 50 per cent goods and 50 per cent bads, whereas the expert would gauge his views around a bad rate of say 10 per cent on the population as a whole
(b) the expert would comment on the bad rate for the attribute in question in the light of the population bad rate rather than in isolation
(c) the expert would be considering real goods and bads, whereas the data is based on pseudo-goods and pseudo-bads.

Point (c) was ignored in the calculations and pseudo-goods and pseudo-bads were treated as being the same as goods and bads, respectively.

Points (a) and (b) were catered for by examining the expert's views on bad rates for each attribute of the characteristic, calculating the bads for each attribute from these views by multiplying the bad rates by the denominators (see section below) and then factoring the denominators for each attribute pro rata so that the overall denominator for the characteristic was twice the number of bads.

15.6.5.4   Estimating the variance of the expert's bad rate. A typical method for eliciting the variance of an expert's distribution is to divide the distribution into intervals that he regards as being equally likely (e.g. quintiles). These intervals can then be used to calculate an approximate variance. This approach was in fact performed by the authors for a couple of characteristics and their attributes in order to verify the main approach that was taken, which was based on the estimation of T [see formula 15.1 above] directly. Formula (15.2) shows that it is not necessary to elicit variances directly from the expert. Instead the focus shifts to measuring a denominator in a ratio. This in fact produces its own set of problems because, typically, a scoring expert will have 'seen' many populations that display various degrees of similarity to the development population and each of these populations will have contained possibly thousands of records. The implicit information that the expert might have derived himself could be, for example, along the lines of the following guidelines:

(i)   no characteristic would be expected to have a bad rate greater than the population bad rate times a factor

(ii)   bad rates for attribute a always exceed those for attribute b

(iii)   'time based' characteristics are usually very predictive, etc.

In the absence of a structural model to soundly evaluate the expert's beliefs the following approach was taken.

1.   A sample size was selected based upon the samples that the expert was bearing in mind when formulating his opinion. The sample size selected differed according to where the information had come from. The following sample sizes were a guide:

Source of information		Sample size
Generally known		2,000
Informed by a few others		1,000
Informed by a credit bureau		10,000
Known from a survey		
sample size known	Use it	
sample size unknown	Use minimum it could be	
Known from correlations with other characteristics	Ignore (but bear in mind in the scorecard build)	

2. A set of Confidence Factors were applied to the sample size to represent the fact that the data which the expert has in mind is of a different nature to the development sample.

The factors used were:

Feature	Factor (to divide sample size by)
Characteristic slightly different	2+
Cannot quite remember bad rates but know approximate direction	4
Different product	3
Different market	4
Bad definitions differ	1.5
Definite cause & effect	0.5
Logical connection	0.7

In order to calibrate the factors, as well as using the quintile method explained above, the characteristic 'Time Business has been Operational' was chosen as this was the one that the expert was most confident with—also nationwide statistics are available on this. The set of factors above gave results that were in accordance with the expert's beliefs on variability of this characteristic. The factors were then applied, as appropriate, to the other characteristics.

Applying the Bayesian Formula. Formula (15.1) was then applied to get combined bad rates for each attribute of the characteristic under study. The data was then weighted to give an overall bad rate of 50 per cent for the characteristic.

Application of the above processes resulted in the elimination of a further three characteristics (because their predictiveness based on the joint data and expert view of bad rates was too low), leaving a total of 10 for the final scorecard. The scorecard was then produced by converting the bad rates to weights of evidence. It was then examined for situations where the data had been at variance with the expert's opinion. On the whole, the scorecard looked reasonable and both the authors and the expert were happy with it.

15.6.6 Validation

The time-based individual characteristics were plotted by time to determine whether the points in the scorecard would reflect the future rather than the past, as the past had

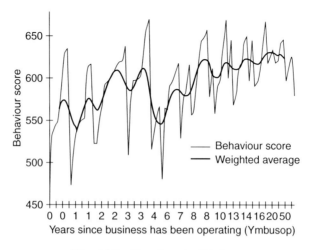

Fig. 15.8   Time-based validation.

included the early 1990s economic recession. Figure 15.8 shows an example of how the recession has affected the average behaviour score for the characteristic 'Years since business has been operational'. The thick line is a moving average of the scores. The points in the final scorecard did not have the dip shown in the graph and hence the characteristic was felt to be reasonably robust.

No independent validation was undertaken. However, the scorecard looked eminently sensible and this alone provided much confidence in the approach and the final answer. Data is currently being collected to verify the approach and to adaptively change the points values.

15.6.7   Final scorecard

The final scorecard had 10 characteristics, all of which referred to the self-employed applicant's business. The actual details of the scorecard are confidential, but may be made available to academics [under a suitable confidentiality agreement].

15.7   Future applications

In today's highly competitive marketplace, situations are arising more and more often where it is necessary to build scorecards on much smaller sample sizes, for example:

(a) when undertaking experiments on new application forms,
(b) when examining atypical niches within existing markets,

Table 15.7 Product strategy.

Markets	Established	New
Established	Market penetration	Product development
New	Market development	Diversification

(c) when the probability of an account defaulting is low, but the seriousness once it
     does is high,
(d) when launching new products,
(e) when moving into new markets,
(f) when diversifying (see Table 15.7).

An example of (c) is 'Commercial Scoring'. This is particularly relevant as there is
a reasonable amount of 'expertise' to draw from.

An example of (e) would be scoring outside of the United Kingdom.

An approach such as that presented in this chapter would be applicable within all
these areas, rationalizing the scoring process by combining what data is available in
a sensible way with expert views. The outcome would be to have more trustworthy
models and hence to be able to make riskier decisions using them, often leading to
quicker actions with less of a wait for experimental results.

15.8   Benefits of the approach

Although the approach taken in this chapter is not pure Bayesian, it has an intuitive appeal and is simple to implement, requiring no complex maths or difficult
simulations. Also, given the rather ad hoc nature of the method to determine the
variance of the expert's views it does not seem too essential to complicate things
too much further. Rather, it is preferable to have a simple, workable, understandable
approach.

A benefit of any Bayesian approach is that the methods allow adaptive calculations
of predictive estimates. In this case the feedback mechanism is particularly easy to
implement. If the final estimated bad rate for an attribute of a characteristic has a
numerator and denominator of 'n' and 'd' respectively, and if the bad rate some
months after implementation is N_1/D_1 (suitably weighted for sample proportions)
then the 'Adaptive' bad rate can be calculated as $(n + N_1)/(d + D_1)$.

The N_1 and D_1 can either be obtained from pseudo bad rates or one can await actual
values. This process can be iteratively applied until such time as there is enough data
to run more traditional scorecard building software. For example, further bads giving
a bad rate of N_2/D_2 lead to a new estimated bad rate of $(n + N_1 + N_2)/(d + D_1 + D_2)$.

Weights of evidence can then be calculated from these bad rates to adjust the scorecard points.

15.9   The correct Bayesian approach

It has been subsequently pointed out to the authors by Bayesian experts that the initial shrinking does not need to be kept separate from the Bayesian analysis. It should be possible, using the latest computer-aided simulation techniques, to build a Hierarchical Bayes model of the situation that would:

be more accurate than that undertaken
be integrated
need no ad hoc components
would deal correctly with some of the conceptual difficulties.

The authors feel that this type of approach needs setting up (preferably by Bayesian experts) so that scorecard developers can use it knowing that it has been endorsed. The challenge to the experts is to produce something that is simple to understand and which ideally is formula based rather than based on simulations.

15.10   Conclusion

In the authors' opinion the call from businesses is for action rather than experimentation. The latter often takes too long and the results can be superceded by more pertinent events. Bayesian techniques supply a way of taking action with increased confidence.

This chapter has shown that it is possible to build a scorecard with very meagre data samples. The approach needs refining and practical testing but, superficially, appears promising. The scorecard that was produced has been implemented and initial indications on its performance are not adverse.

The approach taken in this chapter has bundled together a number of techniques, rather than trying to provide a unified methodology. The next stage of verifying the techniques used could be to verify each component individually. This would mean, for example, undertaking separate analysis to ascertain the merits of using pseudo-goods and pseudo-bads rather than goods and bads as an outcome variable. Alternatively, the approach could be considered holistically—basically only testing if it works as a whole. The authors feel that there is much scope for research by universities into small sample methodologies. They are uniquely placed to devise unusual methods, to provide unified methodologies and to test out sub-components of them, whereas businesses often only have time to produce rather ad hoc models and to do holistic testing only.

Acknowledgements

David Boyes
Sarah Chandler

Appendix 15.A   The calculation of lambda values

Theorem 15.A *Assume a characteristic and an attribute.*
  Let

  N be the number of records with the attribute
  q_a be the actual (true) probability of bad for the attribute
  b be the probability of bad from the sample
  m be the overall bad rate for all the attributes.
  l be any number between 0 and 1 [l is the lambda value]
  q_e be the James–Stein estimate of q_a, that is, $q_e = l \times b + (1 - l) \times m$

then the value of l that minimizes the total squared attribute error for the James–Stein estimate of the bad rate is:

$$l = \frac{(q_a - m)^2}{((q_a(1 - q_a))/N) + (q_a - m)^2}.$$

Proof
  p_a be the actual probability of good for the attribute
  p_e be the estimated probability of good for the attribute
  So $q_a = 1 - p_a$ and $q_e = 1 - p_e$.
  There are $N \times p_a$ goods and $N \times q_a$ bads, thus the total squared error of the estimate of good rate is then:

$$(Np_a)(1 - p_e)^2 + Nq_a(0 - p_e)^2$$

as goods have a value of 1 and bads have a value of 0.
  Dividing by N, the average squared error per record is thus:

$$P_a(1 - p_e)^2 + q_a(0 - p_e)^2 = p_a(1 - p_e)^2 + q_a p_e^2,$$

which, on multiplying, gives

$$p_a - 2p_a p_e + p_e^2,$$

which can be rearranged to give

$$(p_a - p_e)^2 + p_a(1 - p_a)$$

and as $p_a - p_e = q_a - q_e$ and $(1 - p_a) = q_a$ this gives

$$\text{Average squared error per account} = (q_e - q_a)^2 + p_a q_a. \tag{15.A1}$$

The last term represents the irreducible error that occurs even if the bad rate is estimated exactly, and the first term represents the error caused by an incorrect estimate of the bad rate. Only the first term needs to be considered when examining the error minimization. So:

$$\text{let } \alpha_r = q_e - q_a.$$

As $q_e = lb + (1 - l)m$ by definition, we have

$$\alpha = [lb + (1 - l)m - q_a]. \tag{15.A2}$$

Were the sampling to be repeated R times we would have an average error of

$$\alpha^2 = (1/R) \sum \alpha_r^2, \quad \text{where the sum is taken over each } r \leq R \tag{15.A3}$$

where α^2 is now the overall average error and the subscripted terms refer to each sample.

Let $\delta = q_a - m$.

Then from (15.A2) for each sample:

$$\alpha_r = lb_r - lm - \delta.$$

So from (15.A3):

$$\alpha^2 = (l^2/R) \sum b_r^2 - (2l^2m/R) \sum b_r - (2l\delta/R) \sum b_r + l^2m^2 + 2lm\delta + \delta^2. \tag{15.A4}$$

But as $R \to \infty$ $(1/R) \sum b_r \to q_a$ as b_r is a binomial variate. $\tag{15.A5}$

Also, as $\text{Var}(b) = (1/R) \sum (b_r - q_a)^2$

$$= (1/R) \sum b_r^2 - (2/R) \sum b_r q_a + (1/R) \sum q_a^2$$

$$= (1/R) \sum b_r^2 - 2q_a^2 + q_a^2 \qquad \text{[using (15.A5)]}$$

$$= (1/R) \sum b_r^2 - q_a^2$$

and so we can, if R is large enough, replace $(1/R) \sum b_r$ by q_a and $(1/R) \sum b_r^2$ by $\text{Var}(b) + q_a^2$ within (15.A4).

So $\alpha^2 = l^2[\text{Var}(b) + q_a^2] - 2l^2mq_a - 2l\delta q_a + l^2m^2 + 2lm\delta + \delta^2$.

This is a minimum if $d\alpha^2/dl = 0$.

Collecting terms in l we have:

$$\alpha^2 = [\text{Var}(b) + q_a^2 - 2mq_a + m^2]l^2 + 2[m\delta - \delta q_a]l + \delta^2$$

and differentiating with respect to l and setting to 0 we get:

$$l = \frac{2\delta[q_a - m]}{2[\text{Var}(b) + q_a^2 - 2mq_a + m^2]},$$

which, as $\delta = q_a - m$, cancels to:

$$l = \frac{\delta^2}{\text{Var}(b) + \delta^2}.$$

As b is binomially distributed, $\text{Var}(b) = q_a(1 - q_a)/N$ and so

$$l = \frac{(q_a - m)^2}{((q_a(1 - q_a))/N) + (q_a - m)^2}$$

as required.

Appendix 15.B   Derivation of the posterior distribution

It will be assumed that only one attribute of one characteristic is being considered.
  Let:

x be the number of bads for the attribute
k be the number of customers that have the attribute
q_a be the true bad rate for the attribute
$b(x; k; q_a)$ is the binomial distribution for the number of bad customers who have the attribute.

Then the probability of getting x bads is $P(x \mid q_a)$, which is binomially distributed with distribution $b(x; k; q_a)$.
  From Bayes Theorem

$$P(q_a \mid x) \propto P(x \mid q_a)P(q_a), \tag{15.B1}$$

where $P(q_a)$ is the prior distribution and $P(x \mid q_a)$ is the likelihood.
  If the expert bases his prior view on a data sample of size 1 with y bads then

$$P(q_a) = P'(q_a \mid y)$$

for a probability density P', and so 15.B1 can be rewritten as

$$P(q_a \mid x, y) \propto P(x \mid q_a)P'(q_a \mid y) \tag{15.B2}$$

Again, from Bayes Theorem:

$$P'(q_a \mid y) \propto P'(y \mid q_a)P'(q_a). \tag{15.B3}$$

Assume $P'(q_a)$ is a uniform distribution [i.e. all the knowledge of the expert has been encapsulated in the density $P'(y \mid q_a)$]. Then substituting (15.B3) into (15.B2):

$$P(q_a \mid x, y) \propto P(x \mid q_a) P'(y \mid q_a) P'(q_a)$$

$$\propto P(x \mid q_a) P'(y \mid q_a)$$

If P' is assumed to be binomial too, then

$$P(q_a \mid x, y) \propto b(x; k; q_a) b(y; 1; q_a)$$

[note, the probability of success in the binomial distribution is the same because we are effectively viewing the expert's belief in terms of a random sample from a distribution with true mean q_a].

Approximating both binomial distributions by the normal distribution, bearing in mind that the mean and variance of a binomial with probability of success q_a out of k trials are kq_a and $kq_a(1 - q_a)$, respectively, leads to:

$$P(q_a \mid x, y) \propto \exp[-(x - kq_a)^2/2kq_a(1 - q_a)] \exp[-(y - 1q_a)^2/21q_a(1 - q_a)],$$

which equals

$$\exp\left[[-(x - kq_a)^2/2kq_a(1 - q_a)] + [-(y - 1q_a)^2/21q_a(1 - q_a)]\right].$$

Putting the term in the brackets over a common denominator and completing the square leaves:

$$P(q_a \mid x, y) \propto \exp[-(q_a - (x + y)/(k + 1))^2/2v + \text{constant}],$$

where $v = q_a(1 - q_a)/(k + 1)$ which implies

$$P(q_a \mid x, y) \propto \exp[-(q_a - (x + y)/(k + 1))^2/2v], \quad \text{where } v = q_a(1 - q_a)/(k + 1)$$

Thus q_a is normally distributed with mean $(x + y)/(k + 1)$, as required to be proved.

Appendix 15.C

Definitions
A *'Characteristic'* is otherwise denoted as:

A 'Feature'
A 'Variable'
A 'Data Item'
A 'Question' (on an application form)

An *'Attribute'* is a range of values of a Characteristic. An alternative way of viewing this is that it is a range of 'Answers' to a 'Question' on an application form.

Table 15.C1

Characteristic:	Business type	Bads	Goods	Bad rate
Attribute 1	Limited company	3	4	42.9
Attribute 2	Partnership	4	19	17.4
Attribute 3	Sole trader	43	31	58.1
Total		51	54	49.0

The '*Bad Rate*' for an attribute is the proportion of bad accounts for the attribute, that is the number of 'bads' divided by the [number of 'goods' + the number of 'bads']. The '*Weight of Evidence*' for an attribute is calculated by the formula:

$$\log (g/b) - \log (G/B)$$

where 'g' and 'b' are the goods and bads, respectively, for the attribute; 'G' and 'B' are the overall goods and bads; and 'log' is the natural log (to the base e). Thus for attribute 2 the weight of evidence is:

$$\log (19/4) - \log (54/51) = 1.558 - 0.057 = 1.501$$

Barclaycard's *Credit Score* for an account predicts the probability of an account not becoming 3 cycles delinquent within the first 15 months of its life. Eight scorecards were used, each for a different sub-population, but each scorecard contained four component scores:

a bank current account score (for Barclays customers)
a generic credit bureau score from one or other of the two major credit bureaux
a score based on application form data
a post code grade reflecting the geographic credit risk of Barclaycard's customers.

The *Behaviour Score* for an account predicts the probability of a Barclaycard account not becoming 3 cycles delinquent 9 months later. It is purely based on the payment, purchase, and balance information within the previous 12 months or since the account was opened (if less than 12 months). There are nine behaviour scorecards (according to sub-population).

References

Lee, P. M. (1997) *Bayesian Statistics—An Introduction*. New York, Arnold.
Bernardo, J. M. and Smith A. F. M. (1994) *Bayesian Theory*. New York, John Wiley & Sons.

Part VI. Alternative Approaches to Scoring Systems

This part deals with alternative approaches to scoring systems. All four chapters have at least two things in common. First, they present a mix of theory and application, combining some mathematics with what happens or needs to happen in the real world. Second, they are not the end of the research. In each case, they are more of a starting point from which both the mathematician and the practitioner can develop their ideas.

In the first chapter in this part, Burt Narain recognizes that survival analysis has been around as a statistical technique certainly since the 1970s but its use had been mainly in medical and engineering applications. This chapter is one of the first to consider using survival analysis in credit scoring and many papers and pieces of research were carried out following the conference presentation and subsequent original publication of this chapter. Thomas *et al.*, Thomas and Stepanova, and Stepanova and Thomas are three examples of these.

The principal idea is that we look not only at whether accounts performed and were classified as good or bad, but also at when they were classified. (There are parallels to be drawn with sequential hypothesis testing which statisticians have used for many years, and especially in cases where the test elements are expensive or where the test is dangerous.) Consideration of the time until classification may allow us to modify or rebuild a scorecard sooner rather than later. Also, it generates many other questions. For example, do high scoring and low scoring bad accounts go bad at the same rate? For example, is there some characteristic that differentiates between early and late bad accounts? In the chapter, Burt also briefly considers the use of survival analysis in the collections area, where time (and hence cost—both operational and funding) may be quite critical.

What this chapter does is not only to explain the principals of survival analysis and also apply it to credit granting problems, but also to show that using the ideas of survival analysis has the strong potential to generate a better scorecard.

The second chapter in this part is by Pete Sewart and Joe Whittaker and discusses the uses of graphical models for portraying the relationships between variables within a data set. The use of these graphical models in relation to the techniques involved in credit scoring, for example, log-linear modelling, was originally introduced in the 1980s and has developed quite slowly since. It is perhaps only since the middle of the 1990s that the application of such techniques has been applied to specific credit-scoring problems. The first purpose of the chapter is to indicate the importance of conditional independence within a credit-scoring context, to show how conditional independence is related to graphical models, and then to develop some of the ideas within graphical models. The chapter does this very well, using the standard credit-scoring problem, that of the relationship between the variables containing the information available at the point of decision and the performance outcome.

The second purpose of the chapter is to explain how undirected graphs can be used to model the joint distribution of the decision point variables. Not only does the chapter do this in total, but it also does it split by the age variable, as an example. Thus, the technique could easily be extended to explore the relationships between the competing application/decision point variables, such as many of the credit reference variables, which are clearly strongly correlated with each other and which a development would only wish to include one at most. A similar problem occurs with age and time variables—where again we would not want too many of these variables in a final model, as there would then be duplication, redundancy, and multi-collinearity. Graphical models will not provide the answer but, as the authors state, graphical models can be utilized as a data exploratory tool.

Perhaps, with time, if the use of graphical models moves out of the statistical laboratory and into management offices, one could use graphical models to explain to non-technical colleagues some of the issues arising with the data used in credit-scoring developments and in lending environments.

In the chapter by Yobas *et al.* the key objective of the chapter appears in the third paragraph:

There is therefore a need for further experimentation to support, or otherwise, the small number of findings so far published. In addition, no published study has compared all four techniques: traditional linear discriminant analysis, neural networks, genetic algorithms and decision trees using the same credit applicant datasets and using a realistic division of cases between 'good' and 'bad' groups.

The chapter does achieve this objective. However, underlying the remit of this and of other chapters is a fundamental hypothesis—that one technique will be significantly better than the others and that this can be proved. Proof of this hypothesis remains outstanding.

In the introduction, the authors suggest that there are few publicly available comparisons and that the published literature suggests mixed results. Perhaps, one explains the other, especially since the academic literature tends only to publish 'positive' results. The chapter then sets out to review the published research and also presents a review of the techniques. With the review of the techniques and the chapter's own analysis come some weaknesses. There is no reject inference, nor is there continuous modelling which is important for pricing and acceptance strategy. Moreover, decision trees cannot generally cope with combinations of application characteristics that have not been seen before.

Despite these weaknesses, the chapter presents a good review of published work and of the available techniques and then applies these techniques to a data set of 1,001 credit-card accounts, divided into 'good' accounts and 'slow' accounts the latter group being those that had missed a payment at any point during the observation period. The advantage of such a wide 'slow' criterion is that it generates a reasonably large sample size of 'slow' accounts. For three of the four techniques, transformations or scaling factors were introduced. Those chosen were sensible but a wide range of alternative factors could have been chosen which could have produced slightly different results.

The results then appear in two sections. The first section looks at comparing results within each technique as in only LDA is there a form of unique model. For the other techniques, there are some lessons to be learned from the comparison of transformations and scaling factors, etc. The second section then considers the comparison among the techniques. While the results are not completely clear-cut, it is evident that the constraint of linearity within linear discriminant analysis does not significantly weaken its modelling power and it performs no worse than neural networks while being computationally simpler. Genetic algorithms are probably placed third with decision trees the weakest technique.

The conclusion from the chapter is that further research is required, probably on larger data sets, but also with a more business-oriented means of comparison, for example, using actual costs of errors due to misclassification and opportunity costs. The main reasons why this chapter is included in the selection are because it presents a review of the principal techniques and applies these techniques in practice, discussing the difficulties with each. While the chapter reaches some conclusion, it is cloaked in assumptions, ad hoc transformations, and suggestions for future research. Therefore, the chapter represents an excellent starting point for further research and more detailed comparisons.

The final chapter in this part presents a very interesting mix of theory and application. It starts from the fact that Markov chains are used in many risk departments to describe the behaviour of their customers and their accounts. However, rarely are the assumptions supporting the use of Markov chains tested. In one example, these assumptions are tested and found to be far from valid. Modified Markov chains are then built but still the assumptions are not valid. Therefore, the next stage is to identify the fact that the population of customers is not homogeneous.

Previous publications have dealt with populations segmented into movers and stayers; this chapter introduces two other types of customers—shakers and twitchers. The results are that a good fit between model and data is achieved. Other papers have dealt with the heterogeneity including Edelman.

This chapter is important in at least two respects. The first is that it covers the fact that the use of statistical and mathematical models requires some basic assessment of the validity of the assumptions supporting the use of these models. Without this, any predictions and analysis are not only highly suspicious but also potentially damaging to the reputation of modelling in general. The second is that it is possible to modify models to fit the data in a practical way that provides value to the lender.

References

Edelman (1992) An application of cluster analysis in credit control. *IMA Journal of Mathematics Applied in Business and Industry*, 4(1), 81–8.

Stepanova, M. and Thomas, L. C. (2001) PHAB scores: proportional hazards analysis behavioural scores. *Journal of the Operational Research Society*, 52, 1007–16.

Thomas, L. C., Banasik, J., and Crook, J. N. (1999) Not if but when will borrowers default. *Journal of the Operational Research Society*, 50, 1185–90.

Thomas, L. C. and Stepanova, M. (1999) *Survival analysis methods for personal loan data*. Proceedings of Credit Scoring and Credit Control VI, Credit Research Centre, University of Edinburgh.

16. Survival analysis and the credit-granting decision

B. Narain

16.1 Introduction

Credit-scoring systems have traditionally been built on cases which are classified into a number of states (usually two, goods and bads). Associated with each case are a number of measures or predictors (e.g. age, occupation, repayment history of previous loans, etc). The predictor variables are grouped into bands, for example, the variable 'residential status' could be grouped into the three bands 'owner', 'tenant', and 'others'. An indicator variable (0, 1) is created for each band. The problem is now to construct a weighted sum of the indicator variables such that this sum or score distinguishes good from bad cases. Methods used to solve this problem include discriminant analysis, multiple regression analysis, and iterative techniques which maximize some 'information' function. More recently experts systems and decision trees have also come into the picture. Clearly the ability to predict which individuals from a set of applicants are likely to be bad is of great value. However, when a case is classified as bad no regard is taken of the length of time the account has been on the books. I think we would all agree that there is a relationship between the probability of an account being classified as bad and the time that the account has been on the books. In this chapter an attempt is made to model the 'time' taken for an account to be classified as bad. I suspect that we would be more interested in identifying those accounts that make a significant number of payments before being classified as bad. What is classified as significant will depend on a number of factors, for example, interest rates, type of loan, cost of administering each account, etc. We will use the methods of *Survival Analysis* to try and construct this model.

In *Credit Scoring and Credit Control*, (eds. Thomas, Crook, and Edelman), pp. 109–22. OUP, Oxford 2002.

16.2 Basic concepts of survival analysis

Survival analysis is a loosely defined statistical term that encompasses a variety of statistical techniques for analysing the time to some event for a population of individuals. The time to the occurrences are termed 'Survival Times' or 'Lifetimes'. Associated with each individual are a number of predictor variables. Typically a 'survival time' would be the time to failure of a machine or the time a biological unit survives after treatment is administered. These survival times are subject to random variation and are therefore random variables with a probability distribution. The distribution of survival times is usually characterized by three functions:

1. Survival function $S(t) = P(\text{an individual survives longer than } t)$
$$= P(T > t)$$

2. Density function $f(t) = P(\text{an individual failing in the interval } (t, t + \delta t))$
$$= \lim_{\delta t \to 0} \quad P\{t < T < t + \delta t\}/\delta t$$

3. Hazard function $h(t) = P(\text{an individual of age } t \text{ fails in the interval } (t, t + \delta t))$
$$= \lim_{\delta t \to 0} \quad P\{t < T < t + \delta t | T > t\}$$

Figure 16.1 is an example of a survival function which shows that as time increases the probability of survival decreases.

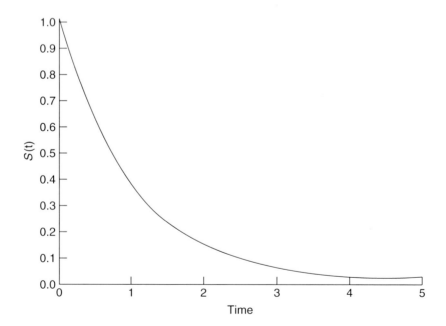

Fig. 16.1 Survival function.

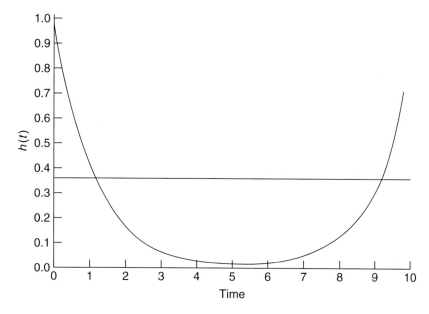

Fig. 16.2 Hazard function.

Figure 16.2 shows two hazard functions, one showing a constant hazard, and the other an example of an individual being most at risk and late in his lifetime.

A feature of survival data is the presence of censored observations. An observation is said to be 'right' censored if the exact value of the failure time is not known but only that it is greater than or equal to 't'. Although other types of censoring are possible (e.g. left and interval censoring), we will only consider right censoring.

The purpose of the analysis is therefore to explore the relationship between failure times and explanatory variables in the presence of censoring.

When the density function is exponential it can be shown that the relationship between the failure times (censored and non-censored) and predictor variables can be expressed as a regression function of the form.

$$Y = XB + ae$$

where Y = vector of failure times (usually the log of the failure times), X = matrix of predictors, B = vector of unknown regression parameters, e = vector of errors with a known density function not necessarily normal, a = unknown scale parameter.

It can also be shown that the hazard function for a given set of predictors X can be written in terms of a base line hazard $h_0(\cdot)$ in the following way:

$$h(t; x) = h_0(te^{-xb})e^{-xb}$$

If a base line hazard function exists then the effect of the predictors is to modify the probability that an individual will survive longer than time t. This is known as the accelerated failure time model since the effect of the predictors is to accelerate or decelerate the time of failure.

In the analysis reported in Section 16.3 we use this idea of accelerated failure time and assume the density function is exponential. Having estimated the unknown regression parameters we use these estimates to modify the base line distribution. For each individual we have an estimate of his probability of surviving to time t (Fig. 16.3; Fig. 16.4).

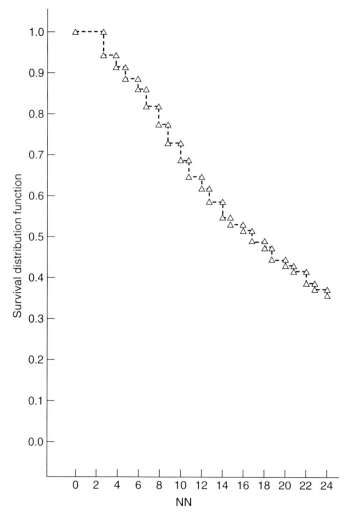

Fig. 16.3 Survival function estimates.

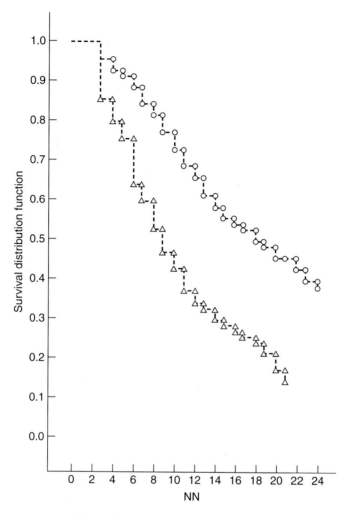

Fig. 16.4 Survival function estimates.

If all we knew about the individuals in our data is their failure time or censored time then all individuals will have the same probability of surviving to t. If we now have further information on each individual, say their age, time at address etc., the effect of this additional information modifies the underlying probability of survival in such a way that some individuals will have a higher probability than others of surviving to time t.

The unknown parameters are estimated by maximum likelihood using an iterative method such as the 'Newton–Raphson algorithm'. This is a parametric solution to the above problem since a known form of the density function is required. The problem can also be solved when the density function is arbitrary and unknown, although this solution will not be explored in this chapter.

The above is a very brief introduction to the concepts of survival analysis. Further details can be found in Lee (1980), Kalbfleisch and Prentice (1980), both of which are aimed at applied workers. The examples in both these texts are taken from the medical field. Readers interested in a more theoretical treatment of the subject should consult Miller (1981) or Cox and Oakes (1984). A number of statistical packages now fit survival models. Two readily available packages are 'GLIM' and 'SAS'. Aitken *et al.* (1989) contains a chapter devoted to the fitting of survival models using 'GLIM'.

16.3   An example of survival analysis applied to a fixed term credit portfolio

The data comprises 1,242 applicants accepted for a 24-month loan between mid-1986 and mid-1988. An account is deemed to have failed if three consecutive payments have been missed. All other accounts are considered to be right censored since failure has not yet occurred. We chose this definition of failure because three payments missed is often used as a definition of a bad account. Note that this analysis assumes that failure is certain if the observation time is long enough. Of the 1,242 cases accepted, 533 failed and 709 are considered right censored. The distribution of failure and censoring times is shown in Table 16.1.

The variables recorded for each applicant were:

Marital status
% Deposit
Home phone?
Residential status
Time at address?
Time with bank?
Time with employer?

All variables except phone and % deposit were grouped in the following manner:

Marital Status
  (i) Married
 (ii) Single
(iii) Other

Residential Status
  (i) Home owner
 (ii) Living with parents
(iii) Other

Table 16.1 Failures and censoring times—total population.

Months	Numbers failed	Numbers censored on books
3	68	41
4	33	32
5	30	44
6	46	30
7	42	27
8	40	31
9	39	37
10	41	49
11	43	57
12	26	27
13	22	36
14	23	28
15	14	27
16	10	30
17	10	28
18	12	24
19	7	16
20	10	22
21	4	20
22	7	24
23	4	34
24	2	45
Total	533	709

Time at address
  (i) Less than 1 year 6 months
 (ii) 1 year 6 months to 4 years 11 months
(iii) 5–7 years 11 months
(iv) 8–14 years 11 months
 (v) 15 years+

Time with Bank
  (i) Less than 2 years 11 months
 (ii) 3–4 years 11 months
(iii) 5–9 years 11 months
(iv) 10–14 years 11 months
 (v) 15 years+
(vi) Not answered

Time with Employer
  (i) Less than 4 years 11 months
 (ii) 5–6 years 11 months
(iii) 7–9 years 11 months
(iv) 10–14 years 11 months
 (v) 15 years+

We begin our analysis by computing a non-parametric estimate of the survival function using the Product–Limit or Kaplan–Meir Method. In the absence of censoring we could estimate $S(t)$ by the proportion of individuals in the sample who survive longer than 't'. The Kaplan–Meir estimate uses the recursive relationship.

$S(t) =$ (proportion of individuals surviving 't' periods, given that they have also survived $t - 1$ periods) $^*S(t - 1)$.

We note that censored information is incorporated into this estimate since censored cases contribute to the calculation of the proportion surviving until they are censored. (See Lee 1980) for further information. Figure 16.3 is plot of this function. Note that failure occurs only after 3 months since our definition of a failure is three payments missed. Figure 16.4 is the estimated, survival functions for two subgroups of the population (A)—'Applicants without a home phone' and (B) 'Applicants with a home phone'. This shows that for a given exposure period an applicant without a phone has a greater chance of failure than one with a phone, or the failure time has been accelerated for applicants without a phone and decelerated for those with a phone.

As indicated in Section 16.2 we will restrict our analysis to fitting parametric models to this data. We therefore need to specify the form of the density function. We make the assumption that the density function follows an exponential distribution. One test of the adequacy of this assumption is a plot of the log of the survival times against $\log\{- \log(\text{survival function})\}$. This should be a straight line if the underlying survival distribution is exponential. It can be shown that if the density is exponential the survival function is of the form $S(t) = e^{ut}$, giving $- \log\{S(t)\} = ut$ which is a linear function of t. (See Aitken *et al.* (1989), section 6.3). This graph is presented in Fig. 16.5 and shows that the exponential distribution assumption seems reasonable.

The *Lifereg Procedure* in the statistical package SAS was used to estimate the 'regression' parameters assuming an exponential distribution for the density function. We use these estimates to modify the base line survival function for each applicant. We are primarily interested in being able to identify the applicant whose survival time is less than 24 months.

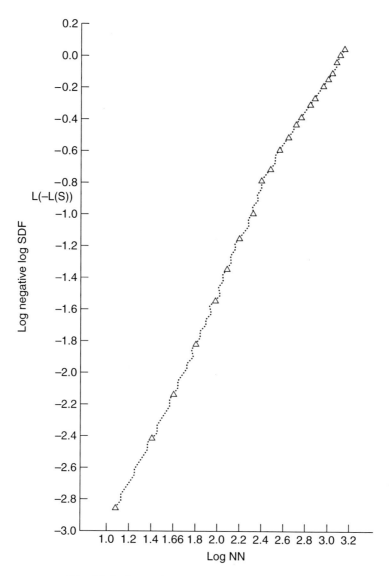

Fig. 16.5   Log($-$log (survival function)) estimates.

We calculate the median survival for each applicant based on the modified survival function. Table 16.2 presents the cumulative percentages for the observed and estimated median survival times for the 533 cases that had failed.

Although the number of variables used in constructing this model is very limited, the results are encouraging. The outcome of the censored cases is unknown and we therefore cannot check the performance of the model for these cases.

Table 16.2 Cumulative % of observed and estimated median survival times for failed cases.

Failure time (months)	Cumulative percentage 'failed cases'	
	Observed	Estimated
<14	80.7	85.9
14	85.0	87.9
15	87.6	89.7
16	89.5	90.6
17	91.4	91.4
18	93.6	92.9
19	94.9	94.2
20	96.8	95.3
21	97.6	95.9
22	98.9	96.4
23	99.6	96.6
24	100.0	97.2

16.4   A traditional scorecard

A scorecard was built on the above sample using multiple regression. A bad case was defined as one that had missed three consecutive payment. A good case was defined as one that had made 10 or more payments and had never been three or more payments in arrears. Bads are therefore all failed cases, and goods are all censored cases that have made 10 or more payments.

The following table presents the ascending cumulative score distribution that resulted from this analysis.

Score	Goods		Bads		Total	
	No.	%	No.	t	No.	t
2	1	0.24	7	1.31	8	0.84
29	11	2.63	52	9.76	63	6.62
56	29	6.94	186	34.90	215	22.61
83	91	21.77	354	66.42	445	46.79
110	185	44.26	461	86.49	646	67.93
137	273	65.31	509	95.50	782	82.23
164	345	82.54	527	99.06	872	91.69
191	395	94.50	532	99.81	927	97.48
232	418	100.00	533	100.00	951	100.00

This table shows that the score discriminates well between bads and goods.

Table 16.3 Payments made between 18 and 21 months.

Payments made	Below cut-off	Above cut-off	Total
Less than 18	233	254	487
18 or more	11	22	33
Total	244	276	520

Of the bad cases, 520 were on the books between 18 and 21 months. Applying the scorecard with a cut-off of 65 (i.e. accept all cases that score 65 and above) we would accept 276 cases and replace 244 (see Table 16.3). If we look at the number of payments made we see that of the 276 cases recommended for acceptance 254 made less than 18 payments. This would suggest that a better credit granting decision could be made if the score was supported by likely survival times.

16.5   Conclusions

Based on this very limited analysis the methods of survival analysis seem to add an additional dimension to that provided by a standard scorecard. The underlying density function assumed is very simple although it seems to fit the data well. Further and more detailed work is required on different data sets with more predictor variables. Although we have looked at the question of whether or not to grant credit, these methods could be equally well applied to any area where there are predictor variables and the time to some event is of interest. In a collections environment we may be interested in the time accounts take to recover under various collection strategies.

The views expressed in this chapter are those of the author and not necessarily those of any organization with which he is associated.

References

Cox, D. R. and Oakes, D. (1984) Analysis of Survival Data. Chapman and Hall, London.

Aitken, M., *et al.* (1989) Statistical Modelling in GLIM. OUP, Oxford.

Lee, E. T. (1980) Statistical Methods of Survival Data Analysis. Lifetime Learning Publication, Belmont, California.

Kaibfleisch, J. D. and Prentice, R. L. (1980) The Statistical Analysis of Failure Time Data. Wiley, New York.

Miller, G. M. (1981) Survival Analysis. Wiley, New York.

17. Graphical models in credit scoring

Pete Sewart and Joe Whittaker

Graphical models simplify the analysis of multivariate observations by summarizing conditional independences in the data. Variables are represented by nodes, and the absence of an edge between two nodes signifies their conditional independence. While graphical modelling has been used in several applications of statistics, credit scoring has only recently been suggested as a suitable candidate.

This chapter suggests the following potential uses for graphical models: to display and interpret the associations between variables taken from a credit-card application form; to compare the credit scoring of sub-populations; to give a description of the credit-scoring selection process in terms of influence diagrams; and to assess the effect of selection bias and stratification on the interdependency of variables.

These methods are discussed in relation to the analysis of a subset of variables from a stratified sample of credit-card applicants. The large number of variables measured in an application form requires the statistical analysis of large sparse contingency tables. It is shown here that tractable graphical models can be extracted from fitting the relatively simple all-two-way interaction model.

17.1 Introduction

Graphical models simplify the analysis of multivariate data: associations between the variables comprising the data are summarized by a graph consisting of nodes and edges. Variables are represented by nodes, and the absence of edges between any two nodes signifies a conditional independence between the corresponding variables. While other techniques designed to analyse multivariate data, such as principle-component analysis (e.g. Krzanowski 1988), reduce dimension by combining the original variables

IMA Journal of Mathematics Applied in Business and Industry, 9, 241–66, 1998.

into a (linear) score, with graphical models the original variables remain distinct, and it is the relationships between the variables that are examined.

The idea of representing log-linear models by independence graphs was originally introduced by Darroch *et al.* (1980). Whittaker (1990) explains in detail the properties of graphical models and includes numerous case studies. Edwards (1995) provides another recent introduction. The area of graphical models is rapidly expanding, with applications in many branches of statistics including regression analysis, log-linear models, time series, and probabilistic expert systems.

Statistical applications in credit scoring have mainly been concerned with the discrimination of 'good' and 'bad' credit risks. These include developing new methods (e.g. Boyle *et al.* 1992), finding ways of comparing these different methods (for a review, see Wilkie 1992), or improving or adapting current systems—for example, by reject inference (Hand and Henley 1993). Fitting logistic regression models is the standard way of building a good discriminant, or credit scorecard. Log-linear models are a closely related technique used for the analysis of multi-way contingency tables (e.g. Agresti 1990).

More recently the field of credit scoring has been suggested as an interesting application area for graphical models. The standard logistic regression model typically models the conditional distribution of Y given by $X = (X_1, \ldots, X_k)$, where in the credit-scoring context, Y is behavioural performance such as the Good/Bad indicator, and X denotes the variables extracted from the application form. We contend, however, that the distribution of X is of interest (a) in its own right, and (b) because it determines the statistical properties of the fitted regression for Y. A graphical model for X allows this distribution to be visually summarized, allows sub-populations to be compared, and relates independence and dependence to orthogonality and collinearity. An advantage of using a graphical model to describe the process is that it allows easy imputation of any missing responses in the X variables, which are a common occurrence in application forms and credit-bureau information.

Another interesting application of graphical models is to model the complete credit-scoring process, including the outcome variables of interest such as behavioural performance and revenue. Marshall and Oliver (1995) describe influence diagrams, which are directed independence graphs incorporating decision nodes and provide the necessary framework for a credit-scoring model. A similar avenue is pursued by Hand *et al.* (1997) who use a mixture of directed and undirected graphs to model the credit-scoring process. We do not consider such an exercise in this chapter and instead utilize graphical models as a data-exploring tool to improve understanding of the credit-card applicant population.

The first purpose of this chapter is, through illustration, to indicate the importance of conditional independence in credit scoring; to show how conditional independence relates to graphical models; and to distinguish between the use of directed graphs, undirected graphs, and influence diagrams.

The second purpose is to explain how undirected graphs may be used to model the joint distribution of the application-form variables. To illustrate the method, the analysis concentrates on modelling a subset of variables taken from the application form. There is much that can be gained from examining even a relatively small subset of variables. The undirected graphical model of these variables allows an improved understanding of the interrelationships between the application characteristics. This is useful for analysts keen to learn about the social, demographic, and economic behaviour of the population of interest. An insight into the differences between distinct populations is gained if they are modelled separately and their graphs compared. This highlights the extent of any differences, which in turn may suggest whether separate scorecards are likely to be necessary for each sub-population.

Section 17.2 describes the properties of graphical models with definitions of conditional independence, and gives examples of Simpson's paradox, which emphasizes the importance of modelling the joint distribution. In Section 17.3 a discussion of the selection processes that occur in credit scoring is explained in terms of an influence diagram and conditional independence. The effects on measuring interaction are noted, and a similar discussion is given for the effect of using stratified samples. The use of the all-way log-linear model is described in Section 17.4, along with an explanation of the edge-exclusion deviance, which is used to select acceptable models.

Section 17.5 shows that attempts to apply the log-linear all-way interaction model prove to be impractical for modelling a large number of variables. This problem is partially solved by constraining interactions of order higher than two to vanish, which still retains the conditional independence structure. Finally, in Section 17.6, our modelling approaches are illustrated on a stratified sample of credit-card applications to the credit-card division of a major bank. It is still necessary to reduce the dimension of the data, by decomposition, in order to construct the graphical model. To illustrate the methods, three graphical models are produced for the subset of application variables: the first constructed using all individuals in the sample, the second constructed on the sub-population of 'young' applicants and the third on the separate sub-population of 'old' applicants. Inferences are drawn from the first graph, and the other two graphs are briefly compared.

17.2   Conditional independence and graphical models

Graphical models are concerned with summarizing association and dependence between the variables in a multivariate data set. It is useful here to define independent and conditionally independent events.

17.2.1   Independence

Events A and B are independent, written $A \perp B$, if and only if $P(A\cap B) = P(A)P(B)$, where $P(*)$ is the probability. An equivalent formulation is $P(A/B) = P(A)$, which states that the outcome of event B has no influence on the outcome of event A.

In applications, it is necessary to work in terms of the probability density or mass functions and use random variables or vectors rather than events. The random vectors X and Y are independent if and only if the joint density function $p_{xy}(*,*)$ satisfies $p_{xy}(x, y) = p_x(x)p_y(y)$ for all x and y. It is straightforward to represent two random variables as graphs, as Fig. 17.1 illustrates.

Directed independent graphs (Bayes nets and influence diagrams) represent the dependence of Y on X as opposed to the association between X and Y. Interest lies in the distribution p_x and the conditional distribution $p_{y/x}$, rather than their joint distribution p_{xy}. This is shown in Fig. 17.2.

17.2.2   Conditional independence

The definition of independent events can be rewritten, by replacing the unconditional probabilities with conditional probabilities, to give the definition of conditional independence. Events A and B are independent, conditional on C, written $A \perp B/C$, if and only if $P(A \cap B/C) = P(A/C)P(B/C)$. Expressed in terms of probability density functions, the random vectors X and Z are independent, conditional on the random vector Y, if and only if $p_{XZ/Y}(x, z/y) = p_{X/Y}(x/y)P_{Z/Y}(z/y)$ satisfies $p_{XZ/Y}(x, z/y) = p_{X/Y}(x/y)p_{Z/Y}(z/y)$ for all x, y, and z. With three random variables, the conditional independence is signified by the absence of a connecting edge, as in Fig. 17.3.

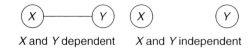

X and Y dependent   X and Y independent

Fig. 17.1   Graphical models representing dependent and independent events.

Y is dependent on X

Fig. 17.2   An example of a directed graph.

Fig. 17.3   Representing the conditional independence of $X \perp Z/Y$ in an undirected and in a directed graph.

More generally, in an arbitrary undirected graph, two subsets of variables are independent conditional upon any *separating* subset of variables. To predict the outcome of a variable, it is only necessary to use those variables that are directly joined to it with an edge. Variables that are separated from the outcome variable in the graph, in other words those that are not connected by an edge, are conditionally independent given the separating variables and hence provide no additional information for prediction.

17.2.3   Simpson's paradox

It is important to understand the difference between marginal and conditional independence. Examples 17.1 and 17.2 illustrate Simpson's paradox (Simpson 1951). It refers to seemingly contradictory interpretations of independence and association present simultaneously in the marginal and conditional distributions.

Example 17.1 *Marginal dependence does not imply conditional dependence.*
Consider a simple (though contrived) example related to sexual discrimination. A sample of 1,200 bank-loan applicants are classified according to gender (male/ female), loan status (rejected/accepted), and bank ($A/B/C$) to which they applied. Examining the marginal table between gender and loan status suggests that sexual discrimination is taking place; see Table 17.1. If the three bank categories refer to different branches of the same national bank, and a decision is made centrally on whether to grant loans, then this is the whole picture, and the conclusion of sexual discrimination is a valid one. The variables' gender and loan status are marginally correlated, and the graph of their distribution is shown in Fig. 17.4.

However, it may well be the case that the banks are competitors, or deal with different types of loan, and hence have different loan-granting policies. It is sensible

Table 17.1   Loan applications by gender.

	Rejected	Accepted	% Accepted
Male	250	350	58
Female	350	250	42

Gender   Loan status

Fig. 17.4   The marginal dependence between gender and loan status.

Table 17.2 Loan applications by gender and bank.

		Rejected	Accepted	% Accepted
Bank A	{Male	75	25	25
	{Female	225	75	25
Bank B	{Male	100	100	50
	{Female	100	100	50
Bank C	{Male	75	225	75
	{Female	25	75	75

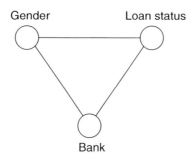

Fig. 17.5   Gender and loan status independent, given bank.

then to break down the figures by bank, since the decision to grant loans is made locally, see Table 17.2. The truth is now that gender and loan status are independent conditional on the bank applied to. The suggestions of sexual discrimination is shown to be false, and instead it is apparent that males tend to apply to the banks with high acceptance rates and females to the banks with low acceptance rates. The reason the banks have different sex ratios applying for loans might perhaps be explained by the bank's marketing strategy, for instance, if directed towards a particular gender. Another possibility is that the banks specialize in loans designed for specific items, which are traditionally gender-orientated. The acceptance rates for the three banks are likely to be predetermined by the bank's history, or the type of loan specialization.

It is evident that gender no longer provides any information about the outcome of the loan decision once it is known which bank the application was made to. The full graph, illustrating the conditional independence, is shown in Fig. 17.5. Collapsing the full table over bank applied to gives the initial marginal table and induces the observed dependence between gender and loan status.

Example 17.2 *Marginal independence does not imply conditional independence.*
This fictional example illustrates how certain characteristics might influence the probability of defaulting on credit-card repayments. A sample of 4,764 credit-card holders are classified according to wealth (poor/rich), default status (no/yes), and credit-card usage (light/heavy).

First, consider the effect of wealth on defaulting. Equal percentages of defaulters in both categories indicates that wealth provides no information about defaulting; see Table 17.3. The subgraph of Fig. 17.6 displays the marginal independence of the variables.

Breaking this table down by light and heavy credit-card users reverses the previous conclusion that wealth and defaulting are independent: they *are* dependent, conditional on credit-card usage; see Table 17.4. If it is known whether an individual is a light or a heavy user, then their wealth becomes an important factor in predicting whether

Wealth   defaulting

Fig. 17.6 Wealth independent of default status.

Table 17.3 Defaulting against wealth and usage.

Wealth	Defaulted		% Default
	No	Yes	
Poor	2,450	60	2.4
Rich	2,200	54	2.4

Table 17.4 Effect of wealth on defaulting.

Usage	Wealth	Defaulted		% Default
		No	Yes	
Light users	{Poor	2,210	10	0.45
	{Rich	110	1	0.9
Heavy users	{Poor	240	50	17.2
	{Rich	2,090	53	2.5

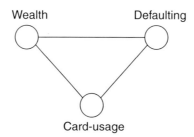

Fig. 17.7   Wealth and defaulting dependent in the joint distribution.

they are likely to default or not. The graph of the three variables, shown in Fig. 17.7, has no edges missing.

These two examples emphasize the importance of examining the whole picture. It is the joint distribution that is of interest if an understanding of how all the variables interact is desired. When only the marginal distributions are examined, interesting associations may be missed and spurious relationships may be unintentionally discovered.

17.3   Selection processes

The statistical analysis of a sample of data on credit-card applicants has to contend with the problem of selection. This may occur for several reasons, of which one, inbuilt into the credit-scoring process, is whereby applicants are accepted (selected) or rejected on the basis of their scorecard value. Another form of selection is the differential selection (or stratification) of cases on the basis of an observed variable, such as the Good/Bad indicator. We examine both these topics in this section.

17.3.1   Selection in the credit-scoring process

The graphical models discussed above relate only to random variables. An adequate description of the credit-scoring process requires the introduction of decision variables, as well as a variable to denote the resulting value of the outcome in the decision process. An influence diagram (Marshall and Oliver 1995) extends the directed graph described above to three types of node: square nodes to represent decisions, with an associated set of choices; circular nodes to represent random variables, each with an associated set of outcomes; and diamond nodes to represent results of the decision process. The direction of the arrows reflects the direction of the influence, and a missing edge portrays lack of direct influence or equivalently a conditional independence, as illustrated in Fig. 17.8.

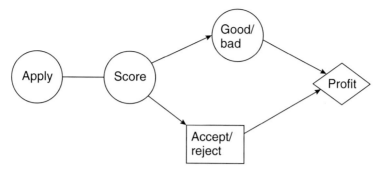

Fig. 17.8 An influence diagram representing the credit-scoring process.

There is a temporal sequencing from left to right. From the credit company's point of view, the 'Accept' node is a decision while the 'Apply' node is a random or chance variable. That there is no edge leading from Apply to Good signifies that Good ⊥ Apply/Score, and supposes that the Score contains all the information from the application form needed to predict the eventual status of Good. That there is no edge leading from Apply to Accept indicates that it is only the score that influences the decision. That there is no edge from Accept to Good states that the underlying probability of Good is not affected by accepting or rejecting the applicant. The only variables influencing profit are the decision Accept and whether the applicant turns out to be Good or Bad.

The influence diagram has an associated decision tree (Fig. 17.9) where every individual in the general population traverses along one of the branches with certain probabilities. These probabilities satisfy the independence constraints displayed in the influence diagram. It is apparent from the diagram that there are two selection processes occurring in the credit-scoring process. The accepted population is selected by the credit-card company from the through-the-door population via the credit-score forecasts of behavioural performance. This through-the-door population is itself self-selected from the general population, by the 'random' decisions of individuals to apply for a credit card. In constructing a graphical model of the application variables, as in the next section, it is important to be clear which is the population of interest. Graphical models of the through-the-door population or the population of accepted applicants are possibly of most interest, but these populations have been conditioned on the decision variables.

The issue to consider here is the implication that this inbuilt conditioning has on the dependence structure (or the independence graph) of the accepted or through-the-door populations. The structure of the graph may differ according to which sub-population is being examined, as the following example shows.

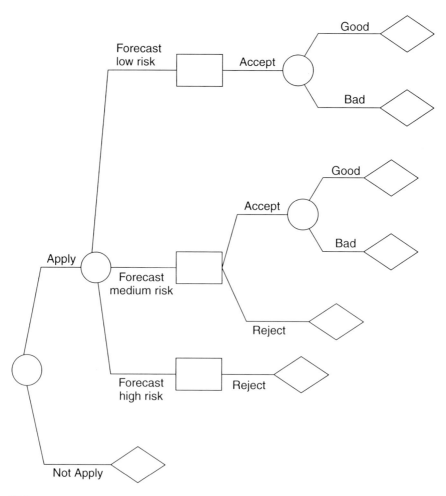

Fig. 17.9 The decision tree of the credit-scoring process. The profit resulting from each branch is recorded at the diamond nodes.

Fig. 17.10 Marginal independence of X_1 and X_2 in the overall population.

Example 17.3 *How selection can influence the joint distribution.*
Consider a contrived example of reasons for applying for a credit card: X_1, the desire for credit (required/not required), and X_2, need for an alternative to cash (yes/no). The selection variable Y also has two levels (apply for card/do not apply). It is reasonable to suppose that the two reasons X_1 and X_2 are marginally independent in the overall population, and the graph is simple; see Fig. 17.10.

We represent the negative events (credit or alternative to cash not required, card not applied for) by 0, and the corresponding positive outcomes by 1. Let $P(X_1 = 1) = 0.7$ and $P(X_2 = 1) = 0.4$. By independence, $p(x_1, x_2) = p(x_1)p(x_2)$, and the marginal table of probabilities can be constructed (Table 17.5).

Another reasonable assumption is to suppose that the probability of the event that an individual applies or does not apply for a credit card, Y, jointly depends on X_1 and X_2. Let

$$P(Y = 1/X_1 = 0, X_2 = 0) = 0.2, \quad P(Y = 1/X_1 = 0, X_2 = 1) = 0.5,$$
$$P(Y = 1/X_1 = 1, X_2 = 0) = 0.7, \quad P(Y = 1/X_1 = 1, X_2 = 1) = 0.9.$$

The directed graph, shown in Fig. 17.11, displays this information.

However, when the population observed consists only of those individuals who applied for a credit card, we obtain an observed distribution, $P(x_1, x_2/Y = 1)$, as shown in Table 17.6. These two observed variables are now dependent in this selected subpopulation, even though they are independent in the general population. For example, compared with 46.2 per cent of those who require credit, of those who do not require credit, 62.4 per cent require a cash alternative. In the general population, 40 per cent required a cash alternative, regardless of whether they required credit or not.

The fact that X_1 and X_2 are marginally independent is no longer observable when their dependence is examined conditional on whether they applied for a credit card as

Table 17.5 $P(x_1, x_2)$ for the whole population.

		x_2, Cash alternative		%
		Not required (0)	Required (1)	
x_1	{Credit not required (0)	0.18	0.12	40
	{Credit required (1)	0.42	0.28	40

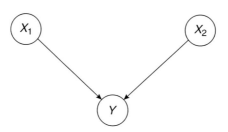

Fig. 17.11   The directed graph of the reasons for applying for a credit card.

Table 17.6 $P(x_1, x_2/Y = 1)$ for the applicant population.

		x_2, Cash alternative		%
		Not required (0)	Required (1)	
x_1	{Credit not required (0)	0.056	0.093	62.4
	{Credit required (1)	0.458	0.393	46.2

$X_1/y=1$ $X_2/y=1$

Fig. 17.12 Loss of independence of the two reasons in the subpopulation of credit-card applicants.

shown by the graph in Fig. 17.12. One effect is that the independence graphs of the through-the-door or accepted subpopulations are likely to appear more complicated than graphs constructed on data from the general population.

17.3.2   Stratification

Although random sampling is the simplest method of sampling from a population, better estimates are obtained by stratification, where minority populations are over-sampled in order to ensure a larger number of exceptional individuals in the sample. This is the case in credit-scoring samples (Lewis 1992), where, although the Bads make up only a small proportion of the total population, a large proportion of the sample includes Bads in order to better estimate the regression coefficients in the score card.

The graphical model analysis of a sample of applicants requires several tests of independence and conditional independence. The test statistic—for example, Pearson's chi-squared or the likelihood-ratio test (here called the edge-exclusion deviance; see later)—not only provides a test of the hypothesis but also gives a scale to measure the relative importance of the dependence or association. Stratification may well affect the values of these statistics and so influence the choice of model and the graph.

Example 17.4 *How stratification can affect the observed relationships between the variables.*
Consider the perceived strength of association between creditworthiness and residential status under various stratification policies. Residential status has been classified

into a binary variable with levels corresponding to renting and owning accommodation, and creditworthiness is classified as Good or Bad. Assume that a sample of 5,200 is to be stratified into various proportions of Bad individuals. We examine the effect of stratifying a sample of 5,200 individuals into various proportions of Goods and Bads.

If the sample was chosen randomly from the population, the proportion of the Bads in the sample might be as low as 5 per cent; see Table 17.7.

The deviance against independence equals 24.7, and on the null hypothesis is to be compared against the chi-squared distribution on 1 df. Choosing equal numbers of observations for each level is a common method of stratification. The deviance, in fact, may grow when this is the case as illustrated in Table 17.8. The deviance increases dramatically from the random sample case to 134.2.

Stratification can have major implications if the number of observations in each level become dissimilar. Consider the case of Bad customers making up only 0.7 per cent of the sample, shown in Table 17.9. The deviance is now 3.6, which is in fact too low to be confident enough to reject the independence hypothesis. Although it appears that stratification actually increases or decreases the strength of the association, it should

Table 17.7 Random sample of the population.

Creditworthiness	Residential status	
	Rent	Own
Bad	195	65
Good	2,964	1,976

Table 17.8 Data for equally weighted stratification.

Creditworthiness	Residential status	
	Rent	Own
Bad	1,950	650
Good	1,560	1,040

Table 17.9 Data for unweighted sample with few Bads.

Creditworthiness	Residential status	
	Rent	Own
Bad	27	9
Good	3,098	2,065

only affect the amount of information available to confidently reject the hypothesis of independence between the variables. When constructing the graph, the edge strengths and missing edges should be tested for sensitivity to the stratification. A random sample is perhaps best if the relative edge strengths are to be compared sensibly. It is possible to infer back to the original sample from a stratified sample if the stratification proportions are known.

17.4   Modelling the joint distribution

There are various features of the credit-scoring process that can be described by graphical models. We consider some of these here. Let X_a, X_b, and X_c denote three, subvectors of application variables used to build the scorecard, with X_d denoting a variable subvector not used in the construction. For example, if $b = (4, 6, 8, 11)$, then: $X_b = (X_4, X_6, X_8, X_{11})$. Let Y be the eventual credit performance indicator and S the Score or credit performance prediction.

The simplest situation is one which examines the joint distribution of the application variables X_a, X_b, X_c, and X_d using undirected edges; see Fig. 17.13. Since the X variables are known for all applicants, inferences can be made about the through-the-door population. Inclusion of the credit performance indicator Y in the model only allows analysis of the accepted population, unless reject inference is successfully applied.

Including the performance indicator (see Fig. 17.14) requires a mixture of directed edges and undirected edges. Such a model allows interpretation of which variables directly influence credit behaviour, for example, to check whether the variables X_d do not predict performance Y.

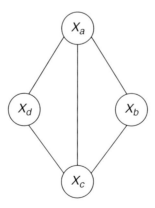

Fig. 17.13   Graph of the application variables.

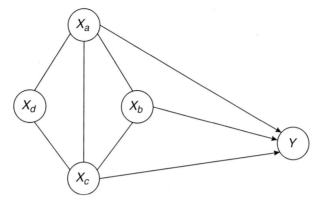

Fig. 17.14 Graph of the application variables and credit performance indicator.

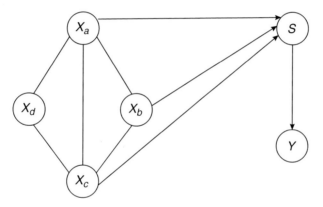

Fig. 17.15 Graph of the application variables, credit performance indicator, and the score.

By further including the Score in this model (see Fig. 17.15), the main focus of interest is in checking whether credit performance is conditionally independent of the application variables given the Score, or whether the X variables contain additional information which could have improved the predictions. The Score is a deterministic function of the observed application variables.

An alternative way of modelling the relationship between X and Y is by a latent-variable analysis. Essentially it is assumed that people possess an unobserved underlying characteristic that determines their credit behaviour. This variable, Z, is such that credit performance, Y, is conditionally independent of the X variables, given Z, as Fig. 17.16 illustrates.

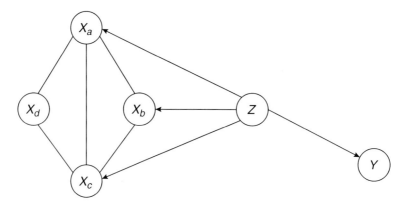

Fig. 17.16 Latent-variable model, showing the application variables' independence of credit performance, conditional on a latent (random) variable Z underlying credit behaviour.

17.4.1   Log-linear models

We concentrate on the simplest situation of building an undirected graphical model from the joint distribution of a subset of the application variables, the X's, as in Fig. 17.13. A systematic way of checking for conditional independences is to fit a log-linear model to the joint distribution (Agresti 1990); within the log-linear parametrization, the specification of independence graphs is relatively straightforward (Whittaker 1990).

To summarize this briefly, we note here that the log-linear all-way-interaction expansion for a three-way table is

$$\log p(x_1, x_2, x_3) = u_{\emptyset} + u_1(x_1) + u_2(x_2) + u_3(x_3) + u_{12}(x_1, x_2) + u_{13}(x_1, x_3)$$
$$+ u_{23}(x_2, x_3) + u_{123}(x_1, x_2, x_3) \qquad (17.1)$$

where, for example, $u_{12}(x_1, x_2)$ is the two-way interaction term between X_1 and X_2. To avoid overparametrization, constraints on the parameters are necessary.

A table in which the conditional independence, $X_2 \perp X_3/X_1$ is satisfied has all interaction terms containing x_2, and x_3 set to zero, that is, $u_{23} = 0$ and $u_{123} = 0$. The density function corresponding to this conditional independence is then

$$\log p(x_1, x_2, x_3) = u_{\emptyset} + u_1(x_1) + u_2(x_2) + u_3(x_3)$$
$$+ u_{12}(x_1, x_2) + u_{13}(x_1, x_3). \qquad (17.2)$$

The parametrization is easily extended from three to k dimensions.

Undirected independence graphs are defined by the correspondence between a missing edge and the pairwise independence of two variables conditioned on the rest. Within the log-linear model, this corresponds to setting to zero all two-way and higher-order interactions containing that pair. Empirically these u terms are estimated by maximizing the appropriate likelihood function, and general-purpose software is widely available (e.g. SPSS, SAS, S+).

17.4.2   Model selection

For any contingency table, especially those in high dimensions, there are a large number of possible models to choose from. It is useful to have a technique to help select an acceptable model. A simple but rather naive model-selection procedure is to fit the saturated model, determine which u terms are negligible, and then use this to deduce the structure of the independence graph. An improvement is to drop the edge according to the site of the edge-exclusion deviance.

The deviance is just the maximized log-likelihood-ratio test statistic and measures the divergence between the observed values and the fitted values:

$$\text{Deviance} = 2 \sum_{\text{cells}} \text{observed log (observed/fitted)}.$$

The fitted values are calculated from the specified log-linear model. Under the null hypothesis that the model specification is correct, the deviance has an asymptotic chi-squared distribution. The degrees of freedom are determined by the number of parameters which have been set to zero in the saturated model's log-linear expansion in order to derive the specified model.

Edge-exclusion deviances are those deviances corresponding to testing a pairwise conditional independence, and are calculated for each of the existing edges in a model, M, say. To calculate any one edge-exclusion deviance, that particular edge is dropped from the model M and a new model, M_1, is defined. The deviance calculated by fitting the model M_1 is then compared with the deviance from the fitted model M. The difference between these two deviances defines the edge-exclusion deviance, and is effectively a measure of how important that edge is in determining a good fit to the observed data. Small edge-exclusion deviances correspond to near conditional independences while large deviances correspond to conditional dependences. The 'strength' of the edge reflects how confidently the null hypothesis that the conditional independence exists can be rejected. When a conditional independence is discovered, the corresponding edge is dropped from the graph and an updated model is defined. Edge-exclusion deviances are then calculated from this new model, and the process continues until a final model is chosen. These edge strengths are used to highlight the important interactions in the fitted graphs.

To add edges to the graph, edge-inclusion deviances can be calculated in a similar manner by comparing the deviances in the models with and without the edge of interest. The edge is added to the graph if a large drop in deviance is apparent in the model which includes this edge.

17.5   Sparsity in the contingency table

17.5.1   The log-linear all-way interaction model

First attempts to find a graphical model were carried out by fitting the all-way log-linear model to arbitrary subsets of application variables. This dataset, described in Section 17.6, includes 7,702 credit-card applicants, and most of the variables contain between 2 and 5 levels. Subsets of between 4 and 8 dimensions were modelled, and an important problem soon became evident.

When attempts were made to drop edges from the saturated model containing all edges, by comparing the edge-exclusion deviance with a chi-squared distribution on the relevant number of degrees of freedom, it turned out that almost all the edges were significant, even at the 1 per cent level. More worryingly it also appeared that the edge-exclusion deviances increased disproportionately when additional variables were introduced to the model, even after accounting for the extra degrees of freedom due to higher dimensions. Although this is theoretically possible, as Simpson's paradox illustrates, it is usually expected that the extra information an additional variable provides reduces the strength of the dependence between the two variables on that specific edge.

Bootstrapping can be used to estimate the variance of a function of the data by repeated replacement sampling from the empirical or the fitted distribution (Efron and Tibshirani 1993). By taking 100 bootstrap samples from the observed data and calculating the edge exclusion deviances for each sample, it is apparent that the sampling distribution of the deviance is misleading. The plots in Fig. 17.17 compare the edge-exclusion deviances from the bootstrapped samples with the edge-exclusion deviances calculated from the actual data.

The first plot in Fig. 17.17 illustrates the bias existing in the distribution of edge-exclusion deviances. The bootstrap calculations of the deviances for the same edge should be symmetrically distributed about the straight line (the empirical edge-exclusion deviance); however, a positive bias for most edges is apparent. The second plot in Fig. 17.17 reveals that the edge-exclusion deviance for most of the edges is increasing as an additional variable is included in the model. It is expected that the deviances should either be unaffected or reduced upon further conditioning, so that the points lie on or below the line.

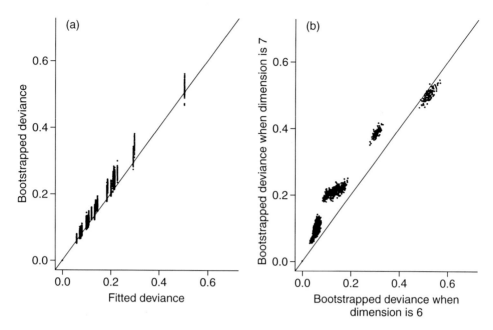

Fig. 17.17   Plot of the edge-exclusion deviances from the actual sample and from the bootstrapped samples: (a) for the original variables, and (b) showing the shift of the deviances when the dimension is increased from 6 to 7; the deviances have been divided by sample size.

Since the number of cells in the contingency table increases with increasing dimension, it is sparsity that is causing the problems.

17.5.2   Sparsity

Sparse tables are caused by relatively small sample sizes, or by a high number of categories classifying the variables, or by a large number of variables. The failure to satisfy the large-sample assumptions causes the deviance to drift from the asymptotic chi-squared distribution and hence induce misleading model selection.

Example 17.5 *How sparsity may cause the deviance to increase upon further conditioning.*

Consider the edge-exclusion deviance between variables X_1 and X_2. As the dimension of the table is increased, each partial table is divided over the levels of the additional conditioning variable. Each partial table contributes to the edge-exclusion deviance. Consider one such sparse observed partial table between the two variables, as in Table 17.10. This partial table's contribution to the edge-exclusion deviance is 0.138. Further conditioning on a variable X_3, independent of X_1 and X_2 with $P(X_3 = 1) = 0.5$, should not effect the edge-exclusion deviance between X_1 and X_2. However, the expected table includes non-integer cell counts, which cannot arise

Table 17.10   Observed incidences of X_1 and X_2.

	$X_2 = 0$	$X_2 = 1$
$X_1 = 0$	1	1
$X_1 = 1$	1	2

Table 17.11   Expected incidences conditional on X_3.

	$X_3 = 0$		$X_3 = 1$	
	$X_2 = 0$	$X_2 = 1$	$X_2 = 0$	$X_2 = 1$
$X_1 = 0$	0.5	0.5	0.5	0.5
$X_1 = 1$	0.5	1	0.5	1

Table 17.12   A possible integer realization.

X_2:	$X_3 = 0$		$X_3 = 1$	
	0	1	0	1
$X_1 = 0$	1	0	0	1
$X_1 = 1$	0	0	1	2

Table 17.13   A possible integer realization.

X_2:	$X_3 = 0$		$X_3 = 1$	
	0	1	0	1
$X_1 = 0$	0	1	1	0
$X_1 = 1$	0	1	1	1

(Table 17.11). The sparsity of the table therefore forces the observations into one or the other of the levels of X_3, and dependences are induced. Two such possible tables are Tables 17.12 and 17.13.

The contribution to the edge-exclusion deviance is 1.73 and 1.05, respectively, from these two tables. By considering all possible tables, the expected edge-exclusion deviance is calculated as 1.71: a large increase from the expected value of 0.138. A larger sample size would avoid this problem. However, with a fixed sample size, high dimensions induce many sparse partial tables, which inevitably increase the edge-exclusion deviances. We propose the examination of the all-two-way log-linear model as a remedy.

17.5.3   Two-way interactions

A method for dealing with sparse data is to restrict models to the class of all two-way interactions. All-way interaction models have the complete table as a sufficient statistic, but the two-way interaction class only requires the set of two-way marginal tables. In general these are not sparse. The number of parameters to estimate is correspondingly and drastically reduced. The conditional distributions derived from a two-way interaction model are necessarily additive in the log-odds-ratio scale, which is often assumed as a working hypothesis in logistic regression.

The two-way interaction models are constructed by constraining to zero all terms of interaction order higher than two in the log-linear expansion. So, in three dimensions, (4.1) becomes

$$\log p(x_1, x_2, x_3) = u_\emptyset + u_1(x_1) + u_2(x_2) + u_3(x_3)$$
$$+ u_{12}(x_1, x_2) + u_{13}(x_1, x_3) + u_{23}(x_2, x_3),$$

and more generally, in k dimensions,

$$\log p(x_1, \ldots, x_k) = u_\emptyset + \sum_i u_i(x_i) + \sum_{i<j} u_{ij}(x_i, x_j). \tag{17.3}$$

It is easily shown (e.g. Whittaker 1990) that the conditional independence $X_1 \perp X_2/ (X_3, \ldots, X_k)$ is equivalent to $u_{12} = 0$, and so the independence graph is determined by the nonzero u_{ij} terms. Due to the reduced number of parameters to estimate, the tests for conditional independences in the two-way interaction model are determined by relatively small degrees of freedom yielding more powerful tests, and better asymptotic approximations.

A further justification for applying a two-way interaction model to the data is its close similarity with the linear logistic regression model commonly used in the credit-scoring discrimination process. The price to pay is that, if higher-order interactions are nonzero, this may not necessarily be recognized and the model may fit parts of the table poorly.

17.5.4   Applying two-way interaction models to the application data subset

In practice, unlike the all-way interaction models, the two-way interaction model gives sensible results. The same subset of application-form variables is used here as was used with the all-way interaction models. Bootstrapping shows that the deviances are no longer biased and now reveals small edge-exclusion deviances indicating conditional independences. This is shown in the first plot of Fig. 17.18, where the edge-exclusion deviances from the bootstrapped samples are plotted against the edge-exclusion deviances calculated from the actual data. The second plot in Fig. 17.18 shows that the

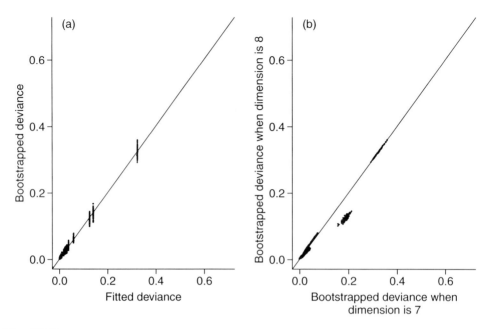

Fig. 17.18   Bootstrapped edge-exclusion deviances revealing (a) no bias and (b) no increase upon further conditioning.

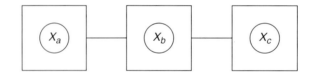

Fig. 17.19   Decomposition of X into subvectors X_a, X_b, and X_c.

addition of further variables into the model now has the desired effect of either not affecting or of reducing the deviance.

17.5.5   Decomposition

Current computational constraints limit the dimension of log-linear models that can be fitted. One strategy for building the independence graph for all the variables is to search for a decomposition into subvectors (X_a, X_b, X_c). A decomposition requires that these subvectors be exclusive and exhaustive, that $X_a \perp X_c / X_b$, and that the subgraph on X_b is complete as illustrated in Fig. 17.19.

To construct the whole graph, it is necessary to model only the subvectors (X_a, X_b) and (X_b, X_c). The joint distribution can then be obtained from the factorization $p_{abc} = p_{ab} p_{bc} / p_b$.

17.6 Modelling the application data

17.6.1 The application data

The data analysed in this section relate to a stratified sample of current account holders of a major bank who applied for a credit card to the bank's credit-card division between June and November 1992. The total sample size is 7702 which includes 'Goods', 'Bads', 'indeterminates', and 'rejects'. Note that the data are for a sample of the through-the-door population. Hence the credit performance variable is not known for some of the applicants, namely the rejects, and we do not consider it here.

The variables analysed in this chapter, taken from the application form, are (1) bank account type, (2) own cheque guarantee card, (3) children, (4) employment status, (5) own telephone, (6) income band, (7) marital status, (8) residential status, (9) time at address, (10) time at employment, and (11) age.

The subset of variables selected here are not only potential scorecard covariates, but also more importantly are chosen to describe the social and demographic characteristics of the population. The variables have been coarsely classified into the credit-card company's usual groupings in order to reduce the number of categories, and most variables contain between 2 and 5 levels.

The initial problem is to discover whether a decomposition as described in Fig. 17.19 exists. In practice we achieved this by reducing the number of categories within each variable so that all of the variables could be simultaneously modelled. The ordinal variables age, income, children, time at address, and time at employment were dichotomized into young/old, low income against high income, no children against children, less than 3 years against more than 3 years, and less than 1 year against more than 1 year, respectively. Residential status was classified as rent/own, and marital status was dichotomized as married against single or separated. Only the categories for employment and bank-account type were not combined. Although many of the complexities of the relationships may be disguised in this reduced classification, it should give an approximation to the structure of the graph.

Trial and error, together with guidance from credit-scoring experts, suggested the decomposition given below and illustrated in Fig. 17.20.

X_a = children (3),
X_b = (employment status (4), income band (6), marital status (7), age (11)),
X_c = (residential status (8), time at address (9), time at employment (10)),
X_d = (bank-account type (1), own cheque guarantee card (2.), own phone (5)).

The results of further modelling the subvectors (X_a, X_b), (X_b, X_c), and (X_c, X_d), using the original variables, reveals the graph in Fig. 17.21.

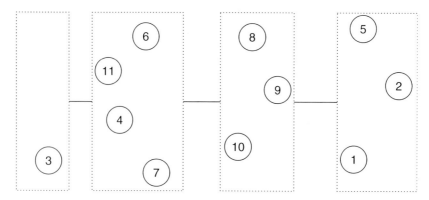

Fig. 17.20 A particular decomposition of the application variables into subsets. The decomposition was suggested by simultaneous modelling of the dichotomized variables.

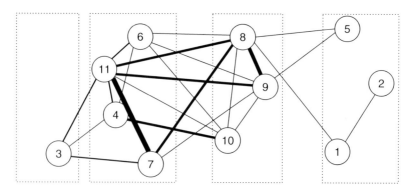

Fig. 17.21 Approximate independence graph of the categorical application variables constructed in two stages. First the decomposition was derived using the dichotomized variables, and then from further modelling using the original variables.

There are a number of observations worth noting.

1. The banking variables, bank account type (1) and own cheque guarantee card (2), are conditionally independent from the rest of the variables given residential status. People who possess their own property are more likely to have both deposit and current accounts; tenants are more likely to have deposit accounts; and people who live with their parents are less likely to have both types of account. People with deposit accounts are less likely to have cheque guarantee cards. The other variables provide no additional information about the banking variables.
2. Owning a telephone (5) depends only on residential status (8) and time at address (9). People who rent property are less likely to have their own telephone, as are people who have only recently moved into a new property.

3. Once information is known about an individual's employment status (4), marital status (7), and age (11), the other variables have no additional power in predicting whether the person has children (3).

4. Marital status (7) and age (11) are very strongly dependent. It is obvious that very young people have a lower probability of being married, let alone separated, divorced, or widowed.

5. Residential status (8), time at address (9), and age (11) are strongly dependent. We can explain this association by considering that young people who live with their parents have generally lived at the same address for a number of years. Apart from this subpopulation, we would expect to see that, in the main, time at address increases linearly with age.

6. Marital status (7) is conditionally independent of employment status (4), given income (6), residential status (8), and age (11).

7. Note that age (11) and residential status (8) have important roles in the graph.

17.6.2 A comparison of distinct age groups

We now compare graphical models built for distinct subpopulations based on young and older age groups. It is apparent in Fig. 17.21 that age has an important role in the model. It is also likely that the two-way interaction model is not sufficient to explain some of the associations, and that some of the more complex relationships could be modelled by considering age groups separately. For example, the relationship between time at address and residential status is dependent on age: young people have not had the opportunity to live in rented or owned accommodation as long as older people. By modelling age groups separately, three-way interactions with age are included.

A separate scorecard is often used for applicants under a certain age. The graphs of the two distinct age groups can reveal the differences between the structure of the two populations, and hence suggest the importance of using separate scorecards. To carry out this comparison, the data have been split into two approximately equal-sized groups of 'young' and 'old' applicants.

The same decomposition is used as before in order to model the subsets. The graphs of the 'young' and 'old' applicants are shown in Figs 17.22 and 17.23, respectively. Note that edges present in the graph in Fig. 17.21 almost always exist in at least one of the subpopulation graphs. While the graphs are substantially similar, there are a number of evident differences, confirming that the interrelationships between these variables change with age. A discriminant function, built without including higher interactions with age, would not succeed in modelling these differences.

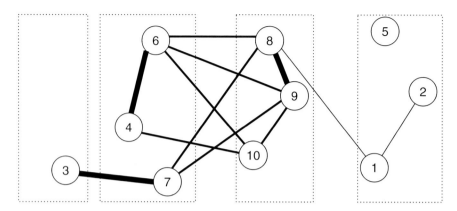

Fig. 17.22   Approximate independence graph of the young subpopulation. The model is built using the decomposition used previously, and edges with small edge-exclusion deviance are removed.

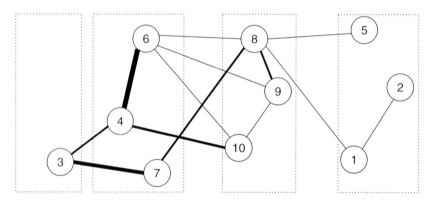

Fig. 17.23   Approximate independence graph of the older subpopulation. The model is built using the decomposition used previously, and edges with small edge-exclusion deviance are removed.

We comment on some of the differences between the two graphs here, although this list is by no means comprehensive:

1. Bank-account type (1) and residential status (8) are independent of the other variables in the young subpopulation. This perhaps reflects a difference between generations and the more open attitudes of banks allowing all young people the same banking opportunities. The older subpopulation are perhaps more reluctant to change their ways and are less often targeted by the banks' marketing departments, and hence older tenants are less likely to have deposit accounts.
2. The conditional dependence between children (3) and employment status (4) is only apparent in the older population, where the self-employed and nonworkers are more

likely to have children. There are obviously less young people with children, so it is difficult to judge whether a relationship exists.

3. Owing a telephone (5) and residential status (8) are independent in the young sub-population. Young people are just as likely to have a telephone wherever they live.

4. The relationship between income band (6) and residential status (8), time at address (9), and time at employment (10), is strong in the young population. For young people, a high income increases the opportunity for moving out of the parental home.

5. Marital status (7) and time at address (9) are conditionally independent in the old population. People tend to change residence or ownership when they get married. In the young population, married people have only been married for a short time, and so marital status is associated with a short time at address.

6. In the young population, time at employment (10) is associated with residential status (8), and is conditionally independent of time at address (9). The converse is true in the old population. We hypothesize that living with parents is associated with not having worked very long. Older people are more likely to live with their parents for reasons other than waiting to find a new job.

Extending the graphs to include the performance indicator is obviously of great importance to scorecard builders, though it raises the question of whether the graph is a model of the joint distribution of application variables X and credit performance Y, or of the conditional distribution of Y given X. In the latter case, the graph can be calculated from the logistic regression of Y on X. The credit performance variable cannot, however, be included in this investigation since the data analysed here were a sample of the through-the-door population, and, without making some kind of reject inference, we are without the performance realizations for the rejected applicants.

17.7 Summary

Graphical models and their associated conditional-independence statements have a role to play in credit scoring. We have argued that, to avoid interpreting spurious relationships and to understand the more complex associations, it is necessary to examine the joint probability distribution of the variables of interest. Through didactic and practical examples set in the credit-scoring context, we have shown that graphical models provide the following advantages.

1. They enable the display and interpretation of multivariate interactions between variables taken from a credit card application form.

2. They allow the direct comparison of credit-scoring subpopulations. In the example given, the comparison of young and old subpopulations highlights a number of differences. It is necessary to include higher interactions or to consider age groups separately in order to model these differences, and we suggest that it is worth investigating the use of separate scorecards based on age groups.
3. They give a simplified description of the credit-scoring selection process in terms of influence diagrams, used in collaboration with decision trees.
4. They illustrate possible effects of selection bias and stratification on variable inter-dependency.
5. Furthermore we note that, while practical difficulties still remain in fitting graphs in high dimensions, we have shown that this is a feasible proposition.

There is further potential for the use of graphical models to model various aspects of the credit-scoring process, for example, by including the score, credit performance indicator, or latent variables. In this chapter we have only considered an application to the through-the-door population in order to improve understanding of the inter-relationships between the variables that characterize the applicants. Hopefully our results should lead to further investigation of the role of graphical models in scoring technology.

We end on a technical note. Modelling in high dimensions inevitably leads to sparsity and misleading model selections from fitting the all-way log-linear interaction model. The asymptotic approximation to the chi-squared distribution becomes invalid and it is not possible to obtain reasonable parameter estimates. The all-two-way model overcomes the problems of sparsity while still retaining the conditional-independence structure. It has strong links with logistic regression, the interactions are easily inter-pretable, and it provides sensible estimates of the edge-exclusion deviances. On the downside, it may neglect higher-order interactions.

There are computational difficulties with large numbers of cells, since most algorithms for fitting the two-way interaction model require storage of the complete contingency table. Even when the categories have been reduced into coarse categories, a typical contingency table of eight variables may consist of around 50,000 cells, and a table with ten dimensions has around 750,000 cells. Seven or eight dimensions with a variety of levels appears to be the limit for the current generation of workstations. However, we believe these constraints will rapidly prove less onerous as time goes by.

Acknowledgements

This work was carried out in collaboration with the credit-card division of a major bank and support from the ALCD (Analysis of Large and Complex Datasets) initiative of the ESRC, grant no. asa6116. We should like to acknowledge the comments of a referee which have led to very substantial improvements in this chapter.

References

Agresti, A. (1990) *Categorical Data Analysis*. Wiley, New York.

Boyle, M., Crook, J. N., Hamilton, R., and Thomas, L. C. (1992) Method of credit scoring applied to slow payers. *Credit Scoring and Credit Control*. Oxford University Press, Oxford.

Darroch, J. N., Lauritzen, S. L., and Speed, T. P. (1980) Markov fields and log-linear models for contingency tables. *Annals of Statistics*, 8, 522–39.

Edwards, D. (1995) *An Introduction to Graphical Modelling*. Springer Verlag, Berlin.

Efron, B. and Tibshirani, J. (1993) *An Introduction to the Bootstrap*. Chapman & Hall, London.

Hand, D. J. and Henley, W. E. (1993) Can reject inference ever work? *IMA Journal of Mathematics Applied in Business & Industry*, 5, 45–55.

Hand, D. J., McConway, K. J., and Stranghellini, E. (1997) Graphical models of applicants for credit. *IMA Journal of Mathematics Applied in Business & Industry*, 8, 143–55.

Krzanowski, W. J. (1988) *Principles of Multivariate Analysis*. Oxford University Press, Oxford.

Lewis, E. M. (1992) *An Introduction to Credit Scoring*. Athena Press, San Rafael.

Marshall, K. T. and Oliver, R. M. (1995) *Decision Making and Forecasting*. McGraw-Hill, USA.

Simpson, C. H. (1951) The interpretation of interaction in contingency tables. *Journal of the Royal Statistical Society Series B*, 13, 238–41.

Whittaker, J. C. (1990) *Graphical Models in Applied Multivariate Statistics*. Wiley, Chichester.

Wilkie, A. D. (1992) Measures for comparing scoring systems. *Credit Scoring and Credit Control*. Oxford University Press, Oxford.

18. Credit scoring using neural and evolutionary techniques

Mumine B. Yobas, Jonathan N. Crook, and Peter Ross

18.1 Introduction

The aim of this chapter is to compare the predictive ability of linear discriminant analysis (LDA), neural networks (NNs), genetic algorithms (GAs), and decision trees (DTs) in the classification of credit card applicants. All four techniques have been applied to the same dataset and the results of the three evolutionary techniques are compared with the LDA results published in Crook *et al.* (1992).

Whilst many credit-scoring agencies have experimented with the latter three techniques, few offer products which use them (Desai *et al.* 1997) and the same applies to credit-granting organizations. Because of the commercial value of particular models there are very few publicly available comparisons between these techniques in the credit-scoring context. The published literature suggests mixed results: some find that traditional techniques correctly classify a greater proportion of applications than AI techniques, others the reverse. For example, using data from three credit unions Desai *et al.* (1996) found that when classifying accepted loans into goods and bads, neural networks correctly classified a greater percentage of both the total samples, and of the goods, than either linear discriminant analysis or logistic regression. But when *generic* models were estimated neural nets were superior only in the prediction of the bads. King *et al.* (1994) compared a large number of algorithms including linear discriminant analysis, neural networks, and decision trees (but not genetic algorithms) and found that linear discriminant analysis predicted less well than various types of decision trees and a smooth additive multiple regression technique, but better than neural networks. However, their data oversampled the 'bad' payers, which can affect

IMA Journal of Mathematics Applied in Business and Industry, 11, 111–25, 2000.

the performance of certain techniques, even if it is the norm in commercial scorecard development. On the other hand, Desai *et al.* (1997) applying the same dataset as in their 1996 paper, to a three-group classification (goods, poors, and bads) and including genetic algorithms into the contest, found that logistic regression was superior to the other methods except for the classification of the poors, where neural networks were best. In classifying the total sample they found that the performance of linear discriminant analysis was almost identical to that of neural networks and slightly better than that of genetic algorithms.

One conclusion, which is often expressed by those assessing the accuracy of neural networks, is that their performance depends on the values of certain parameters that are under the control of the investigator. Whilst there are certain heuristics to aid the choice of these values, the fact that neural networks and genetic algorithms allow for certain non-linearities, which are not possible in the traditional techniques, does not always seem to be reflected in a superior performance. There is therefore a need for further experimentation to support, or otherwise, the small number of findings so far published. In addition no published study has compared all four techniques: traditional, neural networks, genetic algorithms, and decision trees using the same credit applicant datasets and using a realistic division of cases between the 'good' and 'bad' groups. It is the aim of this chapter to do this.

The structure of this chapter is as follows. In the following section we briefly outline the four classification techniques, which are to be compared. In Section 18.3 we describe the data used. In Section 18.4 we present some implementation details and comparative measures and in Section 18.5 the results. Section 18.6 concludes.

18.2 Four classification techniques

18.2.1 Linear discriminant analysis

The principles of LDA have been rehearsed elsewhere (Fisher 1936; Tatsuoka 1970; Eisenbeis and Avery 1972; Choi 1986). Essentially, suppose for each application we have a $(p \times 1)$ column vector of characteristics, X, and suppose we wish to divide the total population of applications into two groups, J_1 and J_2. If the allocation rule chosen is to minimize the expected costs of misclassifying a case into the group of which it is not a member then we wish to minimize:

$$L = P_1 L_1 \int_{J_2} f_1(X) \, dx + P_2 L_2 \int_{J_1} f_2(X) \, dx$$

where $P_1(P_2)$ is the prior probability that a case is a member of set 1 (2); $L_1(L_2)$ is the cost of misclassifying a member of set 1 (2) into set 2 (1); $f_1(X)(f_2(X))$ is the probability density function that a vector X will occur given that a case is a member of set 1 (2).

If it is assumed that $L_1 = L_2 = 1$, that the values of X are normally distributed with the same covariance matrix, C, in both sets, then it can be shown (Thomas 1997) that it is optimal to classify a case into set 1 if

$$(X - 0.5(m_1 + m_2))^T C^{-1}(m_1 - m_2) > \log\left(\frac{P_2}{P_1}\right) \qquad (18.1)$$

where m_1 (m_2) is the $(p \times 1)$ vector of mean values of the characteristics for set 1 (2).

Fisher (1936) deduced the same linear rule as equation (18.1) but in a different way. He argued that the greatest difference between the groups occurred when the between groups sums of squares divided by the within groups sums of squares was maximized. This may be represented as:

$$\lambda = \frac{W^1 B W}{W^1 A W} \qquad (18.2)$$

where W is a column vector of weights, B is the between groups sums of squares and cross products matrix, and A is the within groups sums of squares and cross products matrix (Tatsouka 1970). Differentiating equation (18.2) with respect to each weight separately and equating each resulting equation to zero gives, eventually, in the case of two groups a single set of weights for which λ is maximized (Tatsouka 1970).

18.2.2   Neural networks

A multilayer perceptron feed forward neural network consists of an input layer, a number of hidden layers, and an output layer. In the credit-scoring context the input layer consists of p characteristics, $X_j, j = 1, \ldots, p$. A weight is applied to each characteristic and the resulting products are summed to give

$$U_k^{[1]} = \sum_{j=1}^{p} W_{kj}^{[1]} X_j, \qquad (18.3)$$

where $W_{kj}^{[1]}$ is the weight connecting variable j and neuron k in layer 1. Each $U_k^{[1]}$ value is transformed non-linearly to give an output of neuron k:

$$y_k^{[1]} = f\left(U_k^{[1]}\right) \qquad (18.4)$$

The $y_k^{[1]}$ values are then weighted by a new set of weights and the procedures repeated to yield a new layer of neurons in layer 2. In the credit classification problem, with two groups, the final layer would consist of a single neuron and a case would be classified according to whether $y_n > < c$ where c is the critical value of O_n such that cases with $y_n > c$ are allocated into one group and cases where $y_n < c$ are allocated into the second group.

In general we may write equations (18.3) and (18.4) as

$$U_k^{[s]} = \sum_j^{z^{[s-1]}} W_{kj}^{[s]} y_j^{[s-1]}$$

and

$$y_k^{[s]} = f(U_k^{[s]}) \quad \text{where } k = 1, \ldots, z^{[s]}$$

where $z^{[s]}$ = number of neurons in layer $[s]$ and $z^{[s-1]}$ = number of neurons in layer $[s-1]$.

The only requirement of equation (18.4) is that it is differentiable. Examples are the logistic and hyperbolic tangent functions. In supervised learning networks the predicted group membership is compared with the observed membership to produce an error, $e(i)$:

$$e(i) = d(i) - y(i) \tag{18.5}$$

where $d(i)$ denotes the observed group membership, and $y(i)$ the predicted group membership, for case i. The error is transformed to give

$$\varepsilon(i) = 0.5e(i)^2 \tag{18.6}$$

and the mean value of $\varepsilon(i)$ across all N cases is calculated to give the 'average squared error', E:

$$E = \frac{1}{N} \sum_{i=1}^{N} 0.5e^2(i).$$

Initially a set of weights in each neuron is chosen randomly. The value of $\varepsilon(i)$ is calculated for each case and the weights are altered. The procedure is repeated for each case with the aim of adjusting the weights to minimize E.

For each case, i, the weights in each neuron in each layer are altered by a magnitude, which is proportional to their marginal effect on $\varepsilon(i)$, that is, by a magnitude which is proportional to

$$\partial \varepsilon(i)/\partial W_{kj}^{[s]}.$$

Thus

$$\Delta W_{kj} = \eta \frac{\partial \varepsilon(i)}{\partial W_{kj}^s} \tag{18.7}$$

The precise formula for the modification of W_{kj} depends on whether the weights are in the final layer or a hidden layer. Given equations (18.3)–(18.6), the $\partial \varepsilon/\partial W$ term in equation (18.7) can be written as

$$\frac{\partial \varepsilon}{\partial W_{kj}^{[s]}} = \frac{\partial \varepsilon}{\partial e_k} \frac{\partial e_k}{\partial y_k} \frac{\partial y_k}{\partial u_k} \frac{\partial u_k}{\partial W_{kj}} \tag{18.8}$$

where all variables relate to case i and so the '(i)' term is dropped. Calculating the partial derivatives, equation (18.8) gives

$$\frac{\partial \varepsilon}{\partial W_{kj}^{[s]}} = -e_k^{[s]} f^1 \left(u_k^{[s]} \right) y_j^{[s-1]}. \tag{18.9}$$

In the output layer, d_k is known and so, therefore, is e_k. Given the functional form of equation (18.4), $f^1(U_k^{[s]})$ can be found and the $y_j^{[s-1]}$ are known, so equation (18.9) can be evaluated, and given η, ΔW_{kj} can be calculated.

In a hidden layer e is not observable. Instead the error values from the final layer are back propagated to the weights in earlier layers. The formula used is

$$\Delta W_{kj}^{[s]} = \eta \delta_j^{[s]} y_i^{[s-1]} \tag{18.10}$$

and

$$\delta_j^{[s]} = f_j^{1[s]} \sum_k \delta_k^{[s+1]} W_{kj}^{s+1} \tag{18.11}$$

where $\delta_k^{[s+1]} = \partial \varepsilon_j / \partial U_j^{[s+1]} = e_k^{[s+1]} f_k^{[s+1]}$ which is derived from applying the chain rule to equations (18.4), (18.5), and (18.6) and substituting into (18.8). Thus if $[s+1]$ were the final layer, and $[s]$ a hidden layer, the value of δ_k would be known. If both $[s+1]$ and $[s]$ were hidden layers then from equation (18.11) it can be seen that $\delta_j^{[s]}$ is derived from $\delta_k^{[s+1]}$ and so, recursively, from $\delta^{[s+n]}$ where $[s+n]$ is the final output layer. Equation (18.10) is known as the 'delta rule' and δ the 'local gradient'.

As explained, the back propagation technique leads the weights to converge on those values that minimize E. However, for various reasons the rate of convergence is slow (Haykin 1994: p 190). Jacobs (1988) has outlined four heuristics to accelerate the rate of convergence. The method used in this chapter is to allow the learning coefficient, η, to alter according to the delta-bar-delta method as new cases are fed through the network.[1]

18.2.3   Genetic algorithms

Consider a population of possible alternative solutions to a problem. Each solution may be represented as a collection, or string, of numbers. Each such number is known as a 'gene'. Each specific value that a gene can take on is known as an 'allele'. A collection

---

[1] To explain this method, define

$$P_{ji}(n) = (1 - \lambda)\frac{\partial \varepsilon(n-1)}{\partial W_{ji}(n-1)} + \lambda P_{ji}(n-1).$$

The change in η between one case and the following case is then equal to a constant if $P_{ji}(n-1)$ and $\partial \varepsilon^{(y)}/\partial W_{ji}(n)$ have different signs, equals $-\beta \eta_{ji}$ if P and $\partial \varepsilon/\partial W_{ji}$ have the same signs, and equals zero otherwise. These properties fulfil two of Jacob's heuristics.

of such numbers, arranged in specific positions, is known as a 'chromosome'. Genetic algorithms essentially evaluate the success, called 'fitness', of each possible solution in achieving a given objective, and by the processes of mutation and crossover, they alter potential solutions to improve their fitness. Crossover involves selecting, say, two potential solutions and exchanging portions of these solutions. The probability that a solution is selected is positively related to the fitness of the solution. The resulting 'children' replace members of the population with the lowest fitness and the procedure is repeated. At some stages various values (called 'alleles') in a chromosome are mutated: they are replaced by a different value. The probability that a string is selected for crossover is proportional to its fitness. The probability that an allele is mutated is also stochastic. GAs were first devised by Holland (1975) and have been used in a variety of contexts: optimization, classification, and clustering problems (Goldberg 1989, Albright 1993).

In the credit applicant classification problem, two approaches have been followed. Albright (1993) estimated the parameters of a polynomial scoring equation where each chromosome consisted of estimated parameters. A case was classified according to whether or not the value of the function exceeded a critical value. An alternative method is to estimate ranges of values of each characteristic and a switching value that indicates whether a characteristic is to enter the classification or not.

There are few direct comparisons of classificatory accuracy in the credit-scoring context involving GAs. Fogarty and Ireson (1993) compared the performance of a GA, a decision tree approach, a nearest neighbour approach, and a Bayesian method. They concluded that the GA was superior to the other methods, although with only 6 per cent of the sample classified as bads none of these methods were superior to classifying all cases as goods. Albright (1993), in an application of a GA to 918 credit union loans, correctly classified 76 per cent of the sample. Desai *et al.* (1997) found that GAs were inferior to traditional techniques and neural networks. King *et al.* (1994) using a data set with 8,900 cases found that a decision tree method gave a percentage correctly classified greater than either neural networks, GA or a range of many different statistical techniques.

18.2.4   Decision trees

In these techniques a characteristic is chosen and a particular value of the characteristic is chosen to partition the cases into a number of subsets, typically two. The characteristic becomes a decision node and each decision, indicated by a particular value of the characteristic, forms a branch. Each branch leads to a different characteristic. Again a particular value of this characteristic is chosen to partition the subsets into further subsets and so on. After successive partitions the members of the final subsets will be members of only one group. This is known as a Recursive Partitioning Algorithm

(RPA). New applicants can be classified by successively applying the partitioning criteria to identify the predicted group membership.

Different tests have been used to determine the appropriate characteristics and critical values for each decision node. In this chapter we used an information criterion (Quinlan 1993) whereby different characteristics and different critical values of each are examined, and those which maximize the difference between the information required to partition a set before the test and that information after the test are chosen for partitioning. The details are as follows.

Suppose a test with k outcomes partitions a training set into T_i $(i = 1, \ldots, k)$ subsets. Call the probability that a randomly chosen member, i, of any subset, T_k, will be a member of a particular class, C_j, $P(C_j)_{i \in T_k}$. According to Quinlan 'the information conveyed by a message depends on its probability'. Hence the information relating to class membership is:

$$I(T_k) = -\sum_{j=1}^{l} P_i(C_j) \cdot \log_2(P_i(C_j)).$$

This is the entropy of set T_k.

If applied to the whole training set, T, we gain the average information needed to correctly classify a randomly chosen case.

Suppose a test with n outcomes is used to divide the training sample, T, into T_k subsets $(k = 1, \ldots, n)$. Then the average information needed to correctly classify a case, $I_x(T)$, is: $I_x(T) = \sum_{k=1}^{n} p_k \cdot I(T_k)$ where p_k is the proportion of all cases which is in subset T_k, and $I(T_k)$ is as above.

The method then chooses the characteristic and cut-off values to maximize:

$$\text{Gain Ratio}_x = G_x / S_x$$

where

$$G_x = I(T) - I_x(T)$$

and

$$S_x = -\sum_{k=1}^{n} p_k \cdot \log_2 p_k.$$

G_x is the information gained by partitioning the training set using test X over that gained from allocating members of the training set at random. S_x is the information gained by randomly dividing the training set into n groups.

The RPA will create splits until neither further improvement is possible nor each leaf contains only one group: goods or bads. Quinlan argues that such a tree may 'overfit' the data in the sense that the optimal partitions for the training sample may not give the best classification in the test sample. To reduce the degree of overfit the optimal tree is constructed for the training sample and branches are then pruned off.

Quinlan (1993) describes a technique to transform a decision tree into propositional-like production rules. The rules are in the form: $L \rightarrow R$ where the left-hand side is a conjunction of attribute based tests and the right-hand side is a class. The technique used involved four stages as follows. First the initial rules are obtained by following the path from the root to each leaf. The rule's left-hand side contains the conditions and the right-hand side is the class of that leaf. The path from the root to a leaf gives an initial rule. Second, the initial rules are simplified by removing conditions that do not seem to be useful in discriminating this class from others. Third all the rules for a class are examined and the ones that do not contribute to the accuracy of the set of rules as a whole are removed. This selection process is applied to each class. Finally the set of rules for the classes are ordered in order to minimize the false positive errors and then a default class is chosen.

18.3   Data preparation

18.3.1   Sample

The data set consists of 1,001 individuals who had been issued with a credit card, who had used it and whose repayment history was known. A case was defined as a 'slow' if the individual had missed one or more repayments in the sample period and 'good' otherwise. This is a relatively stringent criterion; most credit grantors would be concerned only if an accumulated three payments were missed, and would then target the account for collection procedures. However, given the small sample size available such a criterion would give a very small number of 'bad' cases, whereas the discrimination between slows and goods results in many more cases in the smaller group.

Furthermore, such a small sample size may be all that would be available, in practice, from some sectors of the US consumer credit market, such as credit unions. In addition, it might represent the size of the first available sample after the introduction of a new product.

The same fourteen characteristics were used in all four methods as described in Table 18.1. However many of the variables were transformed in different ways between the four algorithms. These transforms are explained below.

18.3.2   LDA

The LDA results have been reported in Crook *et al.* (1992) using the same data set as has been used with the evolutionary techniques in this chapter. One way of transforming nominal level data is to use dummy variables. However, given the relatively small

Table 18.1 Characteristics variables.

Applicant's employment status
Years at bank
Home mortgage value
Number of children
Years at present employment
Residential status
Types of account
Other cards held
Outgoings
Estimated value of home
Home phone
Applicant's income
Spouse's income
Major credit cards held

number of degrees of freedom that would result, we used an alternative approach, the weights of evidence method. Values of nominal variables were banded together according to similarity of $g_i/(g_i + b_i)$ where g_i and b_i are, the number of good and slow cases, respectively, in the nominal category i. The alphabetic values were then replaced by X_j where:

$$X_j = \log(g_i/b_i) + \log(B_T/G_T)$$

where

$$b_j\ (g_j) = \text{number of slow (good) cases in band } j,$$

$$B_T\ (G_T) = \text{total number of slow (good) cases in the dataset.}$$

In the case of ratio level data, for consistency, a similar procedure was followed.

18.3.3 Neural networks

Large numeric values will make the values of $U_k^{[1]}$ in equation (18.3) very large and the value of f^1 in equation (18.9) close to zero. This would result in slow learning. Therefore to speed up learning the data was scaled to give a fairly even distribution in the $[0:0.9]$ range. The scaling procedure varied between the variables. As an example, in the case of income where the vast majority of values were less than £35,000, the following transformation was used:

$$x' = \log\left(\frac{x}{35{,}000}\right) + 1 \quad \text{if income} \leq £31{,}699$$
$$x' = 0.9 \quad\quad\quad\quad\quad\quad \text{if income} > £31{,}699.$$

In the case of nominal level data, one-of-N coding was used. That is where such a variable had N possible alphabetic values, N separate inputs were presented to the network with the digit 1 in one of the N digits used to represent the value for each input variable.

18.3.4   Decision trees

No transformations were required with this technique since the minimum level of measurement required is nominal.

18.3.5   Genetic algorithms

Genetic algorithms require numeric values at nominal level or higher. Therefore alphabetic variables were replaced by adjacent natural numbers. For example, residential status, with six possible alphabetic values, was recoded with a numeric value between 0 and 5 replacing each alphabetic value. Finally four of the ratio level variables were scaled by dividing by a constant.

18.4   Implementation issues

The LDA results, drawn from Crook *et al.* (1992) were derived after applying a stepwise routine to an initial data set of 21 variables. The 14 significant variables that resulted were used in the alternative methods reported in this chapter. The validity of the model was tested using the jack-knife method. That is the models were estimated for all cases except for one that was used as the test sample. This was repeated for all 1,001 cases. The LDA was estimated using SPSS.

18.4.1   Neural networks

Different network topologies, learning and momentum rates, activation functions and epoch numbers were experimented with. The number of iterations ranged between 40,000 and 200,000. The learning rule used was delta-bar-delta as explained in Section 18.2 above. The number of nodes used in the input layer was usually 29 although in a few experiments we used 23 when only eight fields were included. Either one or two hidden layers were used. The number of nodes in the first hidden layer ranged between 18 and 5; the number in the second hidden layer ranged between 3 and 5. The number of nodes in the output layer was 2. The number of epochs, that is, number of times the datasets were presented to the network ranged between 50 and 500.

The networks were built using a randomly selected sample of 501 cases and tested on the remaining 500 cases. The networks were estimated using NeuralWorks Professional Plus.

18.4.2   Genetic algorithms

In this application each chromosome consisted of a string of adjacent blocks of adjacent digits (genes). Each block related to a particular applicant characteristic, such as years at address. In the case of continuously measured variables each block consisted of three genes: the maximum, minimum, and outcome value, respectively. The values of the outcome variables were coded 0 for 'do not use this variable to imply an outcome', or 1 for 'use this variable such that if a case meets the conditions indicated by the range in the preceding genes, classify the case as a good'. In the case of a binary variable a block consisted of a single value and an outcome value. The reason why the outcome variable was used to imply two joint conditions (whether to use and, if used, group membership) is that this allows the GA to generate predictive conditions that relate only to a subset of the attributes, rather than all of them.

A chromosome therefore consisted of l genes where $l = 2 \cdot b + 3 \cdot c$ where b is the number of binary attributes and c is the number of continuously measured attributes. An (simplified) example is shown below

No of children	Credit card	Years at present employment
3 0 0	0 1	6 12 1

This chromosome indicates that having between 0 and 3 children implies the condition relating to the number of children is not to be used to predict group membership, and that having no credit card and between 6 and 12 years at present employment implies a case is a good.

A chromosome thus represents a solution in the form of a number of predictions. The predictions take the form whereby first, the values of the variables with an indicator value of 1 implying a joint condition associated with a case being used to make a prediction and that prediction being that the case is a good, and second, values of variables with an indicator value of 0 implying that the attribute is not to be used to predict group membership. Mutation occurred by changing any of the three (or two in the case of binary variables) genes representing a characteristic.

The fitness of the model was estimated using the following steps. First, identify those characteristics where the outcome gene has the value 1, that is, it indicates that the characteristic should be used and that a case which fulfils the condition would be classified as a good. Second, for each case compare the observed characteristic values with those of the condition in the chromosome. If the observed values fulfil the conditions in the chromosome predict that the case is a good, and if this is a correct prediction increase the number of hits by one. If the observed values do not fulfil the conditions in the chromosome but the case is actually a slow, also increase the number of hits by one. This implies that the success of the rule contained in the chromosome is equally 'high' if it correctly classifies goods as if it correctly classifies slows. The fitness (Φ) of the chromosome is then calculated as: $\Phi = (r_h)^{0.5} - \alpha/N_h$ where r_h is the ratio of the number of hits to the total number of training cases, N_h is the total number of hits and α is a constant. The second term represents a penalty for achieving a small number of hits, implying unreliability of the first term.

The GAs were estimated using a package called PGA (Ross and Ballinger 1993).

18.4.3   Decision trees

The models were tested using ten way cross-validation. The data was divided into $N = 10$ datasets such that each set contained an equal distribution of goods and slows. Then N different models are built, in each case using an aggregation of $N - 1$ sets as the training set and the remaining single set as the test set. This ensures that each case appears in only one test set. The overall proportion of test cases correctly classified is then the average value over the N test sets.

The trees were estimated using C4.5 (Quinlan 1993).

18.5   Results

18.5.1   Comparisons within techniques

As explained in Section 18.4 a large number of experiments were performed with the evolutionary techniques.

In the case of neural networks we experimented with the transformation function (tanh or sigmoid), the topology (number of input nodes and number of hidden layers), the epoch number, and the number of iterations. The greatest total proportion of cases correctly classified came from a sigmoid transformation function with all variables included, one hidden layer an epoch number of 500 and 40,000 iterations.

Our experiments suggest a number of general conclusions, as follows.

1. Whilst increasing the number of iterations above 40k did not always increase the proportion of total test cases correctly classified, it often increased the proportion of goods and decreased the proportion of slows correctly classified.

2. Increasing the epoch size to 500 generally, but not always, increased the predictive accuracy. For example, given a sigmoid transfer function, two hidden layers and 40k iterations, increasing the epoch size from 50 to 100 increased the proportion of the test sample that was correctly classified from 61.90 to 63.31 per cent. Increasing the epoch size to 250 and to 500 resulted in the performance deteriorating to 61.90 per cent correctly classified.

3. Increasing the number of inputs in the first hidden layer and removing the second hidden layer increased the proportion of cases that were correctly classified. For example, again consider a sigmoid transfer function, an epoch number of 500 and 40k iterations. Changing from a 29-8-3-2 (number nodes in the input layer, in the first hidden layer, in the second hidden layer, and in the output layer, respectively) to a 29-12-2, increased the proportion correctly classified from 61.90 to 64.20 per cent. (However, changing from 29-8-3-2 to 29-6-2 led to a marginal reduction in predictive performance.)

4. The tanh transformation function generally gave inferior results compared to the sigmoid function.

Turning to the RPA, ten different trees were built on 901 cases each and each tested on the remaining 100 cases. For each tree a set of production rules were derived and tested, again on test datasets of 100 cases. The size of the trees ranged from 421 to 470 leaves and decision nodes in the training samples. After pruning, the number of leaves and decision nodes ranged from 154 to 233. In 8 out of the 10 trees pruning reduced the proportion of the test set misclassified. This suggests that the prepruned trees overfitted the training dataset.

In all cases the error rate in the training sample increased after pruning as one would expect. The range of proportions of the training sets correctly classified by production rules was 72.9–61.9 per cent. The corresponding figures for the test sets were 67.0–59.0 per cent. These differences are due to differences between the selected training and test samples.

In the case of GAs various experiments were conducted. We initially used steady state reproduction whereby children were added to the population of possible solutions. We then used various combinations of (a) one child or twins produced by each crossover, (b) generational reproduction, whereby the new child is placed in a new population which replaces the old one when n children (n being the number of solutions in the population) are produced, (c) with or without mutation and (d) with or without crossover.

The maximum fitness was gained with generational reproduction, with twins, with mutation, and crossover. The lowest fitness occurred with steady state reproduction, without twins, no mutation, and with crossover turned on. In general, producing twins rather than not doing so, and applying crossover rather than not applying it, increased the fitness of the resulting solution. The maximum proportion of the test cases correctly classified occurred over several combinations of parameters including that which gave the greatest fitness.

The advantage of generational reproduction is that to some extent it improves a weakness of steady state reproduction. This weakness is that in steady state reproduction a fit solution takes over the population very quickly and does not allow variations to stay in the population long enough to contribute to the final solution.

18.5.2　Comparison across techniques

Table 18.2 shows the relative performance of each technique and the proportion of cases that could be correctly classified by chance (C_{prop}). In the case of LDA, the proportion correctly classified was calculated using the jack-knife technique. For NNs the proportion given is the highest proportion given by any experiment. For decision trees the proportion is the mean proportion over ten trees. In the case of GAs, the proportion is that corresponding to the highest mean fitness over 50 runs of each experiment.

The most successful technique in terms of the proportion of the total number of cases correctly classified is that reproduced from Crook *et al.* (1992): LDA. GAs and NNs appear to classify approximately the same proportion of cases, but the success of GAs is probably overemphasized because the reported result is based on the classification of the training sample. This was a constraint imposed by the software. Decision trees performed least well of the four methods.

Comparisons of the proportions of goods and slows correctly classified are possible only between LDA and NNs. Nets were found to be marginally less successful than LDA in classifying slows and considerably less successful at predicting the goods. Given that nets are computationally more time consuming, the findings of this chapter suggest that LDA appears to dominate nets in terms of both accuracy and cost.

Table 18.2　Comparison of results: percentage correctly classified.

Techniques	Total test sample	Goods	Slows
LDA[a]	68.4	85	40
NNs	64.2	79	39
Decision trees	62.3		
GAs	64.5		
C_{prop}	46.8		

[a] From Crook *et al.* (1992).

Given that neural networks and GAs allow for far more non-linearities in the relationship between an individual's characteristics and his or her repayment performance than LDA, the superior performance of LDA may seem surprising. Possible explanations for these differences are: that the training samples and test samples differ between the techniques, that the transformations applied to the characteristics variables in LDA result in superior predictive performance, and that the evolutionary techniques have found local, but not global, optimum solution sets. Considering the first possibility it is likely that, everything else equal, the larger training sample used (1,000 cases) in the case of LDA would give estimated parameters with lower variances about the population values than the smaller samples (500 cases) used to estimate the neural nets. This explanation would apply to a lesser extent to the decision trees where the training samples consisted of repeated samples of 900 cases each. The explanation would not apply to the GAs since they were trained and tested in the training sample, as this is known to overestimate the predictive performance.

The validity of the second possible explanation for the different results is difficult to assess. On the one hand aggregating responses across different alphabetic values for each characteristic constrains the estimated coefficients compared with using dummy variables for each alphabetic value; on the other hand, the transformed value used relates to the value closely correlated with the dependent variable in the discriminating equation. Therefore the effect of the transformation on the predictive power of LDA versus GAs or trees is difficult to disentangle because neither of the latter two methods involved transformed values.

The third explanation is always applicable to any of these techniques. We experimented with a number of parameters under our control in all three evolutionary techniques as explained above.

Our results are consistent with those of certain other studies when credit-scoring data is used, but inconsistent with others. For example, in a three way classification, Desai *et al.* (1996) found that when considering the predictive performance for their total sample, LDA was almost identical to that of neural networks and slightly better than GAs. But neural networks (with a best neuron rule) gave the greatest predictive performance when predicting poor payers (rather than goods or chargeoffs and bankrupts) and GAs were superior when predicting chargeoffs and bankrupts. King *et al.* (1994) found that LDA gave a greater predictive performance than neural networks, but a poorer performance compared with decision trees. On the other hand, Desai *et al.* (1996) in a two-way classification found that LDA was *inferior* to neural networks at predicting both good and bad payers (separately). In addition Khoylou and Stirling (1993) using a sample of 2,000 cases, found that neural networks performed considerably better than multiple linear regression, although the latter was not included in our comparison. In terms of ranking decision trees and GAs, the ranking we obtained is exactly the same as that gained by Fogarty and Ireson (1993).

The differences between our results and those of other studies could be explained in a number of different ways: differences in the types of individuals in the samples, differences in the sample sizes, differences in the ranges of controllable parameters used in the experiments, differences in the transformations applied to the data, and so on.

18.6   Conclusion

We have compared the predictive performance of LDA, neural networks, GAs, and decision trees using a small sample of credit scoring data. Like other studies we found that LDA was superior to GAs. However, consistent with some studies but unlike others we found that neural networks were inferior to LDA. Unlike other studies we found that neural networks were almost identical to LDA at predicting the slow payers, and that LDA was superior at predicting good payers. Further research is needed particularly to incorporate the relative costs of rejected good applicants and accepted slow payers, using larger datasets, which preserve the proportions of good and slow payers in the population.

References

Albright, H. (1993) *Construction of a Polynomial Classifier for Consumer Loan Applications Using Generic Algorithms*. Mimeo, Department of Systems Engineering, University of Virginia.

Choi, S. S. (1986) 'Discrimination and classification: an overview'. *Computing and Mathematics with Applications*, 12(2), 173–7.

Crook, J. N., Hamilton, R. and Thomas, L. C. (1992) 'A comparison of a credit scoring model with a credit performance model'. *The Service Industries Journal*, 12(4), 558–79.

Desai, V. S., Crook, J. N., and Overstreet, G. A. (1996) 'A comparison of neural networks and linear scoring models in the credit union environment', *European Journal of Operational Research*, 95, 24–37.

Desai, V. S., Conway, D. G., Crook, J. N., and Overstreet, G. A. (1997) 'Credit scoring models in the credit union environment using neural networks and genetic algorithms'. *IMA Journal of Mathematics Applied in Business and Industry*, 8, 323–46.

Eisenbeis, R. A. and Avery, R. B. (1972) *Discriminant Analysis and Classification Procedures: Theory and Applications*. D.C. Heath, Lexington, MA.

Fisher, R. A. (1936) 'The use of multiple measurement in taxonomics problems'. *Annals of Eugenics*, 7, 179–88.

Fogarty, T. C. and Ireson, N. S. (1993) 'Evolving Bayesian classifiers for credit control—a comparison with other machine learning methods'. *IMA Journal of Mathematics Applied in Business and Industry*, 5, 63–75.

Goldberg, D. E. (1989) *Genetic Algorithms in Search, Optimization, and Machine Learning*. Addison-Wesley, Massachusetts.

Haykin, S. (1994) *Neural Networks: A Comprehensive Foundation*. Macmillan, New York.

Holland, J. H. (1975) *Adaptation in Artificial and Natural Systems*. The University of Michigan Press, Ann Arbor.

Jacobs, R. A. (1988) 'Increased rates of convergence through learning rate adaption'. *Neural Networks*, 1, 295–307.

Khoylou, J. and Stirling, M. (1993) *Credit Scoring and Neural Networks*, presented at Credit Scoring and Credit Control III conference, Edinburgh, 1993.

King, R. D., Henery, R., Feng, C., and Sutherland, A. (1994) *A comparative study of classification algorithms: statistical, machine learning and neural network*. In *Machine Intelligence* (eds. K. Furukwa, D. Michie, and S. Muggleton). 13, Oxford University Press, Oxford.

Quinlan, J. R. (1993) *C4.5: Programs for Machine Learning*, Morgan Kaufman, San Mateo, CA.

Ross, P. and Ballinger, P. (1993) *PGA*, software program, University of Edinburgh.

Tatsuoka, M. M. (1970) *Discriminant Analysis*, Selected Topics in Advanced Statistics: An Elementary Approach, Number 6, Institute for Personality and Ability Testing, Illinois.

Thomas, L. C. (1997) Methodologies for classifying applicants for credit. In *Statistics in Finance* (eds. D. Hand and S. Jacka). Edward Arnold, London.

Yobas, M. B. (1996) *Credit Scoring Using Neural and Evolutionary Techniques*, MSc thesis, Department of Artificial Intelligence, University of Edinburgh.

19. Segmentation in Markov chain consumer credit behavioural models

Joseph Ho, Lyn C. Thomas, T. A. Pomroy, and William T. Scherer

19.1 Introduction

Financial institutions have for many years been interested in modelling the behaviour of their customers. One approach has been to develop default based scoring systems (Thomas 2000) which seek to map the behaviour of a customer in the near past to their default states in a year's time. These are based on classification techniques like logistic regression, classification trees, or linear programming. The customer's score is then used to make operational and credit decisions such as increasing the overdraft permitted. An alternative approach is to model the customer's behaviour in terms of the 'state' of their account using Markov chain models. The states usually describe the different stage of delinquency of the customer's accounts, for example, 1 month overdue. Markov chain models have been used mainly in debt provisioning to forecast the expected losses through default in different time periods in the future. However, with the growing importance of customer relationship management (Schniederjans and Loch 1994) and a move in the financial organizations' objectives from minimizing defaults to maximizing profit there is increasing interest in these Markov chain models as a way of modelling the dynamical behaviour of the consumer.

Existing models in the literature assume that a customer's behaviour can be modelled using a first-order stationary Markov chain. This chapter investigates whether this is the case using a large sample of bank customer data and if not, how could the model

Proceedings of Credit Scoring and Credit Control VII, Credit Research Centre, University of Edinburgh, 2001.

be extended and yet the basic simplicity of the Markov assumption be retained. Cyert *et al.* 1962 pioneered the Markov chain approach to describing consumers' credit behaviour. Subsequently extensions to the model and its application were suggested by Cyert and Thompson (1968), Metha (1972), Liebman (1972), Corcoran (1978), Van Kuelen *et al.* (1981) and Kallberg and Saunders (1983). No formal testing of the suitability of the the stationary Markov Chain assumption for those behavioural models was carried out until Frydman *et al.* (1985) despite the existence of formal tests in Anderson and Goodman (1957). Frydman *et al.* (1985) also suggested that a mover–stayer model might be an appropriate way of describing customers' credit behaviour.

In Section 19.2 we recall the methods of testing whether data satisfy the Markovity and stationarity assumptions implicit in the stationary Markov chain model. We also describe the bank data we use and test it for Markovity. Section 19.3 investigates whether the data can be described by higher order Markov chains using an aggregated state space to deal with the exponential increase in state size caused by the higher orders. Section 19.4 looks at how one can use segmentation based on the mover–stayer idea to improve the fit of the model, while Section 19.5 draws some conclusions from the case study.

19.2   Data analysis for Markov chain models

The Markov chain approach to consumer credit behaviour assumes that there is a state space $S = 1, 2, \ldots, M$ consisting of M states and a consumer's status at time t, X_t is described by one of these states for $t = 1, \ldots, T$. The states are usually described by a combination of the consumer's current delinquency, activity, and balance but could also be defined in terms of the consumer's behavioural score, or a combination of these and delinquency states. The simplest models pioneered by Cyert *et al.* (1962) and Cyert and Thompson (1968) assumed this dynamical behaviour of a consumer follows a stationary Markov chain, where $\mathrm{Prob}\{X_{t+1} = j | X_t = i\} = p(i, j)$ is the probability a consumer will move from state i to state j between two observation points (observations usually taken at a fixed time in each month). A more general assumption is that the dynamics is that of a non-stationary kth order Markov chain. In this case one assumes

$$P\{X_{t+k} = j_{t+k} | X_{t+k-1} = j_{t+k-1}, X_{t+k-2} = j_{t+k-2}, \ldots, X_1 = j_1\}$$
$$= P\{X_{t+k} = j_{t+k} | X_{t+k-1} = j_{t+k-1}, X_{t+k-2} = j_{t+k-2}, \ldots, X_t = j_t\}$$
$$= p_t(j_t, \ldots, j_{t+k-1}, j_{t+k}) = \hat{p}_t(\{j_t, \ldots, j_{t+k-1}\}, \{j_{t+1}, \ldots, j_{t+k}\}),$$

where the form of the last term shows that it is equivalent to a first-order Markov chain on a state space with M^k states. With a non-stationary kth order Markov chain one has to estimate TM^{k+1} transition probabilities. The equivalent stationary kth order chain assumes that

$$P\{X_{t+k} = j_{t+k}|X_{t+k-1} = j_{t+k-1}, X_{t+k-2} = j_{t+k-2}, \ldots, X_1 = j_1\}$$
$$= P\{X_{t+k} = j_{t+k}|X_{t+k-1} = j_{t+k-1}, X_{t+k-2} = j_{t+k-2}, \ldots, X_t = j_t\}$$
$$= p(j_t, \ldots, j_{t+k-1}, j_{t+k}) = \hat{p}(j_t, \ldots, j_{t+k-1}), (j_{t+1}, \ldots, j_{t+k})$$

The first-order stationary assumption is often used in practice but is rarely tested. When Frydman *et al.* (1985) tested a sample of 200 storecard accounts, they found their transitions not to be Markov.

The data considered in this chapter is a large sample of a bank's current account population, where the account included overdraft and personal loan facilities. Only those with borrowing facilities who therefore are subject to default risk are included in the sample. The bank had a 10-state categorization of the current state of these accounts and the data was available for a 60-month period. This period was split into two with the first 48 months being used in model building and the remaining 12 months for checking any forecasting.

The first step was to test whether the consumer's credit behaviour is independent of previous states and thus that a stationary Markov chain model (or if necessary a non-stationary model) was appropriate. Let $n_t(i_0, i_1, \ldots, i_k)$ be the number of consumers with the history $X_t = i_0, X_{t+1} = i_1, \ldots, X_{t+k} = i_k$. Similarly $n(i_0, i_1, \ldots, i_k) = \sum_{t=k}^{T-K} n_t(i_0, i_1, \ldots, i_k)$ is the number of times the sequence $(i_0, \ldots, i_k)$ occurs anywhere in the sample of consumer histories while $N(i_0, \ldots, i_{k-1}) = \sum_{i_k} n(i_0, i_1, \ldots, i_{k-1}, i_k)$ is the number of times the sequence $i_0, i_1, \ldots, i_{k-1}$ occurs in the first $T - 1$ periods. The maximum likelihood estimates of the transition probabilities for Markov chains were shown in Anderson and Goodman (1957) to be

$$\hat{p}_t(i, j) = n_t(i, j)/N_t(i) \quad \text{for } i, j = 1, \ldots, M \text{ and } t = 1, \ldots, T - 1$$

if one assumed that the Markov chain was non-stationary and

$$\hat{p}(i, j) = n(i, j)/N(i) \quad \text{for } i, j = 1, \ldots, M$$

if the chain is assumed to be stationary.

The maximum likelihood estimates of multiple stage transitions are given by

$$\hat{p}_t(j_t, j_{t+1}, \ldots, j_{t+k}) = n_t(j_t, j_{t+1}, \ldots, j_{t+k})/n_t(j_t, \ldots, j_{t+k-1})$$
$$\text{for } j_t, \ldots, j_{t+k} = 1, \ldots, M \text{ and } t = 1, \ldots, T - k$$

for non-stationary higher order chains and

$$\hat{p}(j_0, j_1, \ldots, j_k) = n(j_0, j_1, \ldots, j_k)/N(j_0, j_1, \ldots, j_{k-1})$$
$$\text{for } j_0, \ldots, j_k = 1, \ldots, M$$

if the process is assumed to be stationary.

The first question is whether the transitions between states are Markov. The simplest assumption is that the movements form a stationary Markov chain. This corresponds to the hypothesis that for states i, $i = 1, \ldots, M$

$$H_0(i) : p(1, i, j) = p(2, i, j) = \cdots = p(M, i, j), \quad j = 1, \ldots, M.$$

The likelihood ratio criteria can be used to test this hypothesis. The transition frequencies can be placed in a contingency table with the rows corresponding to the previous location k in $p(k, i, j)$ and the columns being the destinations. The null hypothesis $H_0(i)$ assumes the row percentages of the contingency table are all equal.

Under this hypothesis the log of the likelihood ratio

$$Y^2 = 2 \log \left(\prod_{j=1}^{M} \prod_{k=1}^{M} \left(\frac{\hat{p}(k, i, j)}{\hat{p}(i, j)} \right)^{n(k,i,j)} \right)$$

$$= 2 \sum_{j=1}^{M} \sum_{k=1}^{M} n(k, i, j) \log \left(\frac{\hat{p}(k, i, j)}{\hat{p}(i, j)} \right)$$

$$= 2 \sum_{j=1}^{M} \sum_{k=1}^{M} n(k, i, j) \log \left(\frac{n(k, i, j)N(i)}{N(k, i)n(i, j)} \right)$$

has a χ^2 distribution with $(M - 1)^2$ degrees of freedom. Some of the transitions may appear impossible because of the way the states are defined, though it is interesting how often such transitions occur in practice due to data errors. If there are r_i such structural zeros in row i of the transition matrix (r in total) and c_i structural zeros in column i then the number of degrees of freedom is $(M - c_i - 1)(M - 1 - r_i)$.

A more familiar statistic than the likelihood ratio test is the Pearson goodness of fit χ^2 statistic, which has similar distributional properties.

Let

$$e(k, i, j) = N(k, i)p(i, j) = \frac{N(k, i)n(i, j)}{N(i)}$$

be the expected number of transitions (k, i, j) if the hypothesis $H_0(i)$ holds then

$$X^2 = \sum_{k=1}^{M} \sum_{j=1}^{M} \frac{(n(k, i, j) - e(k, i, j))^2}{e(k, i, j)}$$

has a χ^2 distribution with $(M - 1 - c_i)(M - 1 - r_i)$ degrees of freedom.

The hypothesis that the whole system was a first-order Markov chain namely

$$H_0: p(1, i, j) = p(2, i, j) = \cdots = p(M, i, j) \quad \text{for all } i, j = 1, \ldots, M$$

can be thought of as requiring $H_0(i)$ holds for all $i = 1, \ldots, M$. A Pearson goodness of fit test for this is to consider the table of M^2 rows and M^2 columns with entries $n(i, j, k)$ and assume, under this hypothesis that the expected number of transactions in each cell is $e(k, j)$ as defined above. Then

$$X^2 = \sum_{i=1}^{M} \sum_{k=1}^{M} \sum_{j=1}^{M} \frac{[n(k, i, j) - e(k(i, j))]^2}{e(k, i, j)}$$

has a χ^2 distribution with $\sum_{i=1}^{M}(M - 1 - c_i)(M - 1 - r_i)$ degrees of freedom.

One of the reasons the hypothesis may not be true is that the Markov chain could be non-stationary. Thus it is worth checking if the transitions satisfy the hypothesis for a non-stationary Markov chain namely

$$H_0(i, t): p_t(1, i, j) = p_t(2, i, j) = \cdots = p(M, i, j) \quad \text{for } j = 1, \ldots, M$$

for all combinations of $i = 1, \ldots, M$, and $t = 2, \ldots, T - 1$. The equivalent likelihood ratio and Pearson goodness of fit tests for these hypotheses are

$$Y^2 = 2 \sum_{j=1}^{M} \sum_{k=1}^{M} n_{t-1}(k, i, j) \log \left(\frac{n_{t-1}(k, i, j)}{n_{t-1}(k, i)} \cdot \frac{n_t(i)}{n_t(i, j)} \right)$$

which has a χ^2 distribution with $(M - c_1 - 1)(M - 1 - r_i)$ degrees of freedom and

$$X^2 = \sum_{k=1}^{M} \sum_{j=1}^{M} \frac{(n_{t-1}(k, i, j) - e_{t-1}(k, i, j))^2}{e_{t-1}(k, i, j)} \tag{19.1}$$

where

$$e_{t-1}(k, i, j) = n_{t-1}(k, i) \frac{n_t(i, j)}{n_t(i)}.$$

For each (i, t) combination, $i = 1, \ldots, M$ and $t = 2, \ldots, T - 1$ this hypothesis corresponds to X^2 having the χ^2 distribution with $(M - 1 - c_i)(M - 1 - s_i)$ degrees of freedom.

Applying these tests to the bank data set with the full 10 states considered, it was recognized that

$M = 10, r_1 = 3, r_2 = 3, r_3 = 0, r_4 = 2, r_5 = 4, r_6 = 3, r_7 = 2, r_8 = 1, r_9 = 1, r_{10} = 6,$

$c_1 = 5, c_2 = 0, c_3 = 0, c_4 = 1, c_5 = 3, c_6 = 2, c_7 = 1, c_8 = 5, c_9 = 5, c_{10} = 3,$

so there are 25 structured zeros. Using just a 2 per cent randomly chosen sample of the accounts we still have 313,012 transactions which led to an estimated $\hat{P}$ of

$$
\hat{P} =
\begin{pmatrix}
0.904 & 0.086 & 0.007 & 0 & 0 & 0.002 & 0 & \cdot & \cdot & \cdot \\
0.010 & 0.897 & 0.080 & 0.06 & 0 & 0.004 & 0.002 & \cdot & \cdot & \cdot \\
0.003 & 0.253 & 0.676 & 0.027 & 0.003 & 0.023 & 0.014 & 0.001 & 0.001 & 0.000 \\
\cdot & 0.278 & 0.325 & 0.177 & 0.000 & 0.059 & 0.156 & 0.004 & \cdot & 000 \\
0.026 & 0.070 & 0.137 & 0.003 & 0.757 & \cdot & 0.007 & \cdot & \cdot & \cdot \\
0.007 & 0.189 & 0.130 & 0.025 & \cdot & 0.638 & 0.01 & \cdot & \cdot & 0.000 \\
\cdot & 0.47 & 0.242 & 0.037 & \cdot & 0.082 & 0.263 & 0.224 & 0.004 & 0.001 \\
\cdot & 0.082 & 0.156 & 0.017 & 0.001 & 0.105 & 0.078 & 0.070 & 0.492 & 0.009 \\
\cdot & 0.037 & 0.071 & 0.004 & 0.001 & 0.036 & 0.031 & 0.005 & 0.791 & 0.022 \\
\cdot & 0.007 & 0.002 & \cdot & \cdot & \cdot & \cdot & \cdot & 0.007 & 0.982
\end{pmatrix}
$$

However, neither the log likelihood nor the Pearson test remotely suggested that this was Markov. For the individual rows, the only row that came close to satisfying $H_0(i)$ was the 10th row, which is clear from the transaction matrix is close to being an 'absorbing state'. The same results were found when the Markov property was tested with the non-stationary assumption.

Assuming that the Markov chain is completely non-stationary is counterproductive because one cannot then forecast what the future transaction matrices would be. A more limited assumption which overcomes the difficulty is to assume that there is a monthly 'seasonal' effect so that there are different transaction matrices for each of the 12 months of the year, for example, P_{JAN}, P_{FEB}, etc. To check whether $p_{12t+r}(i, j) = p_r(i, j)$ for $t = 1, 2, 3, 4$ and all i, j one can apply the Pearson χ^2 statistic (defined as X^2 in equation 19.1).The results of the test as to whether the transactions can be explained by 12 different Markov transition matrices, are given in Table 19.1. The results of Table 19.1 show the hypothesis is not true.

Table 19.1   Testing Markovity for seasonal non-stationarity.

Month	Value of X^2	Degrees of freedom	Critical 5% value
$r = 1$: January	2818	270	309
$r = 2$: February	10,760	270	309
$r = 3$: March	4303	270	309
$r = 4$: April	3809	270	309
$r = 5$: May	5673	270	309
$r = 6$: June	3236	270	309
$r = 7$: July	8892	270	309
$r = 8$: August	5932	270	309
$r = 9$: September	2953	270	309
$r = 10$: October	9603	270	309
$r = 11$: November	2612	270	309
$r = 12$: December	5771	270	309

Table 19.2   First-order Markovity for three-state model.

Hypothesis	Degrees of freedom $(M - 1)^2$	X^2	Critical value
H_0	12	568,806	21.03
$H_0(G)$	4	374,901	9.49
$H_0(I)$	4	182,173	9.49
$H_0(B)$	4	11,732	9.49

One possible explanation is that the 10 states provide too fine a graduation of the behavioural situation of bank customers. It was common within the organization to aggregate the 10 states into three classes which we will call Good (G), Intermediate (I), and Bad (B) for identification where $G = \{1, 2, 3, 4\}$, $I = \{5, 6, 7\}$, $B = \{8, 9, 10\}$ where each state is defined by a mixture of how overdue, how active, and what balance the customer has at that time. One could then repeat the analysis using this three-state space to check on Markovity. For the three-state space there are no structured zeros and so $c_i = r_i = 0$ for $i = 1, 2, 3$. The maximum likelihood estimates lead to a transition matrix.

$$\hat{P} = \begin{pmatrix} 0.983 & 0.017 & 0.001 \\ 0.360 & 0.583 & 0.057 \\ 0.134 & 0.088 & 0.778 \end{pmatrix}.$$

Testing the hypothesis suggested that the transitions were still not Markov as the results in Table 19.2 indicate.

Testing the monthly 'seasonal' effect on this three-state chain using the Pearson χ^2 statistic (with 18 degrees of freedom) also showed that the Markov assumption was not satisfied in any month.

19.3   Higher order Markov chains

If the first-order Markov chain assumption does not hold, it might still be the case that the dynamics of consumer behaviour can be explained by a second- or third-order Markov chain. In second-order Markov chains, the state of the system at time t is described by (X_t, X_{t-1}), the current and previous state, while in a third-order Markov chain it is described by (X_t, X_{t-1}, X_{t-2}). Thus if one begins with a M-state chain, the second-order Markov chain can be considered as a Markov chain with M^2 states where typical state is (i, j) implying it is in state j now and was in i at the previous time period. Similarly a third-order Markov chain on a M-state system corresponds to a Markov chain with M^3 states.

The exponential increase in the state space size as second- and third-order Markov chains are considered make it unreasonable to consider such versions of the original 10-state model. However, with the aggregated three-state model a second-order Markov chain would only involve nine states, while even the third order would only tend to a 27-state chain. Table 19.3 describes the results of the goodness of fit tests to check if the system is second-order Markov as opposed to third-order Markov. Note that in a second-order chain with nine states there are six structural zeros in each row and column so the degrees of freedom remain the same as in the first-order tests.

Clearly the chain is not second order even if for some of the (less common) states, the Markov assumption is nearer to holding. Tests for non-stationarity because of monthly seasonality with second-order Markovity compared with third-order Markovity also

Table 19.3   Second-order Markovity of three-state chain.

Hypothesis	Degree of freedom	χ^2	Critical value
H_0 (2nd order)	36	225,706	51.0
H_0 (GG, 2nd order)	4	164,853	9.49
H_0 (IG, 2nd order)	4	853	9.49
H_0 (BG, 2nd order)	4	160	9.49
H_0 (GI, 2nd order)	4	4,265	9.49
H_0 (II, 2nd order)	4	47,664	9.49
H_0 (BI, 2nd order)	4	166	9.49
H_0 (GB, 2nd order)	4	109	9.49
H_0 (IB, 2nd order)	4	486	9.49
H_0 (BB, 2nd order)	4	7,150	9.49

could not be accepted at the 5 per cent level, especially for the important states (in terms of frequency of occupation) GG, II, BB.

19.4 Segmenting into movers, stayers, twitchers, and shakers

One explanation for the movement of customers not being Markov is that the population of customers is not homogenous. There is a whole segment of customers whose behaviour is very stable and other segments with much more volatile behaviour. This idea of splitting the population into 'stayers' and 'movers' has been used with positive results in labour mobility and in marketing. Frydman *et al.* (1985) were the first to suggest its use in credit behaviour and we expand on their idea in this section by investigating splitting the population into multiple segments not just the two suggested in (Frydman *et al.* 1985).

The population is segmented initially on the number of times a customer changes between *G*, *I*, and *B* in the 48 months of the sample period. Those whose accounts were closed during this period were assumed to be in the states *G* or *B* for the subsequent periods after closure depending on the 'status' of the account in closure. The percentage of the population in each segment was given by Table 19.4.

It is perhaps surprising that 44 per cent of the borrowing population made 0-moves during the 48 months—the overwhelming majority of these being in the *G* state, with a very few being in the *B* state the whole time. This almost 50–50 split shows why the Markov assumption was so hard to substantiate for the whole population, and proves that having a 'stayer' segment is valid in order to describe the dynamics. The question now is which segments should be used and what order Markov chain should be used in each of the mover segments. For each segment we calculate X^2 for the Pearson goodness of fit test which checks if the transactions can be described by a Markov chain (first order, second order and in some cases third order).

This is then translated into the *p*-value, of the χ^2-test with the appropriate degrees of freedom. This is the likelihood of observing a less extreme value of the χ^2-test statistic if the Markov hypothesis was true than that which was obtained in reality. In order to obtain numbers comparing different combinations of segments, we then weight the *p*-value for each segment by the number of consumers in that segment, so if one has a segmentation $A_1, \ldots, A_m$ then the average Markovity measure for that

Table 19.4 Distribution of state changes.

No. of state changes	0	1	2	3	4	5	6	7	8	8+
% of population	44.4	6.1	16.4	3.7	7.4	2.7	4.4	2	2.8	10.1

segmentation is

$$w = \sum_{i=1}^{m} n(A_i)p(A_i) = \sum_{i=1}^{m} w_i \qquad (19.2)$$

where $n(A_i)$ is the number of consumers in segment A_i and $p(A_i)$ is the p-value of the χ^2-test on that segment. This is equivalent to weighting each segment's p-value by $n(A_i)/\sum_j n(A_j)$—the proportion of the population in that segment—since one is just dividing each term in (19.2) by the total population. However, when comparing two segmentations of the same population there is no difference in the result as the total population is the same in both cases and (19.2) leads to numbers which are large enough to deal with easily. Within a segment one can also calculate the w_i for first-, second- and third-order Markov chains and this gives an indication of the improvements in description that are possible by going to higher order Markovity. Table 19.5 shows these results where the third-order chains were only built on large segments where the difference between the first and second order were considerable. One can then consider the various partitions of the population into segments and the order of the

Table 19.5 w_i values for various population segments.

Mover subset	w_i		
	First-order chain	Second-order chain	Third-order chain
Original segments			
1-Mover	2,321	2,340	
2-Mover	10^{-24}	209	
3-Mover	10^{-66}	39	
4-Mover	10^{-31}	3,335	8,961
6-Mover	0	626	2,213
8-Mover	0	264	2,442
Combined segments			
(1 + 2)-Mover	10^{-12}	803	
(2 + 3)-Mover	0	79	
(1 + 3)-Mover	10^{-80}	92	
(2 + 4)-Mover	10^{-75}	232	
(3 + 4)-Mover	0	180	
(4 + 6)-Mover	0	409	
(6 + 8)-Mover	0	489	
(1 + 2 + 3)-Mover	0	147	
(2 + 3 + 4)-Mover	0	119	
(1 + 2 + 3 + 4)-Mover	0	155	
(4 or more)-Mover	0	6	
(5 or more)-Mover	10^{-24}	16	2,576

Table 19.6 w-values for various partitions.

Scheme	Segmentation	No. of segments	Each segment's order	w-value
1	$(1+2+3)$, (4 or more)	2	2,2	153
2	$(1+2+3+4)$, (5 or more)	2	2,2	171
3	$(1+3)$, $(2+4)$, (5 or more)	3	2,2,2	340
4	$(1+2)$, $(3+4)$, (5 or more)	3	2,2,2	999
5	1, $(2+3)$, (4 or more)	3	1,2,2	2,406
6	1,2, (3 or more)	3	1,2,2	2,555
7	$(1+2+3)$, 4, (5 or more)	3	2,2,2	3,798
8	$(1+2)$,3,4, (5 or more)	4	2,2,2,2	4,192
9	1,$(2+3)$, 4, (5 or more)	4	1,2,2,2	5,751
10	1,2,3,4, (5 or more)	5	1,2,2,2,2	5,920
11	$(1+2)$,3,4,6,8, (rest)	6	2,2,2,2,2,2	5,067
12	1,2,3,4,6,8,res	7	1,2,2,2,2,2,2	6,794

Markov chain in each segment and determine which leads to the best description of the dynamics of the population. Table 19.6 displays those results for a number of partitions.

The judgement of which scheme is most appropriate is not just a matter of choosing the maximum w-value, but also needs to consider the number of segments, the relative size of the segments, the size of the state space in each segment, and the ease of understanding of the system. Thus, for example, the w_i values for the first- and second-order chains on the 1-Movers were so similar that we will use the first-order chain because it is so much smaller. In our case the partition that was considered most useful was scheme 7 which split the population into 4 segments—the '0' movers ('stayers'), the $(1+2+3)$ movers ('twitchers'), the 4 movers ('shakers'), and 5+ movers (movers). In each case describing the movement by a second-order Markov chain seemed appropriate.

Having determined such a segmentation, one needs to be able to assign customers to the segments prospectively rather than retrospectively which was how they were defined. This becomes a four-class classification problem where one seeks to use current information on customers to assign them to one of the four classes described above. Both linear and logistic regression can be extended to multi-class discrimination. The extensions depend on whether there is an obvious ordering of the classes or not. In this case there is an obvious ordering of the four-classes in terms of stability from stayers (class 0) to twitchers (class 1) to shakers (class 2) to movers (class 3). In a logistical approach if $\mathbf{x} = (x_1, \ldots, x_n)$ are the consumer characteristics and K is the variable describing the class of consumer, one assumes

$$p(K \leq k|\mathbf{x}) = \frac{e^{c_k+\mathbf{w}\cdot\mathbf{x}}}{1 + e^{c_k+\mathbf{w}\cdot\mathbf{x}}}. \tag{19.3}$$

The logistic discrimination scorecards were built using only application data and then only behavioural data, on a subsample of 3000 cases. The scorecard based on application data reduced to one involving only four application variables while that using only behavioural data also reduced to one with four behavioural variables. The results were tested using a holdout sample and the results were what might be expected. The behavioural based scorecard performed better than the application based scorecard in terms of discrimination, and the scorecard was most accurate when discriminating between the two extremes (movers against shakers) and least accurate when trying to identify similar groups (twitchers against shakers). The Gini coefficient in the former case was 0.75 while in the latter case, it was just better than chance (Gini of 0.04). This suggests that while this approach has proved encouraging, one will need to include more variables in order to develop a useable system. It may also mean that one should not separate out the choice of segments from the classification decision of assigning customers to segments. Benton and Hand (2002) advocate this strategy for the problem of determining how many scorecards to build when developing a credit-scoring system.

19.5   Conclusions

This chapter investigates how we can expand the first-order Markov chain models of the dynamics of bank customers' behaviours, previously suggested in the literature to adequately model the real behaviour of such customers. It suggests that first-order chains, be they stationary or non-stationary, do not satisfactorily describe their behaviour. Therefore, it may well be necessary to aggregate the original states to obtain a smaller basic state space, so that the exponential increase in the state space does not lead to unmanageable models. The most useful advance in modelling the real data though was to recognize the non-homogeneity of the dynamics of the bank population. This leads to an extension of the mover–stayer model to segment the population according to the volatility of their movements. A statistic for comparing different partitions of the population was developed and a pilot scoring system for classifying customers into different segments of the population constructed. This allows one to take advantage of the simplifying assumptions of the Markov models and yet model the actual dynamics of the population more closely.

References

Anderson, T. W. and Goodman, L. A. (1957) Statistical inference about Markov chains. *Annals of Mathematical Statistics*, 28, 89–110.

Benton, T. C. and Hand, D. J. (2002) Segmentation into predictable classes. Working Paper, Imperial College, London.

Corcoran, A. W. (1978) The use of exponentially smoothed transition matrices to improve forecasting of cash flows from accounts receivable. *Management Science*, 24(7), 732–9.

Cyert, R. M. and Thompson, G. L. (1968) Selecting a portfolio of credit risk by Markov chains. *Journal of Business*, 1, 39–46.

Cyert, R. M., Davidson, H. J., and Thompson, G. L. (1962) Estimation of the allowance for doubtful accounts by Markov chains. *Management Science*, 8, 287–303.

Frydman, H., Kallberg, J. G., and Kao, D. L. (1985) Testing the adequacy of Markov chains and Mover–Stayer models as representations of credit behaviour. *Operations Research*, 33(6), 1203–14.

Ho, J. (2001) Modelling Bank Customers Behaviour using Data Warehouses and Incorporating Economic Indicators, Ph.D. Thesis, University of Edinburgh.

Kallberg, J. G. and Saunders, A. (1983) Markov chain approaches to the analysis of payment behaviour of retail credit customers. *Financial Management*, 12(Part 2), 5–14.

Liebman, L. H. (1972) A Markov decision model for selecting optimal credit control policies. *Management Science*, 18(10), 519–25.

Metha, D. (1972) Markov process and credit collection policy. *Decision Sciences*, 3, 27–43.

Schniederjans, M. J. and Loch, K. D. (1994) An aid for strategic marketing in the banking industry: a Markov analysis. *Computers and Operations Research*, 21(Part 3), 281–7.

Thomas, L. C. (2000) A survey of credit and behavioural scoring: forecasting financial risk of lending to consumers. *International Journal of Forecasting*, 16, 149–72.

Van Kuelan J. A. M., Spronk, J., and Corcoran, A. W. (1981) On the Cyert–Davidson–Thompson doubtful accounts model. *Management Science*, 27(1), 108–111.

Index

accelerated failure time model 238
acceptance 11, 20, 116, 119, 121, 202, 210
  determination of 78
  expected, expected bad rate versus 113–15
  extrapolation from 134–5
  high/low 252
  probability of 79, 85
  self-employed applicants 206
accommodation type 134
account-management package 182
account performance information 96
accounts 94, 182
  blocking 190, 191
  closed 303
  commonly used methods for monitoring 101–2
  differentiation among 34, 38–40, 41–2
  fraud 191
  over limit 33
  premier 192
  right censored 240
  satisfactory 33, 40
  storecard 297
  suspicious 190
  unsatisfactory 40
  see also bad loans; cut-off scores; delinquency
    accounts; good loans; rejection
acquisitions 81, 123
ACS (adaptive control systems) 33–46
action set 44–5
actual values 104
added value 65, 66
  measuring 67–9
addresses 241, 269, 270, 271, 273
adjustment schemes 102, 106, 143
affordability data 63–71
Afifi, A. A. 24
age 10, 17, 18, 66, 99, 134, 198, 269, 271
Agresti, A. 248
Aitken, M. 240, 242
Albright, H. 282
algorithms 140, 239, 284
  genetic 277, 278, 281–2, 286, 287–8, 289, 290
  proprietary 112
  recursive partitioning 282–3, 289
all-way interaction models 267
alleles 281
Altman, E. I. 27
American Express 85

Anderson, T. W. 296, 297
anomalies 102
Apilado, V. P. 27
appeals process 208
application forms 65, 68, 71, 87, 164, 255
  characteristics referred to on 96–7
  large number of variables measured in 247
  need to expand 13
  new style 205
  variables 269
  variables extracted from 248
application-risk model 181
approved borrowers 27
approximations 25, 59, 269
  asymptotic 267
APR (annual percentage rate) 76
arrears 58, 94, 244
  worst 105
associations 10, 250, 251, 258, 271
  interesting 254
attribute based tests 284
attributes 155, 188, 197, 198, 202, 215, 218
  account 38
  bad rate for 208, 223
  binary 287
  calculating the bads for 219
  categorical 51, 96–108
  characteristic with two 217
  continuously measured 287
  design 75
  predictive 201
  ranked according to natural ordering 212
  should be in the right order 104
  weights of evidence of 217, 221, 224
atypical niches 205, 222
augmentation method 28, 138
authorization 190
automated billing systems 33
automated decision systems 64
automobile finance companies 13
autoregression 27
averaging 149
Avery, Robert 11, 12, 27, 28, 135

bad loans/accounts 5, 8, 13, 20, 22, 23, 26, 28, 40–1,
    95–6, 116, 178, 203, 207, 211, 224, 245, 258
  converting to weights of evidence 221
  definition of 240, 244

bad loans/accounts (*cont.*)
  distribution of good and 101
  estimated 218
  estimating the expert's variance 220–1
  expected 113–15, 114
  expected number of goods required to offset loss of
    120
  expert's mean 219
  grand average 217
  identification rates of 155
  'kill ratio' or discrimination of goods to 158
  matching on 100
  measures for comparing distributions 52–7
  net loss from 119
  nominal distributions of 138
  percentage of good rate 98
  predicting the number that turn out to be good 121
  rank assigned according to 214–15
  ratio of goods to 152
  self-employed 219
  shrunken 219
  strategy curve predicts 114
  table of 102
bank cards 12, 161
bankruptcy 112, 156, 291
banks/bank accounts 5, 190–2, 209, 241, 269, 270, 272,
    297
  risk-based pricing 13
Barclaycard 205–29
Barcun, S. 23
Bates, T. 25, 27
Bayesian approach 21, 112, 134–5, 138, 205, 208,
    218–19, 221, 223, 250, 282
  correct 224
behaviour scoring 33–46, 207, 211, 296–307
Belgium 197, 198, 203
benefit–cost ratio 155
Benton, T. C. 306
bias 27, 102, 106, 133, 135, 136, 210, 218
  positive 264
  potential 157, 207
  sample 152, 153, 155, 156, 157, 158
  selection 247
Biden, Joseph 8
Bierman, H. 18, 19, 20
billing cycle 39
binomial distribution 219
bootstrapping 264, 267
borrowing facilities 297
Boyle, M. 248
business cycle 161–75

calibration samples 141–3
Canada 189, 190
canonical correlation analysis 142
capital 58
capitalism 14
Capon, Noel 9, 164
Cardpac 182

cash alternatives 257
categories 134, 208–9, 214, 269
  accounts classified into two 211
  distinct 183
  response-risk 185
categorizations 156, 297
causal observation 152
causality 9–10
CCN 177, 181
  Autoscore system 182, 185
censoring 237, 240, 243, 244
  absence of 242
Central Statistical Office (UK) 163
Champions and Challengers 35, 38, 45–6
chance 290
Chandler, C. G. 11, 17, 23, 25, 27
Chang, P. C. 24
characteristics 95, 134, 136, 137, 161, 167, 169, 172,
    219, 249, 278, 279, 282, 283, 284, 287
  analysis 102
  bank reference 104
  categorical 96
  continuous 96
  correlations between 207
  cross-classification of a number of 142
  demographic 269
  discrete 212
  group 8, 24
  independence of 216
  individual, time-based 221–2
  judged to be medium or highly predictive 214
  no overlap between 211
  people predicted to be good and bad 162
  predictive bureau 203
  rational way to reduce the number of 213
  reduction process 214, 215
  repayment performance and 291
  score distributions for 102
  scorecard 97, 181
  social 269
  suspect 103, 104
  see also attributes
charge-cards 165, 185
charge-offs 13, 153, 156, 291
Chatterjee, S. 23
checks 64
cheque guarantee cards 269, 270
children 269, 272, 273, 282, 287, 289
chi-squared test 5, 165, 258, 259, 264, 299
  asymptotic distribution 263, 265
chromosomes 282, 287, 288
class membership/rules 283, 284
classification 134, 148, 156, 197–8, 202, 235, 277, 278,
    283, 306
  according to wealth 253
  accuracy of 191
  credit applicant problem 282
  error rates 24
  four techniques 278–84
  gender 251–2

good/bad 140
  incremental 158
  predicted, differences in 161
  reduced 269
  simplistic two-valued logic 157
  slow and poor 158
  three way 291
  three-group 278
  training sample 290
  two-way 291
classification matrices 165, 169
classification trees 282–4, 286, 288, 289, 290, 291
classifier design 134
clustering problems 282
coefficients 142
  canonical function 165, 167, 169
  correlation 212, 213
  equal 150
  generic 149
  individual, significance of 25
  learning 281
  regression 143, 148, 258
  see also Gini
Coffman, J. Y. 17, 23, 25, 27
collateral 21, 26
collection:
  account targeted for 284
  administrative costs of 58
  estimates of prior probabilities of 19
  improvements 65
  indignities of 9
  letter 45
  optimal decisions for 19
  partial repayments 20
collectors queue 34
collinearity 10, 164, 248
colour 17
'Commercial Scoring' 223
complications 181–2
computers 6
conditional density functions 112
conditional distribution 248, 250, 251, 267, 273
  cumulative 112
conditional independence 247, 248–54, 258, 261, 267, 273
  pairwise 263
  systematic way of checking for 262
conditional significance 25
conditioning 264, 265
  inbuilt 255
confidence factors 221
confidence interval approach 104, 213
confidentiality 190, 208, 222
consecutive authorizations 190
constrained problem 122
consultancies 207
consumer credit 11, 12, 17–18
  granting models 23
  risk-based pricing 13

segmentation in Markov chain behavioural models 295–307
consumer preferences 73–88
consumers 7, 11
  better off 8
  desirous and deserving 9
  installment credit 6
  policy to benefit 13
  self-employed 213
contingency tables 263, 298
  multi-way 248
  sparsity in 247, 264, 265–6
control 106
convergence rate 281
Corcoran, A. W. 296
correlations 214
  characteristic 216
  measuring 207
correspondence analysis 142
Corrigan, B. 147
costs 23
  acceptance 19
  acquisition 81
  additional decision 19
  bad debt 19
  collection 8, 19, 21, 58
  credit analysis 20
  disruption 191
  error 26
  information 19, 21
  investment 19
  lost sales 19
  marginal 152
  misclassification 22, 24, 26, 121, 191, 278
  modelling 13
  opportunity 18, 21
  processing 20
  rejection 19
  saving 192
  social 10
  startup 20
  sunk 81
  updating 20
counterfeit fraud 189, 192
County Court judgements 137
court tests 25
covariance matrices 138, 279
  common 139
Cox, D. R. 240
C_{prop} 290
credit bureaux 65, 68
Credit Card Redlining 8, 9, 10
credit cards 74, 76, 196, 254, 257, 269, 277–93
  annual fee and annual percentage rate 14
  classification of applicants 277
  detecting fraud 189–93
  installment type lending 22
  major 165
  missing consecutive payments 163–4
  prestigious 11

credit cards (*cont.*)
  probability of defaulting on repayments 253
  reasons for applying for 256
  returns on balances 13
  strategy for reissuing 33
  typical question about preferences 85
  usage 253
  very low ownership 201
  see also Barclaycard; Mastercard; Visa
credit-granting decisions 20, 22, 235–45
credit grantors 94, 284
  policy decisions 163
'Credit Guide Score' (Wonderlic) 6
credit history 95
credit limit setting 182
  strategy for 33
credit lines 49, 76, 77, 78, 80, 85, 261, 273
credit performance:
  eventual indicator 260
  past/future 19
credit record 14, 84, 85
credit scoring:
  agencies 161, 277
  challenges to 7–12
  credit for initiating the concept 5
  measures for comparing 51–62
  traditional system 106
credit-scoring models:
  individually developed 155, 158
  linear 148
  methodology 18–22
  necessary framework for 248
  review of 22–3
  statistical problems in 23–8
credit searches 65
credit unions 148, 153, 155, 157, 158, 277, 282, 284
creditors 7, 19
  competition among 8
  financial and non-financial services 21
  granting more loans to females 12
  may define many strategies 46
  sorting good from bad risks 10
creditworthiness 7, 8, 10, 78, 84, 95, 105, 156, 258–9
  ability of formula to separate two types of 152
  appraising 94
  arraying cumulative percentages for 152
  classified 259
  true good or bad 133
criminals 189
critical values 279, 282, 283
Crook, J. N. 164, 277, 284, 286, 290
cross correlation matrix 214
crossover 282, 289, 290
cross-references 181
cross-tabulations 169
'curse of insensitivity' 147
curve fitting exercise 101
customer relationship 20, 21
  jeopardizing 177, 178, 179
  value of 22

customers:
  acceptable to the lender 71
  anticipated overall response rate 183
  assigning to segments 306
  bad 65, 211
  bank, behavioural situation of 301
  disposable income 63
  good 65, 191
  high response rates and low risk 181
  high-risk 13, 64, 70
  house rate applicable to all 12
  low-risk 13
  loyal 178
  movement of 303
  new 73, 75
  past, purchasing patterns of 19
  potential 74, 75
  probability of gaining 86
  prospective 77, 78, 85
  rejected 65
  special 42
  unmailed and unresponsive 181
  utility preference information from 49
cut-off scores 13, 78, 158, 183, 208, 245
  above/below 210
  effects of changes in 166–72
  optimal 152
  varying 162
cut-off values 283
Cyert, R. M. 296

Darroch, J. N. 248
data 163–4, 208–9
  accounting of 13
  affordability 63–71
  analysis, biased estimation in 156
  application 107, 269–71, 306
  authorization 190
  availability of 12, 95
  behavioural 306
  combining expertise and 206
  conditional independences in 247
  correlations in 207
  credit bureau 65
  deemed to be important 95
  easy interpretation of 211
  estimation 156
  expert 211, 219
  full delinquency 95
  marketing and profitability modelling 13
  missing 140
  multivariate 247, 249
  new and enhanced sources 94
  nominal level 286
  obtained from application forms 96
  pooled 149
  preparation 284–6
  relevant to assessment of Good/Bad outcomes 112
  scorecard development 213

scrutinized in depth 181
sparse 267
survival 237
trial questionnaire 205
unuseable for model building 95
databases 181, 196
payment profile 95
retail credit 197
single European 201
Dawes, R. M. 147
debt:
bad 19, 202–3
low probability of repaying 9
decision area 43
decision-making 203, 254
decision-management system 182
decision trees 119, 235, 255, 277
decomposition 268, 269
mixture 136, 138, 140, 143
default 21, 26, 77, 112, 165, 166, 254
ability of certain variables to predict 162
alternative definitions of 163
average rates 19
both cards 211
likelihood of loans 23
much higher chance of 78
possibilities of 78
probability of 21, 22–3, 207
degrees of freedom 263, 264, 267, 285, 298, 299, 300, 303
delinquency/delinquent accounts 14, 26, 33, 34, 36, 41
actual 208
collections area 43, 44–5
continued 39
current 296
delinquency/delinquent accounts full data 95
differentiation 38
early measurements 207
known, monitoring and adjustments in the light of 102–6
no information can be obtained 95
one-cycle 35, 38
probability of not reaching 3-cycles 211
specific threshold 211
status of 35
delinquency reports 108
delta-bar-delta method 281, 286
demographics 153, 157, 181, 249, 269
Dempster, A. P. 140
density function 236, 237, 242, 245
dependants 198, 201
dependence:
conditional 263, 272
induced 266
marginal 251
scale to measure relative importance of 258
deposit accounts 165
Desai, V. S. 277, 278, 282, 291
deterministic function 261

deviance 259, 268
edge-exclusion 258, 263, 264, 265, 266, 267
differentiation 38–40
differentiators 46
dimensionality reductions 24, 25
direct marketing 178
directed graphs 248, 249
Dirickx, Y. M. 18, 20, 21
discounting 19
discriminant analysis 135, 148, 165, 235
problems in applying 17–32
three-group 139
discriminant functions 5, 271
changes in 165–6
desirable to have more variables in 156
discrimination 8, 10, 67, 69, 138, 139, 152, 244, 248, 267
goods and bads 53–5
indirect 11, 12
perfect 114
prohibited 17
sexual 251–2
slows and goods 284
threat of suits for 13
discriminatory power 153, 155, 161
statistically significant 165–6
dispersions 24–5, 27, 28
distribution 113, 139, 220
asymmetric 135
behaviour score 210, 212
biased 135
chi-squared 259, 263, 264, 265
class-conditional 141
completely specified 140
'conjugate' 219
continuous 60
cumulative 150
empirical 143, 264
equal, goods and slows 288
exponential 61, 242
goods and bads 52–7, 101
marginal 112, 140, 251, 254
nominal 138
normal 59
observed 257
overall 140
probability 236
sampling 264
survival 236, 242
test for equality of 152
see also conditional distribution; joint distribution
distribution functions 59
double inference 180
double reject inference approach 178
Durand, David 5, 6, 23, 25
Durkin, Thomas A. 11
dynamic programming models 20

ECOA (US Equal Credit Opportunity Act 1972) 11, 12, 16, 26, 28, 149
  passage which prohibited discrimination 17
  response to requests for reasons for credit rejection 14
  threat of suits under 13
economic depression 162
economic rationale 5–7
edge-exclusion deviance 258, 263, 264, 265, 266, 267
Edmister, R. O. 18, 20, 21, 27
Edwards, D. 248
'effects test' 23
efficiency 5, 10
  variation over time 20
efficient frontier 74, 75, 122
  cut-off policies 111–31
Eisenbeis, R. A. 24, 25, 135
electoral roll information 65
Elliehausen, Gregory E. 11
EM algorithm 140
empirical evaluation process 6–7
employment 153, 242, 269, 271, 272, 273, 287
  see also self-employed applicants
entropy 283
epoch number 288
Equal Opportunities Commission 11
equations 104, 105, 106–7, 120, 148, 279, 280
  applying the chain rule to 281
  developmental 153
  discriminant 149–50, 157, 158
  generic 149, 150, 152, 153, 155, 156, 157–8
  individually derived 155
  polynomial scoring 282
  principal-components 158
  regression 99–100, 158
Equifax 177, 181, 183, 185
errors 8, 281, 289
  classification 23, 24, 26–7
  costs of 26
  data 298
  false positive 284
  mean square 156
  overall 22
  unbiased estimates of 28
estimates/estimation 104, 158, 164–5, 286
  best possible 100
  biased 27, 156, 157
  classical linear discriminant analysis 139
  classification error rates 24, 26–7
  consistent 28
  default probabilities 23
  good rate 98, 107
  improved 138
  many techniques for 112
  maximum likelihood 297–8, 301
  model-based 135
  obtained by stratification 258
  popular ways of handling 101
  predictive 223
  probability 98, 100–1

regression 100, 156
  reliability of 23
  unbiased 28
  see also James-Stein
ethnic origin 10
Europe 195–204
evaluation 20
Everitt, B. S. 136
evolutionary techniques 277–93
Ewert, D. C. 11, 25, 27
expected profits 77–83, 86, 113
  cut-off policies that maximize 119
  expected losses and 115–17, 121–3
  maximum objectives 119–21
  tradeoffs 123–5
  under perfect information 122
  zero 122
expenditure 63, 66
  elusive 65
  pinning down of what constitutes 64
Experian Scorex 195–204
expert opinions 207–8, 216
expert systems 189, 191–2
  probabilistic 248
experts 213, 214, 218, 219, 235
  Bayesian 224
  credit-scoring 269
  eliciting the mean bad rate 219
  estimating the variance of bad rate 220–1
  in-house 205
exponential curve 103
extrapolation 96, 129, 134–5, 136, 139, 142, 156

face validity 9–10
factorization 268
failure times 237, 238, 240, 242
Fair, William 8, 10
Fair Isaac Corporation 28, 177
  Triad system 182, 183
Federal Reserve Regulation B 18, 23
feedback mechanism 223
financial institutions 21, 119
  financial exposure for 189
  risk exposure limited 191
financial services 177, 178
financial situation/status 78, 85, 87
Fisher, R. A. 279
fitness 282, 287, 288
  highest mean 290
  lowest 289
  maximum 289
Fitzmaurice, G. M. 140
flat-maximum effect 147–60
flexible control systems 106
Fogarty, T. C. 282, 291
forecasting 147, 148, 297
Forgy, E. W. 27
France 197

fraud 112
  detecting 189–93
Frydman, H. 296, 297, 303
full payment history records 65
future period receipts 19

gains 119, 120
gender, *see* sex
generational reproduction 289, 290
generic models 277
  linear scoring 147–60
genetic algorithms 277, 278, 281–2, 286, 287–8, 289,
    290, 291
Germany 197, 198, 203
Gini coefficient 47, 56–7, 59, 202, 306
GLIM (statistical package) 240
global parameters 42–3
good loans/accounts 5, 8, 13, 20, 22, 26, 28, 40–1,
    95–6, 116, 178, 191, 192, 211, 255
  accepted 119
  actual 100, 104
  correctly classified 288
  distribution of bad and 101
  estimated 98, 103
  estimates regression procedure separates out 107
  expected number required to offset loss of bad 120
  false 155
  'kill ratio' or discrimination of bads to 158
  linear by score curve 104
  matching on 100
  measures for comparing distributions 52–7
  net profit from 119
  nominal distributions of 138
  outcomes 112, 114, 115
  predicted 98, 99, 100, 104, 105
  predicting number that turn out to be bad 121
  pseudo-actual 106
  ratio of bads to 152
  re-estimating 101, 102
  score an indicator of 98
Goodman, L. A. 296, 297
graphical models 214–15, 247–75
Greece 197, 198, 203
Greer, C. C. 18, 19, 21
group membership 165, 280, 283, 287

Hand, D. J. 135, 136, 140, 248, 306
Hausman, W, H. 18, 19, 20
Haykin, S. 281
hazard functions 236, 237, 238
Hester, D. D. 21
Hettenhouse, G. W. 27
heuristics 27, 278, 281
HFC (Household Finance Corp) 6
higher-order interactions 263, 267
Hills, M. 24
Hoadley, B. 78, 119, 120
holdouts 27, 153, 163, 167, 169

Holland, J. H. 282
home ownership 99, 100, 104, 240
  average level 198, 201
homogenous subpopulations 64
HopScan function 120, 122
Hsia, D. C. 138

impersonal aspect 7–9
implementation issues 286–8
income 66, 68, 156, 172, 269
  determining 64
  disposable 63
  elusive 65
  residential status and 273
  transfers 9
independence 259, 260
  marginal 251, 253, 256
  pairwise 262
  tests of 258
independence graphs 248, 258
  deducing the structure of 263
  specification of 262
independence models 216–17
indeterminates 95, 96
inference 177–86
  see also reject inference
influence diagrams 248, 249, 250, 254
  independence constraints in 255
INFOLINK 95
information criterion 283
information function 235
information statistic 60, 57
insensitivity 147, 148
integrated models 181
intercept points 97, 99
interest rate 20, 76, 77, 78, 84, 85, 94
  lower 80
investment yields 152
Ireson, N. S. 282, 291
iso-preference curves 77–86
Italy 197, 201, 203
iterations 288, 289
iterative logistic approach 104
iterative techniques 235, 239

jack-knife method 286, 290
Jacobs, R. A. 281
James-Stein Estimators 217–18
joint conditions 287
joint density function 250
joint distribution 249, 250, 254, 256, 268, 273
  modelling 260–4
judgemental approach 7

Kalbfleisch, J. D. 240
Kallberg, J. G. 296
Kaplan-Meir Method 242
Keeney, R. L. 114
Khoylou, J. 291

King, R. D. 277, 282, 291
Klecka, W. R. 164
Kolmogorov-Smirnov statistic 55, 152
Krzanowski, W. J. 247
Kuhn-Tucker optimality conditions 121–2

labour mobility 303
lambda value 217
Lane, S. 23, 25, 27
large development data sets 96
latent-variable analysis 261
LDA (linear discriminant analysis) 93, 161, 164, 278,
        284–5, 286, 290, 291
    classical 134, 139, 140, 141
    comparing the predictive ability of 277
least squares 156
Lee, E. T. 240, 242
Levin (US Representative) 10
Lewis, E. M. 1, 78, 119, 120
Liebman, L. H. 296
Lifereg Procedure 242
'Lifetimes' 236
likelihood 136
likelihood ratio 113, 258, 263, 298, 299, 300
linear analysis techniques 24, 25
linear discriminant functions 24
linear models 102, 148, 205
    perfect 100
linear regression *see* LDA
Linhart, H. 24
loan review and internal control model 23
loans 5, 27
    appraisal of new applicants 6
    business 21, 22
    categorizing 26
    changes in number and quality of applicants 20
    commercial 13, 22
    consumer 22, 152
    credit union 282
    current, applicants with 105
    decision to grant 252
    gender-orientated 252
    granting to fewer than all applicants 18
    indirect 107
    industrial 22
    major feature and indicator of quality 76
    minorities 22
    optimal number of 18
    personal 101, 297
    single period 19, 20
    term 22
    value determined 21
    see also arrears; bad loans; default; good loans;
        rejection; repayment
'local gradient' 281
log-linear models 57, 248, 262–3, 268
    all-two-way 266–7
    all-way 264–5
    low-order 142

log-odds-ratio scale 267
logistic function 148
logistic regression 101, 103, 104, 134, 135, 141, 248,
        267, 273, 277, 278
Long, M. S. 18, 20, 21, 28
Lorenz diagram (*see* ROC curves) 55–6
losses 6, 8, 58
    default 77, 119
    expected 20, 113, 115–17, 120, 121–3
    increasing, to the lender 77
    incremental (marginal) 120
    large 78
    net of risk-free return 119
    relative, on bad accounts 13
Lovie, A. D. & P. 147, 156
Luenberger, D. 121

Mahalanobis (mean) differences 53
mailing lists 177, 178
mailing response/risk matrix 183–5
mailing-risk model 181
management controls 36–7
marginal benefits 152
marital status 10, 17, 240, 269, 271, 273
market share 73, 74, 75, 77, 78–9, 84, 86, 119
    expected contribution to 81
    increases in 123
    increasing 125
    tradeoffs between profits and 85
marketing 13, 64, 94, 117, 182–3, 303
    bank departments 272
    different strategies 185
    direct 178
    niche 206
    strategy 252
Markov chain 19, 295–307
    Rth order 296
    stationary 297
Marks and Spencer Financial Services 177–85
Marquardt, D. W. 156
married people 273
Marshall, K. T. 119, 248
mass functions 250
Mastercard 189, 206, 211
mathematical techniques/analysis 9–10, 96, 211–12
mathematics 218, 219
maximum deviation 55
maximum likelihood 28, 101, 140, 239, 297–8, 301
means 217
    estimates of 28
Mehta, D. 18, 19, 21, 296
Miller, G. M. 240
misclassification 58, 158, 289
    costs of 22, 24, 26, 121, 191, 278
    probabilities of 23
mixture-decomposition approach 136, 138, 140, 143
model selection 263–4
monitoring 94, 95, 97, 101
    and adjustments, new book 106–7

commonly used methods for accounts 101–2
current fraud 190–1
population dynamics and 107–8
monotonically increasing function 101
mortgages 68, 165
movers 303–6
multi-period-multi-decision type models 21
multiple regression analysis 235
multiple stage transitions 297
multivariate multiple regression 142
multivariate normality 135, 140
multivariate observations 247
mutation 282, 287, 289
Myers, J. H. 27
mystique 93–109

National Bureau of Economic Research 5
national origin 17
neighbour techniques 24, 282
neural networks 112, 277, 278, 279–81, 282, 286–7,
    290, 288, 291
NeuralWorks Professional Plus 287
new products 106
Newton-Raphson algorithm 239
niche products 206
nodes 247, 255, 286
    circular 254
    decision 248, 282, 283, 289
    diamond 254
non-affordability 66, 67, 68, 69, 70
non-creditworthness 7
    arraying cumulative percentages for 152
non-discriminatory treatment 12
non-integer cell counts 265
non-linear programming 121
non-linearities 291
non-receipt fraud 189
non-stationarity 300, 302
non-workers 272–3
normality 59, 61, 129
    assumed unrealistic 140
    multivariate 135, 140
notation 112–13
NPV (net present value) 13, 20
null hypotheses 259, 298
number of children 165

Oakes, D. 240
objective or criterion function 20
observations 259, 266
    censored 237
    multivariate 247
odds 39, 98, 119, 120, 126
    alignment of 102
    cut-off 113, 122, 124, 125
    information 112, 113
    posterior 112
    relative 112

Office of Fair Trading 208
Oliver, R. M. 78, 119, 120, 248
'One Free Bite Approach' 8
one-of-N coding 286
OPs (operating points) 114–15
optimal policies 19
optimal price 122
optimality conditions 123
optimization 114, 282
optimum solution sets 291
organizational preferences 85, 86
Orgler, Y. E. 27
orthogonality 248
outcome indicators 211
over-commitment 63, 94
overdraft facilities 297
overindebtedness 63
overparametrization 262

parametric models 242
parametrization 262
part-time work 11, 12
partial derivatives 281
partial equilibrium approach 20
partitioning criteria 282–3
Partnership bad rate 217
payments:
    late 112
    missed 162, 163–4, 240, 244, 284
    overdue 156
    past behaviour 8
    performance 19
payoffs 119
    expected, risky gamble with 120
Pearson's chi-squared test 258
Pearson's goodness of fit test 298, 299, 300, 302
perfect information 120
perfect scoring systems 57
personal management style 84
perverse scoring systems 57
PGA package 288
Pierce, J. C. 21
plots 117–19
points 10, 11, 99, 107, 210
    frozen 96
    making changes to values 95
    owners given too few 100
    recalculated 105
    re-estimated 104
    reflecting the future 221
    summing, in unadjusted scorecard 98
    zero 97
poor payers 156, 164, 291
population dynamics 107–8
population shifts 102, 123
portfolios 34, 42, 73, 86
    acceptance rate 202, 203
    consumer loan, auditing 148
    corporate preferences 85

portfolios (*cont.*)
  efficient frontier cut-off policies 111–31
  fixed term, survival analysis applied to 240–4
  lower volume 125
  reports on 33
  retail-card 178
  retail credit 78
  rogue 196
post codes 197, 209
potential borrowers 27
predictability 6
prediction 41, 98, 102, 142, 147, 148, 161, 205,
    261, 287
  averaging 99
  biased and optimistic 26
  correct 288
  credit performance 260
  good, often destroyed 156
  neural net 112
  no additional information for 251
predictive accuracy 147, 289
predictive models 210–22
  allocating resources to produce 208
predictive patterns 197–8
predictive performance 130, 162, 289, 291
predictive power 157, 158, 213
  four categories 213
  relative 153
predictive strength 67, 68
predictive value 65, 66, 104
predictiveness 214, 217, 221
  lack of 213
predictors 114, 147, 164–5, 235, 237, 238
  most powerful 211
  'nonsignificant' elimination of 157
  quadratic 134
  statistically sufficient 207, 211
  straight-line 134
Prentice, R. L. 239
prepayment 112
principal-components model 156, 158
privacy concerns 12, 14
probability 25, 41, 60, 114, 139, 255, 283
  a priori, inappropriate 24, 26
  acceptance 79, 85
  account will remain in satisfactory condition 39
  adjusted 161
  applicant is good 134, 138
  attribute 99
  collection, estimates of 20
  conditional 99, 106, 112, 113, 138, 167, 250
  default 21, 22–3, 207, 253
  distribution of 141
  equal 77
  estimates of 100–1, 135
  gaining a customer 86
  marginal 99
  misclassification 23
  modified 238
  not reaching 3-cycles delinquent 211

posterior 141, 167
prior 19, 161, 165, 166, 169, 172
stochastic 282
survival 239
transition 297
transition matrix 300
unconditional 250
probability function 134, 136, 278
probability of take 79, 80, 81, 82, 83
product differentiation 206
product offers:
  consequences of 76–81
  win-win 81–4
Product-Limit Method 242
profile 96, 197–201
  non-scored payment characteristics 103
'Profiles' rewards scheme 206
profitability 13–14, 113
profits 73, 74, 75, 86, 122
  expectations of 118
  maximizing 18, 113, 120
  random contribution to 116
  tradeoffs between market share and 85
  see also expected profits
proportions 142
prosperity 162
protected classes 12
Pseudo-bads/Pseudo-goods 212, 219
public assistance benefits 11, 17
purchasing patterns 19

quadratic procedures 25, 27
quality of credit applicants 106
questionnaires 205, 206, 208, 209
Quinlan, J. R. 283, 284

race 10, 12, 17
Raiffa, H. 114
random digits 37, 46
random performance 112
random variation 236
recession 206, 222
reclassification 28
records 216–17, 220
recovery values 26
recursive portitioning algorithm (RPA) *see* classification
    trees
recursive relationship 242
redlining 8
re-estimation 101, 102, 104
references 97
regression 214, 242, 248
  biased techniques 156
  from a new unbiased angle 99–101
  linear 97, 112
  logistic 101, 103, 104, 134, 135, 141, 248, 267, 273,
    277, 278
  mechanics of 97–9
  multiple 244
  multivariate multiple 142

non-linear 112
principal-components 156
procedure separates out 'good rate estimates' 107
ridge 156
stepwise multiple 148
unknown parameters, estimated 238
regression analysis 25, 248
regression coefficients 143, 148, 258
regression function 237
regression models 142
  individually developed 158
  two-class 156
regression weights 147
Reichert, A. K. 139 reject 134
reject inference 95, 133–45, 177, 178, 181, 207, 248,
    260, 273
  biased 106
  formal 106
rejection 8, 11, 28, 58, 65, 96, 105, 106, 150, 161,
    169, 172
  accounts payoff 119
  data not available for 95
  determination of 78
  examining 104
  high rates 64
  increased rates 94
  method used to infer behaviour 98
  requests for reasons for 14
  risk-neutral, indifference to 120
  truncation resulting from 135
reliability of estimates 23
religion 10, 17
Reminder Letters 34
repayment 161, 165
  characteristics and 291
  estimates of probabilities of 19
  factors that can affect 162
  likelihood of 65, 66
  low probability of 9
  missed one or more 284
  partial 20
  performance 20
  probability of defaulting on 253
  regular 205
  unsatisfactory 11
reports 37, 38
  alignment of odds 102
residential status 65, 102, 165, 169, 172, 235, 240,
    258–9, 269, 270, 271, 272, 273, 286
response patterns 136
response-scoring techniques 178
retail credit 197
returns 20
revenues 13, 21
  additional, estimating values of 19
  increasing 8, 77
ridge regression 156
rights 11, 17
risk-based pricing 12–13, 64
risk-management system 14

risk(s) 21, 33, 41
  ability to predict 181
  acceptable 178, 179, 180
  assessing 65
  associated with groups of people 7
  aversion to 119, 120
  current, precise measure of 39
  deciding whether to accept or reject an individual
      121
  decisions that reduce 113
  decrease, as score increases 112
  default 77, 297
  determination of 34
  differentiating good from bad 5, 248
  expectations of 118
  good 134, 137, 141
  high 13, 106, 178, 185
  low(er) 13, 125, 181, 183
  means of reducing 26
  poor 78, 137
  significant 64
  sorting good from bad 10
  'statistically sufficient' predictor of 207, 211
  tools for controlling 205
  tradeoffs between volume and 114
  traditional indicators 68
  women exceptionally good at 6
ROC curves 47, 55–6
RPA (Recursive Partitioning Algorithm) 282–3, 289
rules:
  Champion-Challenger contest 36–7
  classification 26, 139
  cut-off 210
  learning 286
  policy 94, 95, 106
  production 284, 289
rules of thumb 104, 107, 213

sales 18, 19
samples/sampling 18, 27, 138, 163, 284
  arbitrary 141
  biased 152, 153, 155, 156, 157, 158
  bootstrap 264, 267
  calibration 141–3
  developmental 152, 153, 155
  holdout 155, 156, 161, 164, 165, 168, 172, 306
  irregularities 57
  large 205
  partitioned 141
  random 258, 259, 260
  repeated replacement 264
  small 205–29
  sparse 135
  training 164, 283, 290, 291
  truncated 27
SAS (statistical package) 240, 242, 263
Saunders, A. 296
scaling 97
scenario table 45

Schlarbaum, G. G. 18, 20, 21
Scientific American 217
score 59
scorecards 11, 64, 65, 67–9, 136, 137, 141, 143, 205,
    216–17, 220
  adjusting 94
  application-risk 180
  application variables used to build 260
  behaviour 211
  claims of using rejects to improve 138
  country 202, 203
  degradation over the business cycle 161–75
  development data 213
  development of 177, 181
  final 221, 222
  generic 207
  logistic discrimination 306
  more possibilities for improving 138
  point-of-mailing 180
  portfolio 202, 203
  potential covariates 269
  proprietary development software 66
  regression coefficients in 258
  response 179, 183
  risk 179, 183
  separate, importance of using 271
  single European 195–204
  totally new approach for mailing-list selection 178
  traditional 244–5
  updating 93–109
Scorex 177, 178, 181, 182, 183, 195–204
screening 6, 7, 18
seasonality 302
segmentation 64, 295–306
selection 20, 254–60
  mailing-list 178
self-employed applicants 205, 206, 208, 272–3
  bad rates 219
self-interest 12
self-pre-screening 27
sequential decision models 19
sex 10, 11, 12, 17, 251–2
shadow price 122–3
shakers 303, 305, 306
shareholders' equity 20
Shinkel, B. A. 28
shrinkage 217–18, 224
sigmoid transformation function 288, 289
Simpson's paradox 251–4, 264
simulation 218
  computer-aided techniques 224
single-period models 23
single reject inference 181
slow cases 22, 23, 156, 158, 233, 284, 285, 288
Smirnov statistic 55
Snee, R. D. 156
software 181, 290
  general-purpose 263
  scorecard building 223
Southern/Latin Europe 197

sparsity 135, 247, 264, 265–6
Spearman's rank correlation coefficient 212
Spiegel 6
SPSS (software) 263, 286
standard deviations 53, 59
  common 61
stationarity assumptions 296
statistical analysis 37, 254
statistical techniques 141, 282
status 133, 251, 255
  default 253
  delinquent 35
  employment 269, 271, 272
  financial 78, 85, 87
  marital 10, 17, 240, 269, 271, 273
  residential 65, 102, 165, 169, 172, 235, 240, 258–9,
      269, 270, 271, 272, 273, 286
  true good/bad 140
stayers 303, 305
steady state reproduction 289, 290
Stepanova, M. 231
stepwise routine 148, 156, 157, 165, 166, 286
Stirling, M. 291
Stockley Park 182
storecard accounts 297
strategy 33, 34–5, 43–4
  defined 46
strategy assignment table 46
strategy curves 113–15
strategy table 45
stratification 247, 249, 254, 258–60
stream splitter 46
subdividing populations 24
summarizing statistics 142
supplementary information methods 140–1
survival analysis 235–45
survival function 236, 238, 242
  modified 243
'swap set' 178
system decay 20
systems approach 12, 14

telephone ownership 198, 240, 242, 269, 270, 273
  very high 201
temporal sequencing 255
ten way cross-validation 288
tenancy/tenants 98, 100, 104, 169, 172, 270, 272
  high level of 198
terminal branches 119
Thomas, L. 119, 231
Thompson, G. L. 296
three-group model 139
three-way interactions 271
through-the-door applicants 27, 178, 255, 258, 269,
    273, 274
time lags 96
time series 248
tradeoffs 123–5, 142
  market share and profits 85

operational 68, 69
  volume and risk 114
training cases 164, 283, 288, 290, 291
transformation function 288, 289
trial and error 269
triggering event 43
truncation 27, 134, 135, 139
  making explicit 140
twins 289
twitchers 303, 305, 306
two-group model 139
two-way interaction 262, 263, 267, 271

uncertainty:
  classic problem of decision making under 119
  three-dimensional bands 118
unconstrained profit-maximizing problem/solution 113,
    119, 120, 122
uncreditworthiness 95
undirected graphs 248, 249, 262
  arbitrary 251
  unemployment figures 94
United Kingdom:
  Coincident Indicator of state of economy 163
  Euro scorecard 202
  post code statistics 197
  predictive bureau characteristics 203
United States 9, 10, 11, 73
  challenges to the use of credit scoring 7
  consumer credit market 284
  credit unions 148
  movement towards risk-based pricing among
    commercial banks 13
  public relations and political problem 14
unsecured credit balances 68
update policies 20
useless scoring systems 57
utility 34

validation 18, 27, 153–6, 155, 191, 221–2
  ten way cross- 288
validity 25, 135, 286
  face 9–10
Van Kuelen, J. A. 296
variables 5, 26, 59, 97, 99, 161, 240, 243, 268
  ability to predict default 162
  alphabetic 286
  application 248, 249, 255, 260, 261, 262,
    264, 273, 306
  association and dependence between 249
  banking 270
  basically judgemental 6
  behavioural 306
  binary 259, 287
  categorical 24, 140
  characterizing 142
  clear and believable relationship between 9
  common 201
  conditioning 265

country specific 202
credit performance 269, 273
decision 254, 255
discrete 197
distribution 24–5
dummy 12, 25, 284
economic 164
empirically derived 8
explanatory 148, 237
functional forms of 96
global 197
high degree of collinearity among 10
independence between 260
indicator 235
marginally correlated 251
nominal 285
observed 257
ordinal 269
outcome 207, 211, 216, 248, 251, 254, 287
pairwise independence of 262
predictor 148, 149, 155, 156, 157, 164–5, 166, 235,
    236, 237, 245
prohibited 10, 11, 12
random 119, 136, 236, 250, 254, 255
rank ordering 214
re-classifying and re-weighting 198
relationships between 248, 271
represented by nodes 247
socio-demographic 164
stratification on the interdependency of 247
variance 26, 220–1, 264
Virginia 153
Visa 189, 206, 211
volume 118
  expected 120, 123–5
  mailing 183

Wainer, H. 148
Wakeman, L. 18, 20, 21
Washington DC 148
Watro, P. R. 13
Which? 7, 11
wealth 253–4
weighting systems 149
weights of evidence 217, 221, 224, 285
Wells, E. 78
Wentworth, J. R. 27
Whinston, W. 121
Whittaker, J. C. 248, 267
Wilk's lambda 165
Wilkie, A. D. 248
win-win offers 81–4
women 12
  exceptionally good at credit risks 6
  indirect discrimination 11
Wonderlic, E. F. 6
writing off 19

young people 273